iPad® with iOS 10 for Seniors

D1533680

Studio Visual Steps

iPad® with iOS 10 for Seniors

Learn to work with the iPad with iOS 10

www.visualsteps.com

This book has been written using the Visual Steps™ method.
Cover design by Studio Willemien Haagsma bNO

© 2016 Visual Steps
Author: Studio Visual Steps

First printing: October 2016
ISBN 978 90 5905 423 3

Resources used: A number of definitions and explanations of computer terminology are taken over from the *iPad User Guide*.

Do you have questions or suggestions?
E-mail: info@visualsteps.com

Would you like more information?
www.visualsteps.com

Website for this book:
www.visualsteps.com/ipad10

Subscribe to the free Visual Steps Newsletter:
www.visualsteps.com/newsletter

Table of Contents

Foreword

The iPad is an extremely user-friendly, portable multimedia device with countless possibilities. This device is ideal for all sorts of purposes, for instance surfing the Internet, sending and receiving emails, taking notes, or keeping a diary.

But this useful device has much more to offer. There are a number of standard apps (programs) available for working with photos, video, and music. You can even look up addresses and well-known places around the world, with *Maps*.
Also, you can go to the *App Store* and download numerous free and paid apps and games. What about recipes, horoscopes, fitness exercises, and stories to read aloud? You name it, and there will be some useful app to be got.

In this book you will get acquainted with the main functions and options of the iPad, step by step and at your own pace.

You can work through this useful book independently. Put the book next to your iPad and execute all the operations, step by step. The clear instructions and multitude of screen shots will tell you exactly what to do.
This is the quickest way of learning to use the iPad. Simply by doing it. A whole new world will appear!

We wish you lots of fun in working with the iPad!

Studio Visual Steps

PS After you have worked through this book, you will know how to send an email. We welcome your comments and suggestions. Our email address is: info@visualsteps.com

Visual Steps Newsletter

All Visual Steps books follow the same methodology: clear and concise step-by-step instructions with screen shots to demonstrate each task. A complete list of all our books can be found on our website **www.visualsteps.com** You can also sign up to receive our **free Visual Steps Newsletter**.
In this Newsletter you will receive periodic information by email regarding:
- the latest titles and previously released books;
- special offers, supplemental chapters, tips and free informative booklets.
Also, our Newsletter subscribers may download any of the documents listed on the web pages **www.visualsteps.com/info_downloads**

When you subscribe to our Newsletter you can be assured that we will never use your email address for any purpose other than sending you the information as previously described. We will not share this address with any third-party. Each Newsletter also contains a one-click link to unsubscribe.

Introduction to Visual Steps™

The Visual Steps handbooks and manuals are the best instructional materials available for learning how to work with the iPad and other computers. Nowhere else can you find better support for getting to know an iPad, the Internet, *Windows*, *MacOS*, a Samsung Galaxy Tab and computer programs.

Properties of the Visual Steps books:
- **Comprehensible contents**
  Addresses the needs of the beginner or intermediate computer user for a manual written in simple, straight-forward English.
- **Clear structure**
  Precise, easy to follow instructions. The material is broken down into small enough segments to allow for easy absorption.
- **Screen shots of every step**
  Quickly compare what you see on your screen with the screen shots in the book. Pointers and tips guide you when new windows are opened so you always know what to do next.
- **Get started right away**
  All you have to do is turn on your computer, place the book next to your device and execute the operations on your own iPad.
- **Layout**
  The text is printed in a large size font. Even if you put the book next to your iPad, this font will be clearly legible.

In short, I believe these manuals will be excellent guides for you.

dr. H. van der Meij
Faculty of Applied Education, Department of Instruction Technology, University of Twente, the Netherlands

What You Will Need

To be able to work through this book, you will need a number of things:

Suitable for all iPads with iOS 10.

For more information, see the webpage
www.visualsteps.com/ipad10

A computer or a notebook computer with the *iTunes* program installed. In *Appendix B Download and Install iTunes* you can read how to install *iTunes*.

If you do not own a computer or notebook, you may be able to execute these operations on the computer of a friend or family member.

You will need a printer with the *Airprint* option for the exercises about printing. You do not have a printer? Then you can skip the printing exercises.

How to Use This Book

This book has been written using the Visual Steps™ method. The method is simple: you put the book next to your iPad and execute all the tasks step by step, directly on your iPad. Because of the clear instructions and the multitude of screen shots, you will know exactly what to do. By executing all the tasks at once, you will learn how to use the iPad in the quickest possible way.
In this Visual Steps™ book, you will see various icons. This is what they mean:

Techniques
These icons indicate an action to be carried out:

    The index finger indicates you need to do something on the iPad's screen, for instance, tap something, or type a text.

The keyboard icon means you should type something on the keyboard of your iPad or your computer.

 The mouse icon means you should do something on your computer with the mouse.

 The hand icon means you should do something else, for example rotate the iPad or switch it off. The hand will also be used for a series of operations which you have learned at an earlier stage.

Apart from these operations, in some parts of this book extra assistance is provided to help you successfully work through this book.

Help
These icons indicate that extra help is available:

 The arrow icon warns you about something.

 The bandage icon will help you if something has gone wrong.

 The hand icon is also used for the exercises. These exercises at the back of each chapter will help you repeat the operations independently.

1 Have you forgotten how to do something? The number next to the footsteps tells you where to look it up at the end of the book in the appendix *How Do I Do That Again?*

In separate boxes you will find general information or tips concerning the iPad.

Extra information
Information boxes are denoted by these icons:

 The book icon gives you extra background information that you can read at your convenience. This extra information is not necessary for working through the book.

 The light bulb icon indicates an extra tip for using the iPad.

Website

On the website that accompanies this book, **www.visualsteps.com/ipad10**, you will find a Bonus Online Chapter and more information about this book. This website will also keep you informed of changes you need to know as a user of the book. Visit this website regularly and check if there are any recent updates or additions to this book, or possible errata.

Test Your Knowledge

After you have worked through this book, you can test your knowledge online, at the **www.ccforseniors.com** website.

By answering a number of multiple choice questions you will be able to test your knowledge of the iPad. After you have finished the test, you will receive a *Computer Certificate*.
Participating in the test is **free of charge**. The computer certificate website is a free Visual Steps service.

For Teachers

The Visual Steps books have been written as self-study guides for individual use. Although these books are also well suited for use in a group or a classroom setting. For this purpose, some of our books come with a free teacher's manual. You can download the available teacher's manuals and additional materials at:
www.visualsteps.com/instructor
After you have registered at this website, you can use this service for free.

The Screen shots

The screen shots in this book indicate which button, file or hyperlink you need to tap on your iPad screen or click on your computer. In the instruction text (in **bold** letters) you will see a small image of the item you need to tap or click. The line will point you to the right place on your screen.
The small screen shots that are printed in this book are not meant to be completely legible all the time. This is not necessary, as you will see these images on your own iPad screen in real size and fully legible.

Here you see an example of such an instruction text and a screen shot of the item you need to click. The line indicates where to find this item on your own screen:

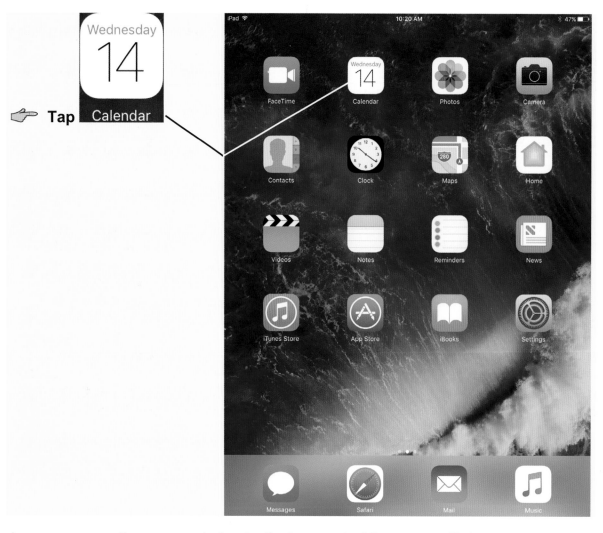

In some cases, the screen shot only displays part of the screen. Below you see an example of this:

At the bottom of the screen:

We would like to emphasize that we **do not intend you** to read the information in all of the screen shots in this book. Always use the screen shots in combination with the display on your iPad screen.

1. The iPad

Since the introduction of the first iPad in January 2010, millions of iPads have been sold. The iPad has now become one of the best selling tablet computers in the world. There are several editions of the iPad available today, but each iPad works in the same way.

The popularity of the iPad is not so surprising if you consider how lightweight and portable the iPad is and how easy it is to use. It has many of the same functions and capabilities of a regular computer. Not only can you surf the Internet and send and receive emails, you can also maintain a calendar, play games or read your favorite book, newspaper or magazine. You can also take pictures or make a movie and view or share them easily with others. You can do all this by using the so-called *apps*, the programs that are installed on the iPad. Along with the standard apps supplied on your iPad, you can easily add more (free and paid) by visiting the *App Store*, the web shop with all the apps.

If you connect your iPad to the computer, you can use *iTunes* to load your favorite music, movies, tv series and podcasts onto it. When you have done this you can use the iPad wherever you want. You can connect to the Internet through a wireless network (Wi-Fi) and with the 3G or 4G version, to the mobile data network as well.

In this chapter you will get to know your iPad and you will learn the basic operations necessary to operate the iPad and the onscreen keyboard.

In this chapter you will learn about:

- turning the iPad on or waking it up from Sleep Mode;
- initial setup;
- the most important components of your iPad;
- updating the iPad;
- the basic operations for the iPad;
- using the onscreen keyboard;
- connecting to the Internet via a wireless network (Wi-Fi);
- connecting to the Internet via the mobile data network;
- connecting the iPad to the computer;
- safely disconnecting the iPad;
- putting the iPad into Sleep Mode or turning it off.

Please note:

You might see a different screens during the setup of your iPad. This depends on the type of iPad you are using.

1.1 Turning the iPad On or Waking it Up From Sleep Mode

The iPad can be turned off or locked. If your iPad is turned off, here is how you turn it on:

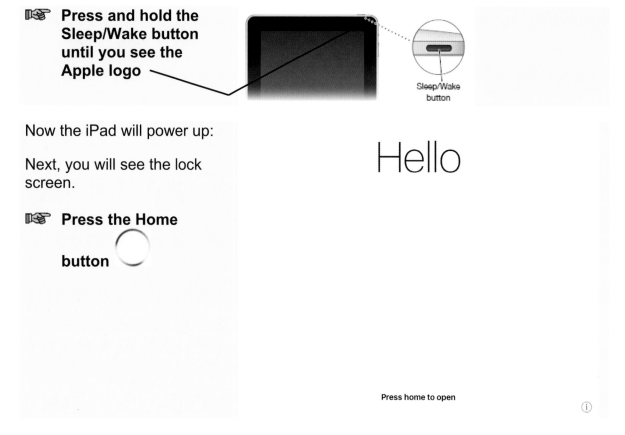

☞ **Press and hold the Sleep/Wake button until you see the Apple logo**

Now the iPad will power up:

Next, you will see the lock screen.

☞ **Press the Home**

button

The iPad may also be locked. This is called Sleep Mode. If your iPad is locked, you can unlock it in the following way:

☞ **Press the Home button**

1.2 Initial Set Up of the iPad

When you start up your iPad for the very first time you will see a few screens where you are asked to enter some basic information. If you have already used your iPad before, you can skip this section and go to page 29. The first thing to do is set the language and country settings for your iPad:

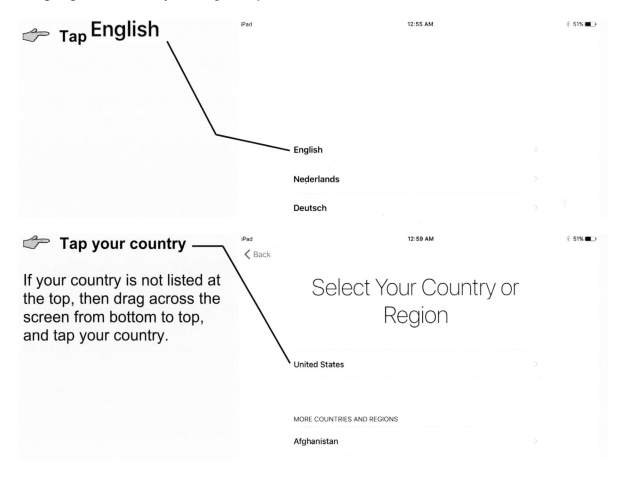

☞ **Tap** **English**

☞ **Tap your country**

If your country is not listed at the top, then drag across the screen from bottom to top, and tap your country.

In the next screen, you will be asked to choose your Wi-Fi network.

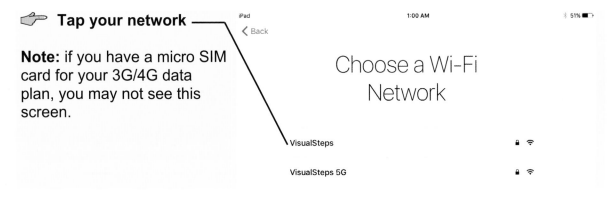

☞ **Tap your network**

Note: if you have a micro SIM card for your 3G/4G data plan, you may not see this screen.

Help! I don't have Wi-Fi.

If you do not have Wi-Fi available or prefer not to use it, then you will need to connect the iPad to *iTunes* on your computer in order to continue. You can use the USB cable that came with the packaging to do this.

In the Wi-Fi Networks screen:

☞ **Tap** Connect to iTunes

A small window will appear:

☞ **Tap** Continue

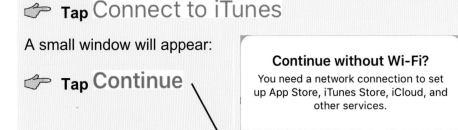

Continue without Wi-Fi?

You need a network connection to set up App Store, iTunes Store, iCloud, and other services.

Continue   Use Wi-Fi

☞ **Continue further with the steps in section *1.9 Connecting the iPad to the Computer***

⌨ **Type the password**

Does your password contain capital letters or numbers? Go to page 41 to read how to type them.

☞ **Tap** Join

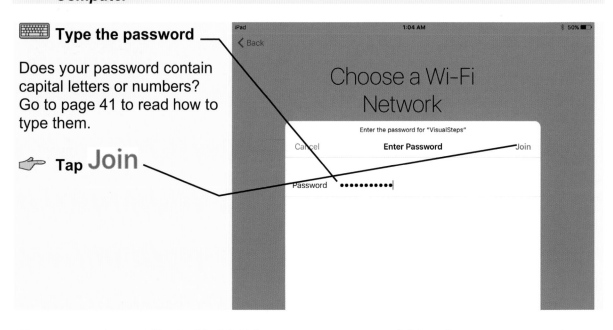

Choose a Wi-Fi Network

Enter the password for "VisualSteps"

Cancel   **Enter Password**   Join

Password   •••••••••

If you are using an iPad with 3G/4G, you may see an additional screen concerning the placement of your SIM card and checking the provider's settings. In *section 1.8 Connecting to the Internet Through the Mobile Data Network* you can read more about inserting a SIM card and connecting through the mobile data network.

☞ **If necessary, tap** Next **or follow the instructions in the windows**

You will be asked if you want to turn on Location Services. Location Services lets the iPad physically locate you using its built-in GPS. You can decide later on if you want to keep this service turned on or off.

To turn Location Services on, at the bottom of the screen:

☞ **Tap**
Enable Location Ser

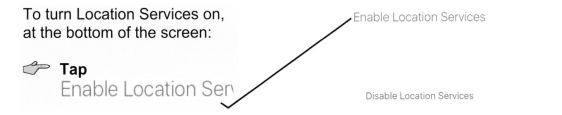

On the latest type of iPads you will see an option to use your fingerprint (Touch ID) in place of a passcode. In this example we will use a passcode:

☞ **If necessary, tap**
Set Up Touch ID La

You will need to confirm this:

☞ **Tap** Continue

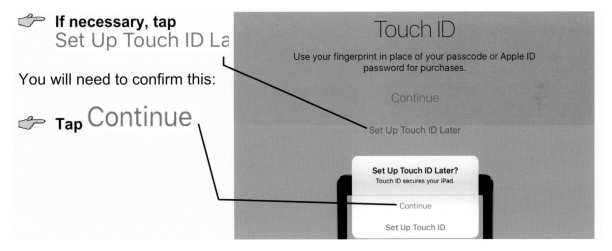

You can enter a passcode with which you can unlock your iPad. This is a security measure that prevents others from using your iPad without your consent. In this example a four-digit passcode is asked. On you iPad you might need to enter six digits.

⌨ **Type the desired passcode**

If you do not want to enter a code, tap Passcode Options and Don't Add Passcode.

You will need to enter the code once more:

⌨ **Type the desired passcode again**

It is also possible to enter a six-digit numeric code, a custom alphanumeric or custom numeric code. You wil find out more about this in the *Tips* at the end of this chapter.

In this example, a new iPad is being set up for the first time

☞ **Tap**
Set Up as New iPad

You will be asked whether you want to sign in with an existing *Apple ID* or if you want to create a new one. An *Apple ID* consists of a combination of an email address and a password. You need to have an *Apple ID* to be able to download apps from the *App Store* and when using certain applications. If you already have an *Apple ID*:

⌨ **By Apple ID and Password enter your *Apple ID* and password**

☞ **Follow the onscreen instructions**

☞ **Continue on page 26, with the Terms and Conditions**

If you do not yet have an *Apple ID*:

☞ **Tap**
Don't have an Apple ID

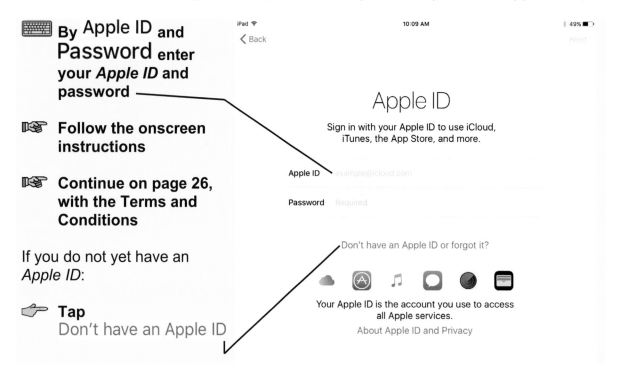

Tap
Create a Free Apple

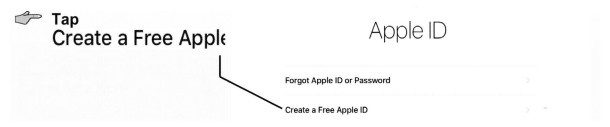

Apple ID

Forgot Apple ID or Password   >

Create a Free Apple ID   >

Tip

Skip
You can also choose not to create an *Apple ID*.

 Tap Set Up Later in Settings
 Tap Don't use
Continue on page 26, with the Terms and Conditions

First, you need to enter your birth date:

 Spin the wheel until you see your month of birth

Do the same for the day and year of birth

After you have selected your birth date:

 Tap Next

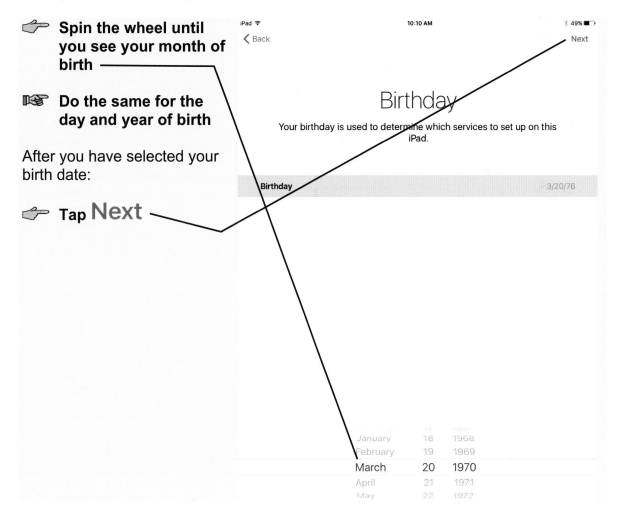

Now you are going to enter your name:

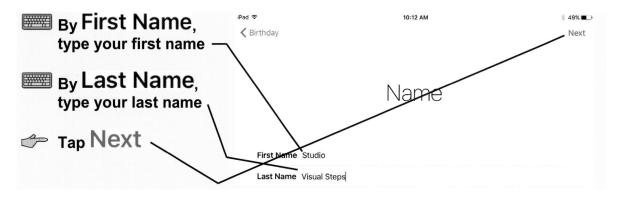

By **First Name**, type your first name

By **Last Name**, type your last name

☞ Tap **Next**

In this book we assume you already have an email address and want to use this address for the options on the iPad. It does not matter if you use this email address on your computer, or on another device:

☞ If necessary, tap **Use your current er**

Now you can enter your email address:

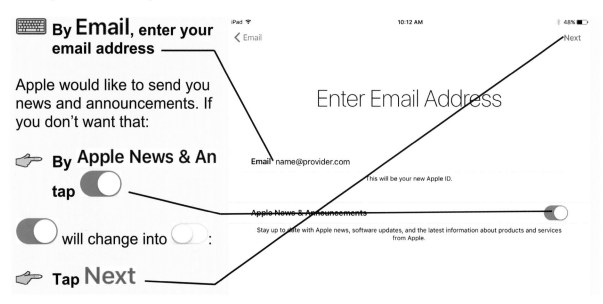

By **Email**, enter your email address

Apple would like to send you news and announcements. If you don't want that:

☞ By **Apple News & An** tap

 will change into :

☞ Tap **Next**

Your password must contain a minimum of 8 characters, at least one digit, an uppercase letter, and a lowercase letter:

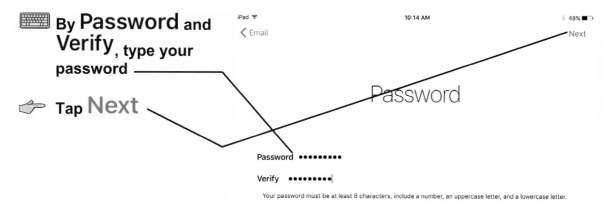

Next, select questions that will act as a hint to help you remember your password. You can use these security questions to retrieve your password, if you forget it:

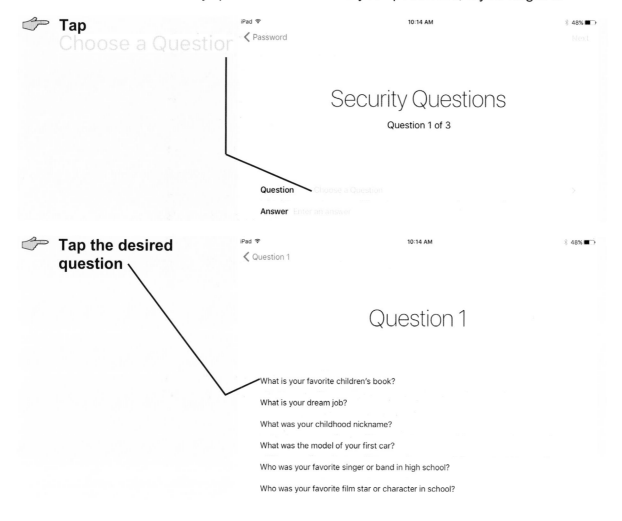

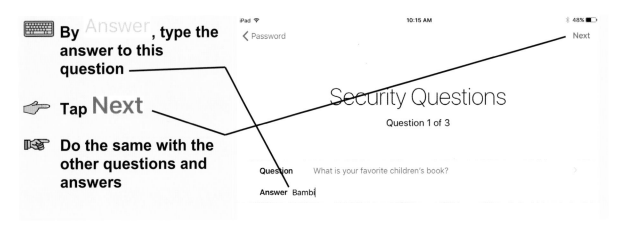

By Answer**, type the answer to this question**

☞ **Tap** Next

☞ **Do the same with the other questions and answers**

The next screen displays Apple's Terms and Conditions. You must agree to these terms in order to be able to work with your iPad.

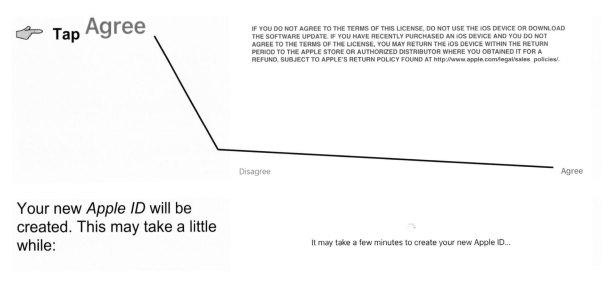

☞ **Tap** Agree

Your new *Apple ID* will be created. This may take a little while:

It may take a few minutes to create your new Apple ID...

You will see a sceen with the option to set up your email. In this example, we will not set up the email account yet. We will do that in *Chapter 2 Sending Emails with Your iPad*.

☞ **Tap** Next

☞ **Tap** Skip

Skip email setup?

Some services will not be available
until you verify your email address.
Setting it up will automatically verify it.

Don't Skip   Skip

🖎 **Please note:**

You might see a couple of different screens. This depends on the type of iPad you are using. Please follow the onscreen instructions.

The iPad might ask you if you want to use *Siri*. With *Siri* you can give the iPad verbal instructions to execute or ask the iPad for information. More about *Siri* in *section 4.10 Siri*.

☞ **Tap** Turn On Siri

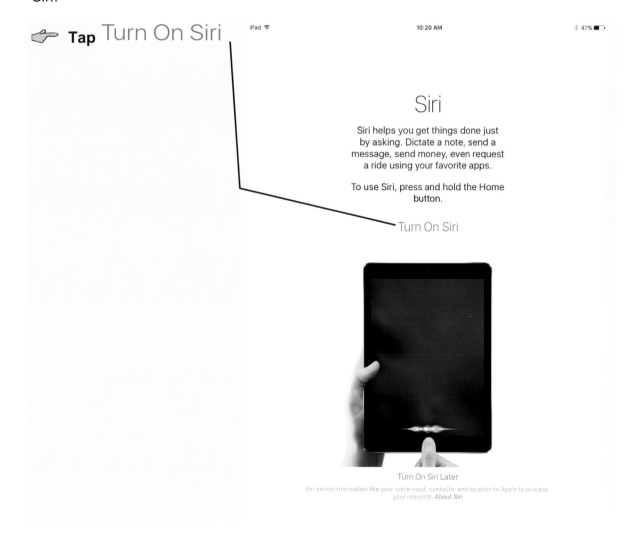

iPad 🔋   10:20 AM   ⚹ 47% 🔋

Siri

Siri helps you get things done just
by asking. Dictate a note, send a
message, send money, even request
a ride using your favorite apps.

To use Siri, press and hold the Home
button.

Turn On Siri

Turn On Siri Later

Siri sends information like your voice input, contacts, and location to Apple to process
your requests. About Siri

In the next window you are asked if you want to assist Apple with the improvement of their products by sending them diagnostic and usage data.

If you don't want to send this:

☞ **Tap** Don't Send

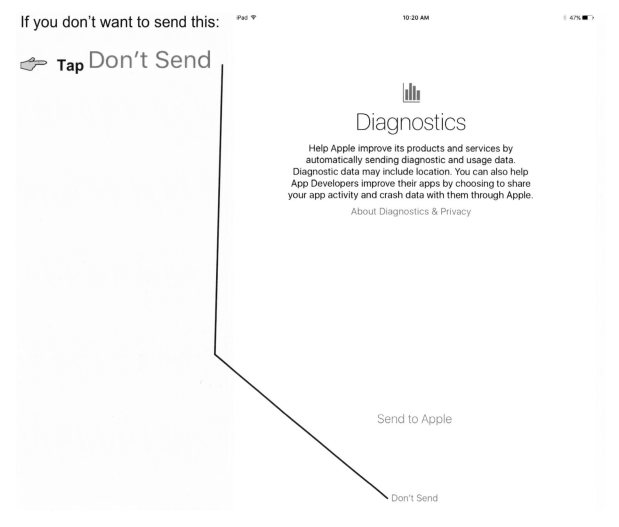

You have now completed the initial set up. There still is a little more to set up, but that comes later.

☞ **Tap** Get Started

Welcome to iPad

Get Started

Now you will see the home screen with all the colored app icons:

The background of your iPad might be slightly different.

Help! My iPad is locked.

If you don't use your iPad for a little while, the home screen will lock itself. This happens after about two minutes of non-activity. You can unlock the iPad like this:

 Press the Home button

 If necessary, enter the code

1.3 The Main Components of Your iPad

In the images below and on the next page you will see the main components of the iPad. When we describe a certain operation in this book, you can look for the relevant component in these images.

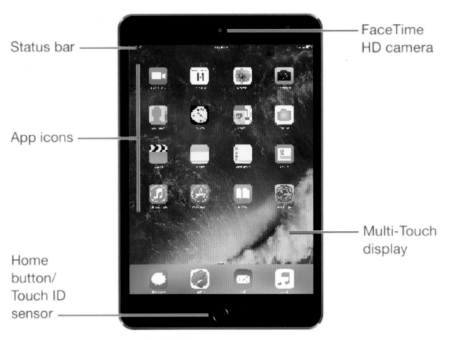

Source: User Guide iPad mini 4.

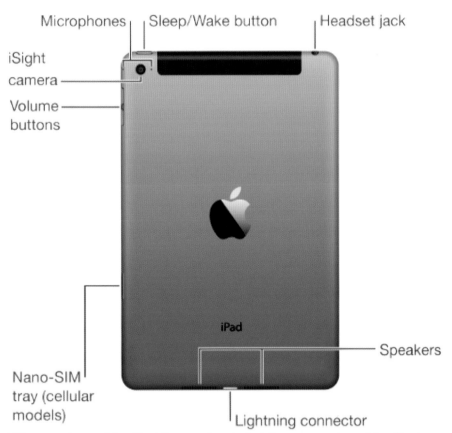

Microphones | Sleep/Wake button | Headset jack

iSight
camera

Volume
buttons

iPad

Speakers

Nano-SIM
tray (cellular
models)

Lightning connector

*Source: User Guide
iPad mini 4.*

* The speakers of the iPad Pro are located at the upper edge of the iPad.
** On the iPad Pro a True Tone Flash is located under the iSight camera.

On the status bar, located at the top of your iPad, various icons display information about the status of the iPad and its connections. Below you see an overview of all the most important status icons you might encounter along with their significance:

	This shows that the screen orientation is locked.
	The iPad is locked. This icon will be displayed when the lock screen appears.
	Battery is charging.
	Battery is fully charged.
Not Charging	The iPad is connected to the computer, but the USB port does not provide enough power for charging the battery.
▶	Shows that a song, audio book or podcast is playing.

- Continue on the next page -

📶	Shows that the iPad has a Wi-Fi Internet connection. The more bars, the stronger the connection.
No SIM	No micro SIM card has been installed (in an iPad suited for Wi-Fi and 3G or 4G).
3G/4G	Shows that your carrier's mobile data network (iPad Wi-Fi + 3G or 4G) is available and you can connect to the Internet over 3G or 4G.
●●●●●	Signal strength of the connection and name of the mobile network carrier currently in use.
E	Shows that your carrier's EDGE network (some iPad Wi-Fi + 3G or 4G models) is available and you can connect to the Internet with EDGE.
GPRS	Shows that your carrier's GPRS network (some iPad Wi-Fi + 3G or 4G models) is available and you can connect to the Internet with GPRS.
VPN	This icon appears when you are connected to a *Virtual Private Network* (VPN). VPNs are used in organizations, for secure sending of private information over a public network.
◁	This icon appears when a program uses location services. That means that information about your current location will be used.
☀	Shows network and other activity. Some apps may also use this symbol to indicate an active process.
✳	Bluetooth icon. If the icon is rendered in grey, it means Bluetooth has been enabled, but no device is connected. If a device is connected, the icon will be displayed in white.
✈	Airplane mode is on. If your iPad is in this mode, you do not have access to the Internet and you cannot use Bluetooth devices.

1.4 Updating the iPad

Apple is regularly issuing new updates for the iPad software. In these updates, existing problems are fixed or new functions are added. Normally, these updates will be downloaded automatically to your iPad.
But we would advise you to regularly check if there are any updates available for your iPad. If necessary, wake your iPad up from sleep:

☞ **Press the Home button**

You will see the locked screen of the iPad. This is how you unlock the iPad and proceed to the home screen:

☞ **Press the Home**

button

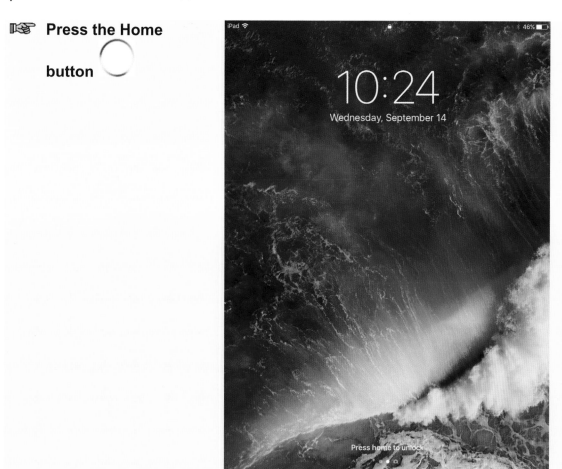

If you have entered a passcode while you were setting up the device, you will need to type this first, before you can continue:

☞ **Tap the code**

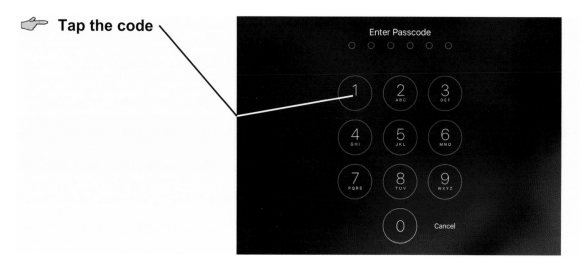

Now you will see the home screen of your iPad. This is how to open the *Settings* app:

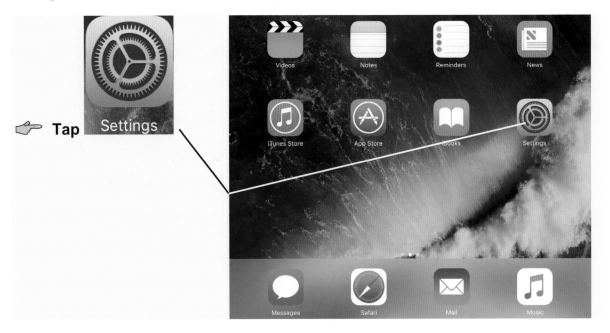

☞ **Tap**
   Settings

Please note:

In this book we always use the iPad in portrait mode, where the longer side is vertically positioned. We recommend using your iPad in portrait mode while you work through the chapters in this book, otherwise you may see a screen that is different from the examples shown.

Here you see the *Settings* app:

The *General* section is already opened: ————

☞ **Tap**
   Software Update

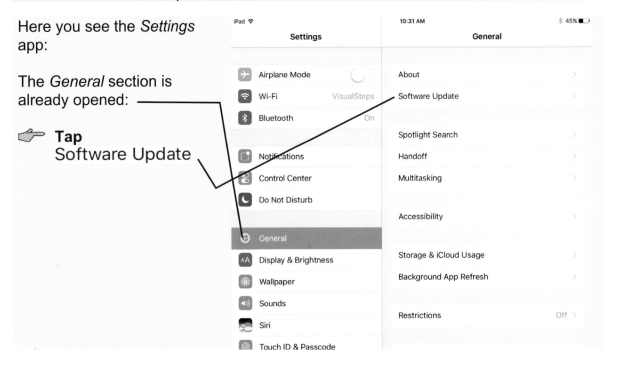

Now the iPad will check if there is any new software available.

In this example, the iPad already has the current software version installed:

To return to the *General* section:

☞ **Tap** < General

If a newer version is found, you will see a message about the update.

☞ **Follow the onscreen instructions**

When the update has been installed, you will return to the home screen.

It is also possible to install a new update with *iTunes*. Then you will need to connect the iPad to your computer. You can read more about this in the *Tips* at the end of this chapter.

1.5 Basic iPad Operations

In this section, you will learn how easy it is to use your iPad. You will practice some basic operations and touch movements. If necessary, wake your iPad up from sleep:

☞ **Press the Home button**

You will see the locked screen of the iPad. This is how you unlock the iPad and proceed to the home screen:

☞ **Press the Home button**

☞ **If necessary, type the code**

You are going to lock the iPad in vertical position with use of the Control Center. You can check to see if this works:

☞ **Hold the iPad upright, in a vertical position**

☞ **Turn the iPad to the right or left towards a horizontal position**

☞ **Hold the iPad upright again**

You will see the home screen of your iPad. This is how to open the Control Center:

☞ **Drag your finger upwards on the screen**

☞ **Tap**

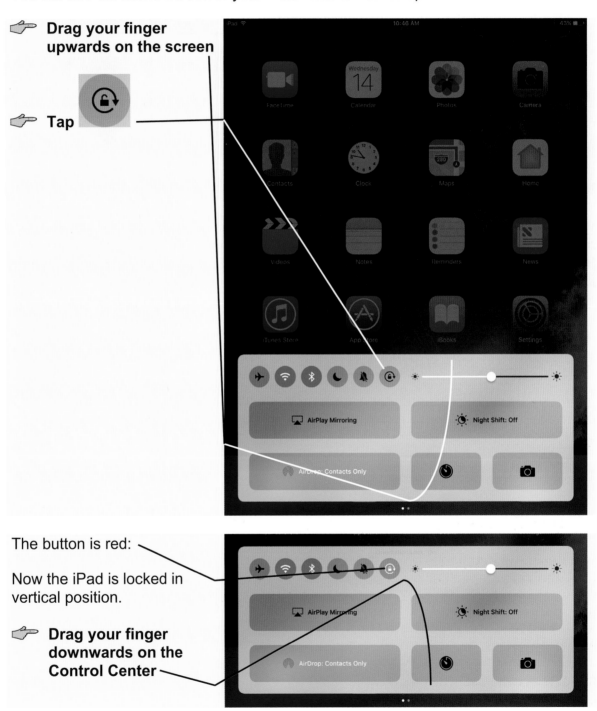

The button is red:

Now the iPad is locked in vertical position.

☞ **Drag your finger downwards on the Control Center**

☞ Turn the iPad across to a vertical position

Now you will see that the image on the iPad screen is not rotating. If you want the iPad screen to rotate:

☞ **Drag your finger upwards on the screen**

☞ **Tap**

☞ **Drag your finger downwards on the Control Center**

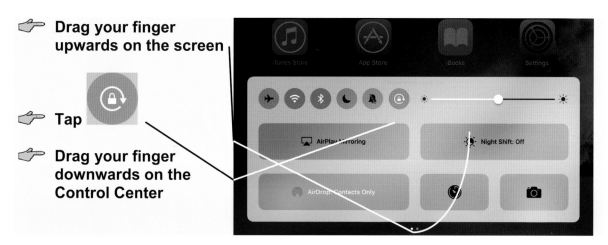

You can adapt the background (wallpaper) of the lock and home screens of your iPad to your own taste, by selecting a different background. You can also adjust the brightness of the screen. Here is how to do that. On the home screen:

☞ **Tap** Settings

☞ **Tap** AA **Display & Brightr**

☞ **Drag the slider**

By default, the brightness of the screen is automatically adapted to the light of the environment. This is indicated by the ⬤ button:

You can also adjust how the text looks on the iPad:

Here is how to change the wallpaper:

☞ **Tap** Wallpaper

☞ **Tap**
Choose a New Wallpa

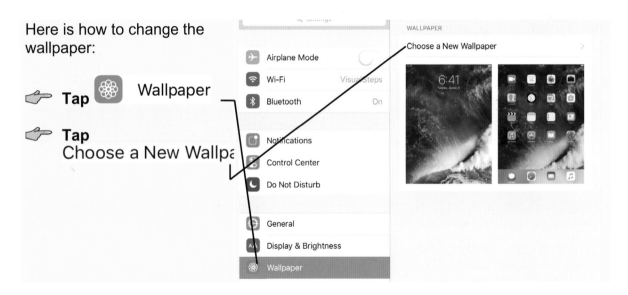

Select a wallpaper from one of the standard still wallpapers:

☞ **Tap the wallpaper by**
Stills

If you do not see this window:

☞ **Continue with the next**
step

☞ **If necessary, drag the**
page upwards

☞ **Tap a wallpaper, for**

instance

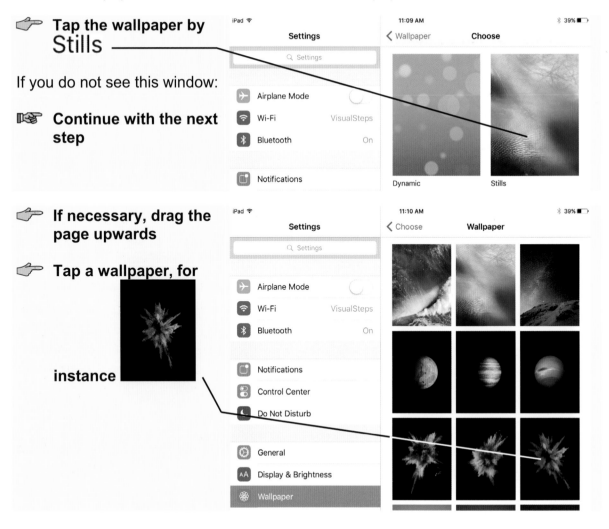

You will see a preview of this wallpaper. Now you can decide if you want to use this wallpaper for the lock screen, the home screen, or both:

☞ **Tap**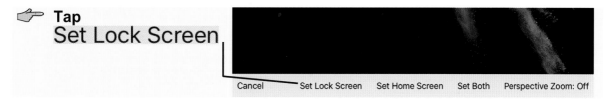

Now you will be back at the *Brightness and Wallpaper* screen. Check to see if the wallpaper of the lock screen has indeed been changed.
Here is how to close the *Settings* app:

☞ **Press the Home button**

Put the iPad in sleep mode:

☞ **Press the Sleep/Wake button**

☞ **Wake the iPad up from sleep mode** $\mathcal{G}\mathcal{G}^2$

Now you will see that the wallpaper of the lock screen has been changed.

1.6 Using the Keyboard

Your iPad contains a useful onscreen keyboard, which will appear whenever you need to type something. For example, if you want to take notes in the *Notes* app. Here is how to open the *Notes* app:

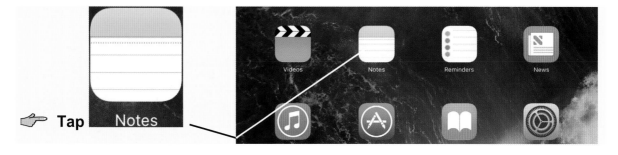

☞ **Tap** Notes

When you open *Notes* for the first time you might see a screen with information about the app.

☞ **If necessary, tap**

You might see a message about *iCoud*. In this example we will not turn on *iCloud* at this moment:

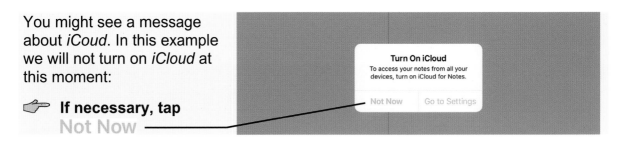

☞ **If necessary, tap**
Not Now

You will open a new note:

☞ **Tap**

You will see a new, blank notes page with the onscreen keyboard. The onscreen keyboard works almost the same way as a regular keyboard. You simply tap the keys instead of pressing them. Just give it a try:

If you do not see the onscreen keyboard:

☞ **Tap the notes page**

⌨ **Type:**
This is a test.

Above the keyboard you see options from the predictive text engine:
You will also see options to change the format of the text and to add a photo or video:

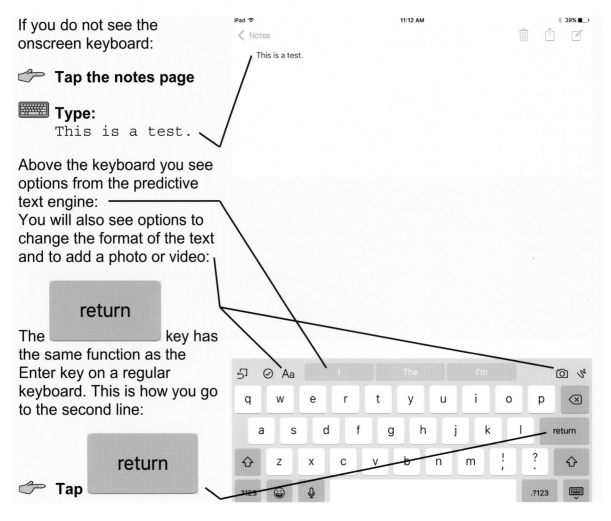

return

The ⬚⬚⬚ key has the same function as the Enter key on a regular keyboard. This is how you go to the second line:

return

☞ **Tap**

Tip

Comma, period, exclamation mark, question mark
The comma and the exclamation mark share a key on the keyboard, just as the period and the question mark. This is how to type the symbol on the lower part of the key, for example, the period:

 **Tap**

And this is how to type the symbol on the upper part of the key, for example, the question mark:

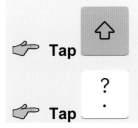 **Tap**

 Tap

 Tip

Capital letters
New sentences will automatically begin with a capital letter. This is how to type a capital letter in the middle of a sentence:

 **Tap**

☞ **Tap the character**

In the standard view of the keyboard, you will not see any numerals. If you want to use numerals, you need to change the keyboard view:

☞ **Tap**

The keyboard view will change and you will see the numerals and some additional special characters:

Type the beginning of an easy sum:

 **Type:** 12-10

To type the '=' sign you need to use the third view of the onscreen keyboard:

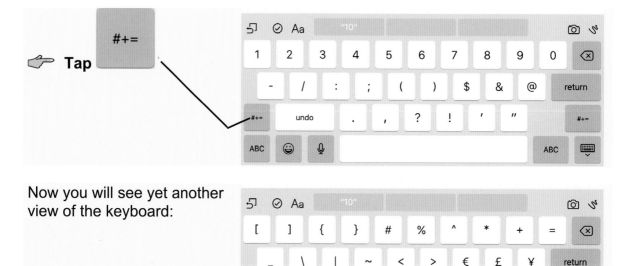

Now you will see yet another view of the keyboard:

Finish the sum:

 **Type:** =

To type the answer, you will again need the numerals. This is how you can return to the keyboard view with the numerals:

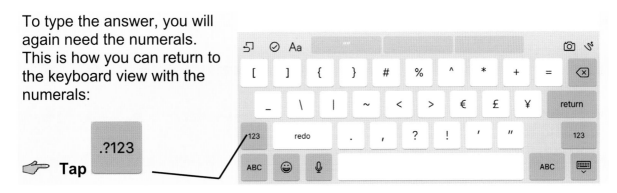

☞ **Tap** .?123

Now you will see the keyboard with the numerals and special characters once again:

Type: 3

If you have made a typing error, you can correct this with the Backspace key:

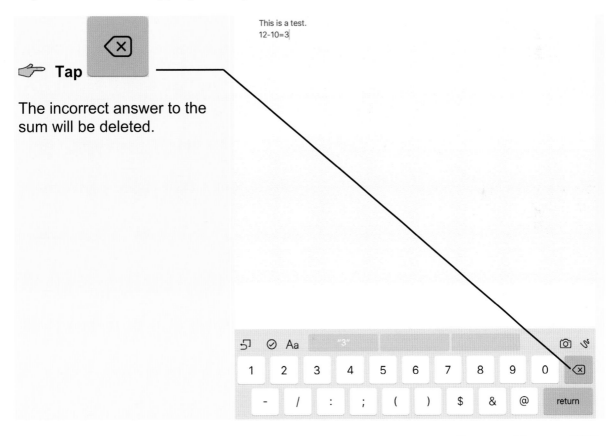

☞ **Tap**

The incorrect answer to the sum will be deleted.

This is a test.
12-10=3

Type: 2

Now the answer is correct.

☞ **Tap**

💡 **Tip**

Return to the standard keyboard view
If you are in the view with the numerals and special characters, you can go back to the standard onscreen keyboard with the letters:

☞ **Tap**

It is also possible to change the format of the text:

☞ **Tap** Aa

You will see the formatting options:

☞ **Tap** **Heading**

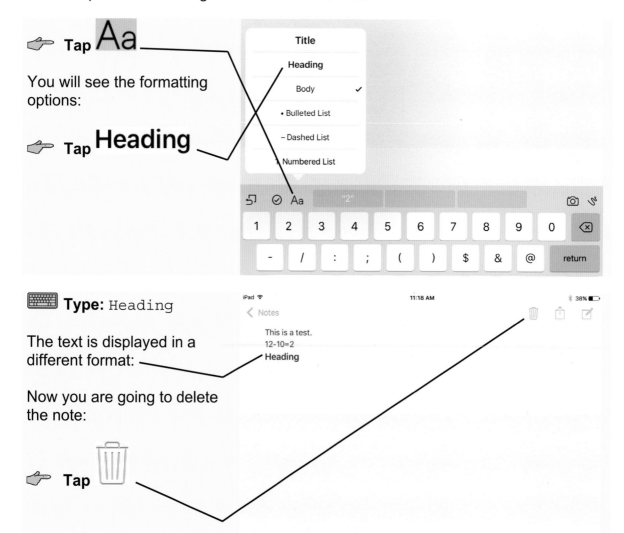

⌨ **Type:** Heading

The text is displayed in a different format:

Now you are going to delete the note:

☞ **Tap** 🗑

A message appears. Deleted notes will be moved to the *Recently Deleted* folder. They will be permanently deleted after 30 days:

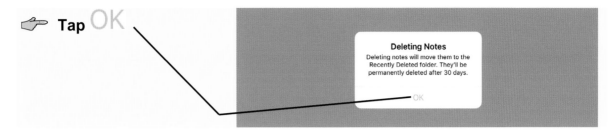

☞ Tap OK

You can open the *Recently Deleted* folder like this:

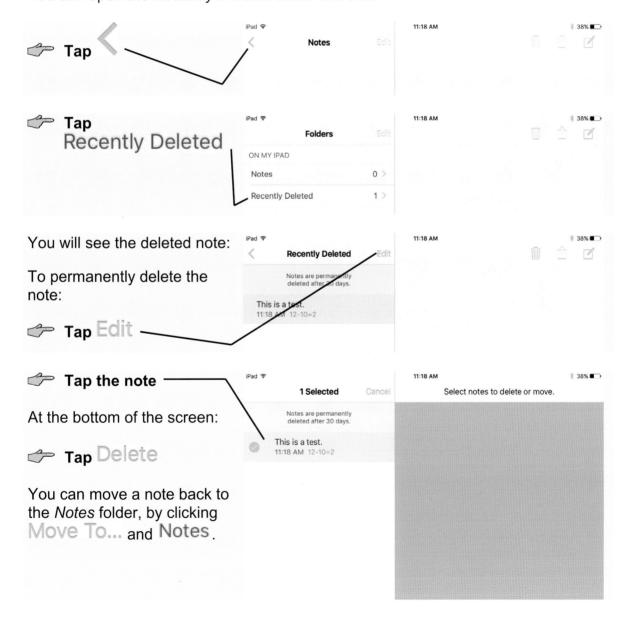

☞ Tap <

☞ Tap Recently Deleted

You will see the deleted note:

To permanently delete the note:

☞ Tap Edit

☞ Tap the note

At the bottom of the screen:

☞ Tap Delete

You can move a note back to the *Notes* folder, by clicking Move To... and Notes.

The note has been permanently deleted. Now you can close the *Notes* app:

☞ **Press the Home button**

By now, you have practiced some of the basic operations and touch actions. There are more touch actions to learn, such as scrolling and zooming in and out. We will discuss these actions in the chapters where you need to use them to perform specific tasks.

1.7 Connecting to the Internet Through Wi-Fi

You may have already connected to the Internet while you were setting up your iPad. But it can happen that the default network is not available. Perhaps you are using the iPad at a different location or your own default network is temporarily down for some reason. If you have access to a wireless network, you can connect to the Internet with that.

➟ **Please note:**

To perform the following actions, you will need to have access to a wireless network (Wi-Fi). If Wi-Fi access is not (yet) available, you can just read through this section.

Now, go back to the *Settings* app you used in previous steps:

☞ **Open the *Settings* app** **6**

To connect to a Wi-Fi network:

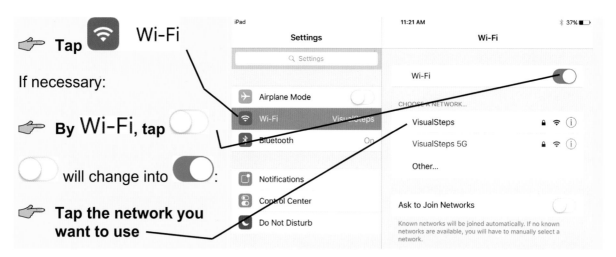

If you see a padlock icon next to the network name, for instance
VisualSteps 🔒 📶 (i) , you will need a
password to gain access to this network.

⌨️ **Type the password**

👉 **Tap** Join

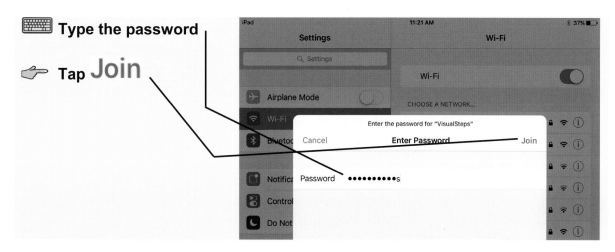

You will be connected to the wireless network:

The 📶 icon on the status
bar indicates that there is a
connection with a wireless
network: ————

You will see a check mark
next to the selected network,
in this case
✓ **VisualSteps**.

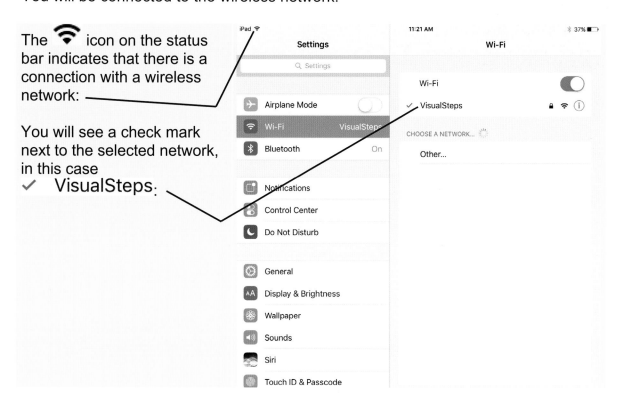

In future, the connection with known wireless networks will be made automatically as soon as you enable Wi-Fi. You can check this out for yourself by disabling Wi-Fi first:

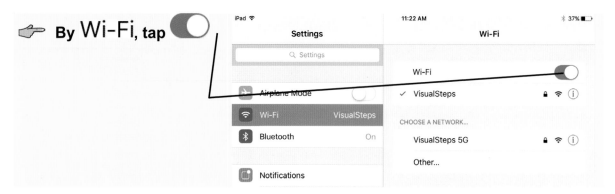

Now, Wi-Fi is disabled and you will see that the button looks like this ⬭. The 🛜 icon has disappeared from the status bar.

Wi-Fi will be enabled once again.

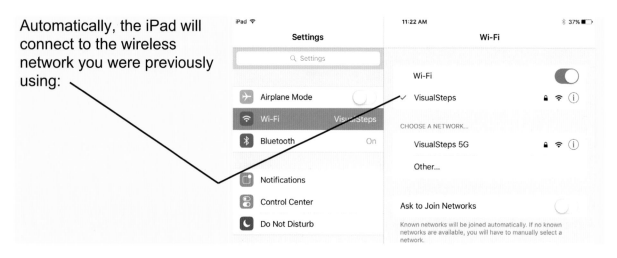

☞ **If you want, you can disable Wi-Fi again**

 **Press the Home button**

1.8 Connecting to the Internet Through the Mobile Data Network

If your iPad is also suitable for the mobile data network, you can connect it to a 3G or 4G network. The 4G network is available in the United States and most of the other countries. Connecting to the mobile data network can be useful when you are in a location where there is no Wi-Fi. You will need to have a micro SIM card with a data subscription or contract, or a prepaid mobile Internet card. If you do not (yet) have these items, you can just read through this section.

 Tip

Mobile Internet
Since the iPad does not have a simlock, you are free to select a mobile Internet provider. Many providers, such as AT&T, Verizon Wireless and British Telecom offer data subscriptions for the iPad, including a micro SIM card. For prepaid mobile Internet plans you can use Virgin Mobile USA, AT&T, Verizon and Vodafone, among others.

The prices and conditions are subject to regular changes. Check out the websites of various providers for more information.

An iPad that is suitable for Wi-Fi and 3G or 4G will be fitted with a micro SIM card tray.

Remove the micro SIM card tray, by using the SIM eject tool (included in the packaging):

If you do not have this tool, you can also use the end of a small paperclip.

Source: User Guide iPad

Place the micro SIM card in the micro SIM card tray

Insert the micro SIM card tray into the iPad

The connection with the mobile data network will start up automatically.

As soon as the connection
has been made, you will see
the signal strength and the
name of the mobile network
provider in use: ———————

If the iPad status bar displays the 3G (**3G**) or 4G (**4G**), EDGE (**E**), or

GPRS (**O**) symbols, the device is connected to the Internet through the mobile data
network.
If necessary, you can temporarily disable the Internet connection through the mobile
data network. This way, you can prevent your children or grandchildren from playing
online games on your iPad and using up all of your prepaid credit. Here is how to do
that:

☞ **Open the *Settings* app** 𝒟𝒟⁶

☞ **Tap**  Cellular Data

☞ **By** Cellular Data, **tap** 🔘

Now you have disabled the
cellular data:

In the status bar, you will just
see iPad:

This means that there is no
Internet connection through a
mobile data network.

🖐 **Please note:**
If you are using cellular data, by default, the Data roaming function will be disabled.
Data Roaming means that you can use the network of a different Internet service
provider, whenever the network of your own provider is out of reach. If you enable
this option abroad, this may result in extremely high costs.

You can activate the cellular network again:

 By Cellular Data, **tap**

 Press the Home button

 Tip

Update for provider settings

When you connect the iPad to the computer, you may see a message in *iTunes* about an update for the carrier settings. These updates for carrier settings are small files (approximately 10 kB) that are downloaded in *iTunes* and installed onto your iPad Wi-Fi + 3G or 4G.

The update is usually an improvement to the way in which your iPad connects to the wireless data network of your provider (carrier). You should install the most recent updates for these carrier settings as soon as they are available.

 Follow the onscreen instructions

1.9 Connecting the iPad to the Computer

You can connect the iPad to the computer. When it is connected, you can use *iTunes* to sync data, music, videos and more from your computer to the iPad. You can even do this wirelessly with *iTunes Wi-Fi Sync*.

 Please note:

If you have not yet installed *iTunes* onto your computer, it is time to do so now. If you go to *Appendix B Download and Install iTunes* at the end of this book you can read how to do this.

You will start the *iTunes* program on your computer, laptop or notebook. On the desktop of a *Windows 10* or *8.1* computer a shortcut is placed:

⊕ **Double-click** iTunes

On a *Windows 7* computer:

⊕ **Click**

Most likely you will see a window asking you to accept the software license agreement.

⊕ **Click** Agree

You may see a slightly different window on your computer. But this will not affect the following operations.

☞ **Close the window** ✂️**11**

Now you see the *iTunes* Start screen:

⊕ **Click** No Thanks

You may see a different window. This will not affect the following operations.

Now you are going to connect the iPad to your computer. This is how you do it:

☞ **Connect the broad end of the white Dock Connector-to-USB-cable to the iPad**

☞ **Connect the other end of the cable to one of the USB ports on your computer**

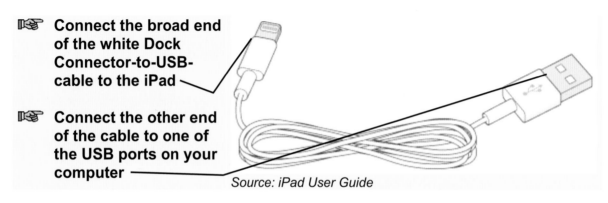

Source: iPad User Guide

In *Windows 8.1* it is possible that a small message appears in the top right of your screen. In *Windows 10* this message might appear at the bottom right of the screen:

You can ignore this message.

In *Windows 7* it is possible that a small message appears in the bottom right of your screen, indicating that a device driver is being installed.

This takes just a few moments and then your iPad is ready for use:

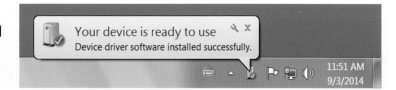

Maybe you will now see the *AutoPlay* window:

☞ **If necessary, close the *AutoPlay* window** 🦶**11**

☞ **If necessary, unlock the iPad, if it is locked with a lock code**

On *iTunes* on the computer:

⊕ **If necessary, click** Continue

After a while you will probably see this window:

⊕ **Click** Continue

If you see a different window, it will probably be the window at the bottom of this page, or the window in the Help frame on the next page. In that case, continue with the relevant window.

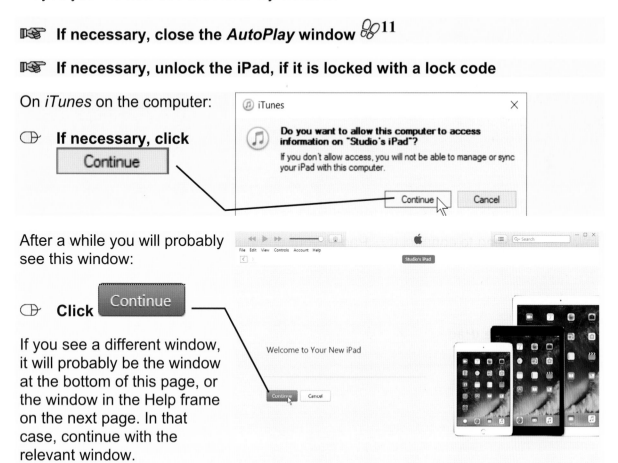

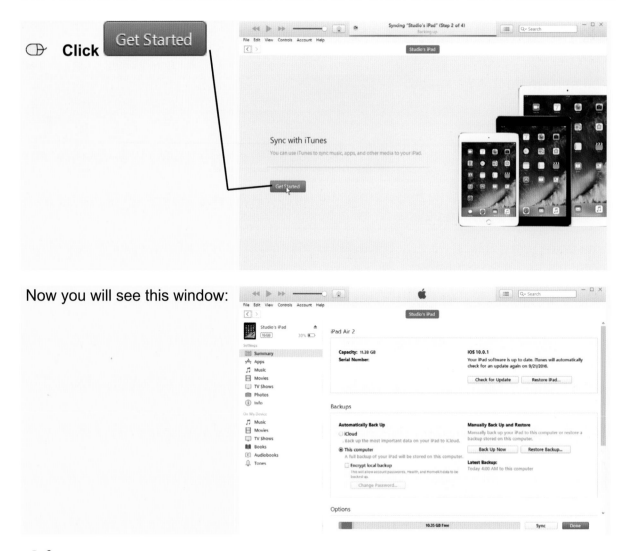

⊕ **Click** Get Started

Now you will see this window:

HELP! I see a different window.

If the iPad has previously already been connected to the computer you will see a different window:

At the top right of the window:

⊕ **Click** ☐

Now you will see the window described on the previous page and you can continue executing the operations on the next page.

HELP! I see a window with a registration message.

If you connect your iPad for the first time, you may even see a different window altogether. You will be asked to register the iPad. It is up to you whether you want to register the iPad; if you do, then just follow the operations in the various windows.

 HELP! My iPad does not appear at all.

If you do not see your iPad appear in *iTunes*, you can try out the solutions below.

☞ **Check whether the plugs of the Dock Connector-to-USB-cable have been correctly connected**

☞ **Charge the iPad's battery if the battery level is low**

☞ **Disconnect any other USB devices from the computer and connect the iPad to a different USB port on your computer. Do not use the USB ports on the keyboard, on the monitor, or on a USB hub**

☞ **Unlock the iPad, if it is locked with a lock code**

If the iPad is still not recognized by *iTunes*:

☞ **Re-start the computer and re-connect the iPad to your computer**

If this does not work, you can re-start the iPad. This is how you do it:

☞ **Keep the Sleep mode button (see section *1.1 Turning the iPad On or Waking it Up From Sleep Mode*) depressed until you see a red slider on your screen**

☞ **Drag this slider to the right, to switch off the iPad**

☞ **Once again, keep the Sleep mode button depressed until you see the *Apple* logo appear**

☞ **Download and install (once more) the most recent *iTunes* version from the www.apple.com/itunes/download website**

☞ **Try to re-connect your iPad, preferably to a different USB port**

Assign an easily identifiable name to your iPad:

iTunes suggests giving your iPad the same name as your user account. You can change this:

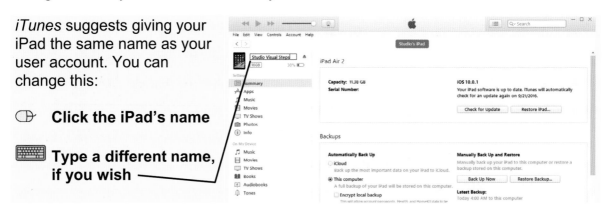

☞ **Click the iPad's name**

⌨ **Type a different name, if you wish**

Although *iTunes* does not automatically synchronize tracks, photos, or other items if you have not started such an operation yourself before, the standard setting is that *iTunes* will still start synchronizing by itself when you connect it to the computer. This happened when you connected the iPad to the pc the first time as well. In that case, no data has been transferred to the iPad, but only a backup copy of the iPad has been created.

During synchronization, at the top of the window a progress bar indicating the progress of the synchronizing operation is shown:

You can continue when you see the Apple logo:

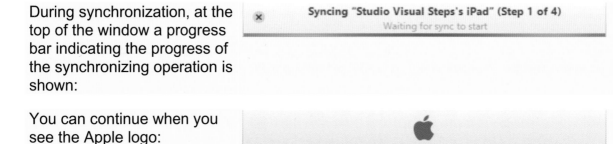

Synchronizing means the content of your iPad will be matched to the content of your *Library*. Tracks, videos, and apps that no longer appear in your *iTunes Library* will be removed from your iPad during synchronization. You will be able to manage the content of your iPad more easily when you disable the automatic synchronization altogether and manually start the synchronization operation whenever you feel like it. You are going to check the settings for automatic synchronization:

☞ Click Edit

☞ Click Preferences...

You will see a window with various sections:

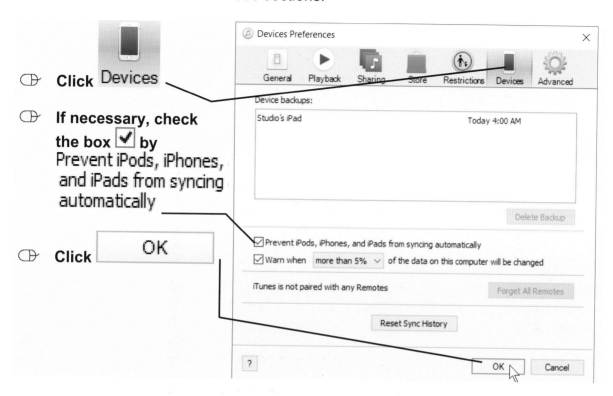

⊕ **Click Devices**

⊕ **If necessary, check the box ☑ by** Prevent iPods, iPhones, and iPads from syncing automatically

⊕ **Click OK**

Now you will see the *Summary* tab:

This iPad's software is up-to-date:

In this example a backup copy of the iPad is made on the computer. You can also make and store a backup copy to *iCloud*:

Here you see the available capacity of the iPad:

☞ **If necessary, drag the scroll box downwards**

☑ **Manually manage music and videos** means that music files and videos will not be automatically synchronized:

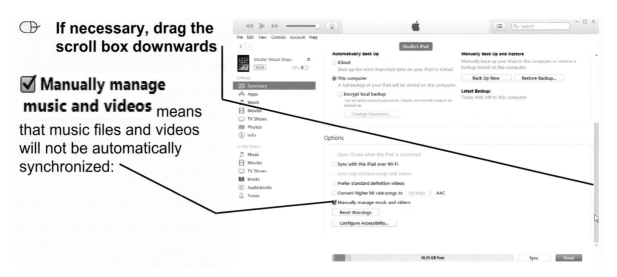

💡 **Tip**

Wireless synchronization of the iPad with iTunes
You have attached your iPad to your computer using the so-called Dock Connector-to-USB cable. You can synchronize your iPad wirelessly using *iTunes*.

On the *Summary* tab:

☞ **Check the box ☑ by Sync with this iPad**

☞ **Click** Apply

From now on, every time the computer and the iPad are connected to the same network, the iPad will appear in *iTunes*.

1.10 Safely Disconnecting the iPad

You can disconnect the iPad from your computer any time you want, unless the device is being synchronized with your computer.

If the synchronization is in progress, you will see this message at the top of the *iTunes* window:

When you see this, you can
disconnect the iPad:

This is how you disconnect your iPad from *iTunes*:

By your iPad's name:

⊕ **Click**

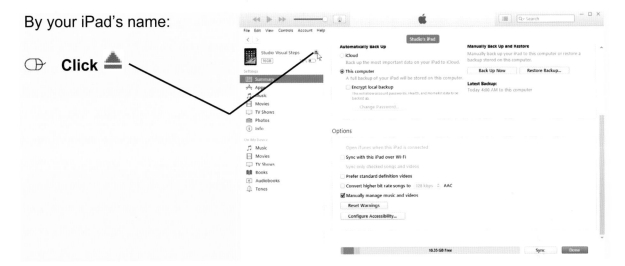

In a few seconds, the iPad is
no longer shown in the
iTunes window.

You can safely disconnect the
iPad.

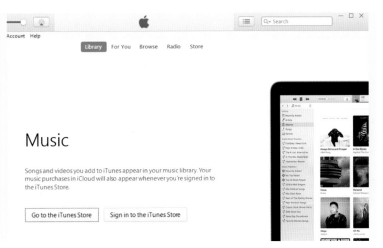

☞ **Disconnect the iPad**

You can now close *iTunes*:

☞ **Close *iTunes*** ✂️11

1.11 Putting the iPad to Sleep or Turning it Off

When you stop using the iPad, you can either turn it off or put it to sleep. When the iPad is in sleep mode, it is not turned off but will use less energy. If you have disabled Wi-Fi or the mobile data network, the iPad will use hardly any energy at all. This is how you put your iPad to sleep:

☞ **Press the Sleep/Wake button**

The screen will turn dark.

If you want to turn the iPad off completely, do this:

☞ **Press the Sleep/Wake button until you see the screen below**

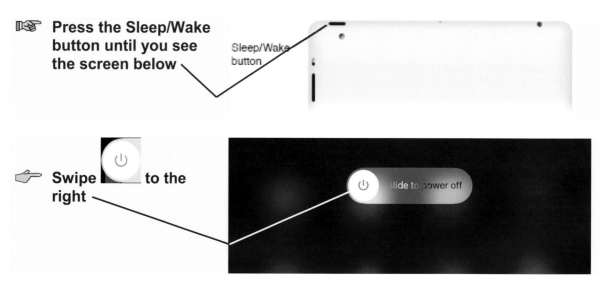

☞ **Swipe** ⏻ **to the right**

The screen will turn dark and the iPad is turned off. In future, you can decide whether you want to put the iPad in sleep mode, or turn it off.

In this chapter you have learned how to turn the iPad on and off, connect and disconnect it to the computer and how to gain access to the Internet. You have also taken a closer look at some of the main components of the iPad and performed basic operations for using the device.

The exercises on the following page will let you practice these operations. In the *Background Information* and the *Tips* you will find additional information for this chapter.

1.12 Exercises

To be able to quickly apply the things you have learned, you can work through these exercises. Have you forgotten how to do something? Use the numbers next to the footsteps 𝒪𝒪¹ to look up the item in the appendix *How Do I Do That Again?*

Exercise 1: Turn On, Sleep Mode and Turn Off

In this exercise you are going to repeat turning the iPad on and off, and putting it into sleep mode.

☞ If necessary, wake up the iPad from sleep mode, or turn it on. 𝒪𝒪²

☞ Put the iPad into sleep mode. 𝒪𝒪¹

☞ Wake up the iPad up from sleep mode. 𝒪𝒪²

☞ Turn off the iPad. 𝒪𝒪¹

Exercise 2: The Onscreen Keyboard

In this exercise you are going to type a short text with the onscreen keyboard.

☞ Turn on the iPad. 𝒪𝒪²

☞ Open the *Notes* app. 𝒪𝒪³

☞ Type the following text: 𝒪𝒪⁴
```
The distance between New York and Boston is 189 miles. The
distance between New York and Buffalo is 395 miles. How
long would that take by car?
```

☞ Delete the note. 𝒪𝒪⁵

☞ If you want, put the iPad into sleep mode, or turn it off. 𝒪𝒪¹

1.13 Background Information

Dictionary

Airplane mode	If your iPad is in this mode, you will not have access to the Internet and will not be able to use Bluetooth devices.
App	Short for *application*, a program for the iPad.
App icons	Colored icons on the iPad, used to open various apps.
App Store	Online store where you can download apps, for free or at a price.
Auto-Lock	A function that makes sure the iPad is turned off and locked after two minutes (by default), if it is not in use.
Bluetooth	Bluetooth is an open wireless technology standard for exchanging data over short distances. With Bluetooth you can connect a wireless keyboard or headset to the iPad, for example.
Data roaming	Using the wireless network of another provider, when your own carrier's network is not available. Using this option abroad may lead to high costs.
EDGE	Short for *Enhanced Data Rates for GSM Evolution*. It allows improved data transmission rates as a backward-compatible extension of GSM. In the UK, EDGE coverage is reasonably widespread and in the USA it is pretty common.
GPRS	Short for *General Packet Radio Service*, a technology that is an extension of the existing gsm network. This technology makes it possible to transfer wireless data more efficiently, faster and cheaper.
Gyroscope	A sensor that measures in which direction the iPad is moving. Some games use this function.

- Continue on the next page -

Home button

, the button that lets you return to the home screen. You can also use this button to wake the iPad up from sleep.

Home screen The screen with the app icons. This is what you see when you turn the iPad on or unlock it.

iPad The iPad is a portable multimedia device (a tablet computer) made by Apple. The iPad is a computer with a multi-touch screen.

iTunes A program that lets you manage the content of your iPad. But you can also use *iTunes* to listen to music files, watch movies, and import CDs. In *iTunes* you will also find the *iTunes Store* and the *App Store*.

iTunes Store Online store where you can download and purchase music, movies, tv shows, podcasts, audio books and more.

Library The *iTunes* section where you can store and manage your music, movies, podcasts and apps.

Location Services Location Services lets apps such as *Maps* gather and use data showing your location. For example, if you are connected to the Internet and have turned on Location Services, data about the location will be added to the photos and videos you take with your iPad.

Lock screen The screen you see when you turn the iPad on. Before you can use the iPad, you need to unlock it by swiping the slider.

Micro SIM card The small SIM card that is used in the iPad Wi-Fi + 3G or 4G, for wireless data transfer. This SIM card is also called a 3FF SIM card (Third Form Factor).

Notes An app with which you can take notes.

Podcast An episodic program, delivered through the Internet. Podcast episodes can be audio or video files and can be downloaded with the *iTunes Store*.

Rotation lock This function takes care of locking the screen display when you rotate the iPad.

- Continue on the next page -

Simlock

A simlock is a capability built into a cell phone or another wireless device that is used to restrict the use of the SIM card for that device. This lock prevents the user from using SIM cards from different providers in the device. The reason many network providers SIM lock their phones is that they offer phones at a discount to customers in exchange for a contract to pay for the use of the network for a specified time period, usually between one and three years. The iPad Wi-Fi + 3G or 4G is simlock free.

Sleep mode

You can lock the iPad by putting it into sleep mode if you do not use it for a while. When the iPad is locked, it will not react when you touch the screen. But you can still keep on playing music. And you can still use the volume buttons. You can activate or deactivate sleep mode with the Sleep/Wake button.

Synchronize

Literally, this means: equalizing. If you sync your iPad with your *iTunes Library*, the content of your iPad will be made equal to the content of your *Library* on your computer. If you delete files or apps from your *Library*, these will also be deleted from the iPad, when you synchronize it again.

Tablet computer

A tablet computer is a computer without casing and a separate keyboard. It is operated by a multi-touch screen.

VPN

Short for *Virtual Private Network*. With VPN you can gain access to private secure networks through the Internet, such as your company network.

Wi-Fi

Wireless network for the Internet.

3G

3G is the third generation of standards and technology for cell phones. Because of its higher speed, 3G offers extensive possibilities. For example, with 3G you can use services such as making phone calls via the Internet, among others.

4G

4G is the fourth generation of standards and technology for cell phones. It is almost ten times the speed of 3G and will offer many new possibilities. 4G is available in the United States and most other countries.

Source: User Guide iPad, Wikipedia

1.14 Tips

 Tip

Setting up Touch ID

Most new models of iPads are equipped with Touch ID. On the device, the Home button contains a fingerprint scanner that allows you to do different things. First, you can quickly unlock your iPad with your finger. Also, you can quickly log on to apps that are suitable for that purpose. Touch ID can be set during the installation of an iPad. But it can also be set up later, by the *Settings* app:

 Tap Settings

 Tap 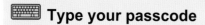 Touch ID & Passcode

Do your *Settings* only offer the option  Touch ID? That means that Touch ID is not available on your device. Only the newer iPad models are equipped with a fingerprint scanner and Touch ID.

⌨ **Type your passcode**

 **Tap** Add a Fingerprint...

Now you see some information on adding a fingerprint. You can proceed:

☞ **Put your finger, for example your thumb, on** ◯

iOS scans your finger. The idea is that you lift your finger briefly and rotate a little when the device vibrates. The red lines in the signed fingerprint indicate how much of your fingerprint is scanned already. Unfortunately, we cannot show any pictures of this process.

☞ **Tap Continue**

iOS will proceed with the scanning. Again, you have to lift and rotate your finger briefly when the device vibrates.

☞ **Tap Continue**

- Continue on the next page -

The fingerprint is now added, and is called 'Finger 1':

The fingerprint is now ready to use. In the future you can unlock your iPad after you press the Home button.

If you wish, you can add more fingers by tapping **Add a Fingerprint...**, from your other hand for example.

 Tip

Auto-Lock

By default, the iPad will lock and go into sleep mode after two minutes, if you do not use it, or it is left unattended. This setting will save energy, but maybe you would prefer to keep the iPad on for a little longer:

☞ **Open the *Settings* app** $\mathscr{GG}^6$

☞ **If necessary, tap**
  AA **Display & Brightn**

☞ **Tap Auto-Lock**

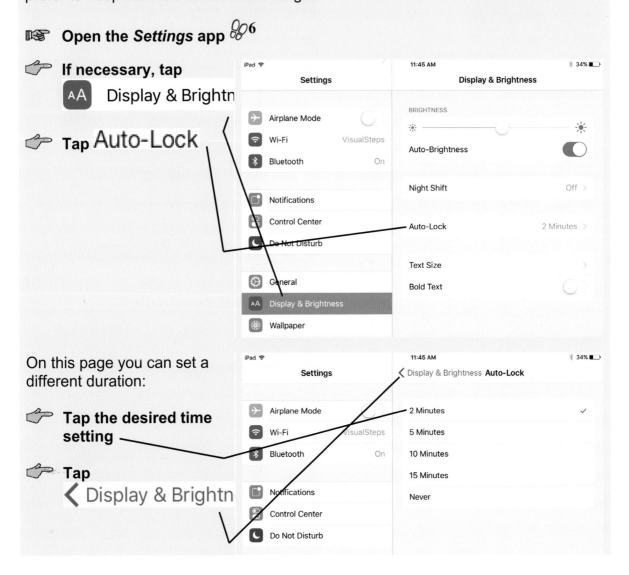

On this page you can set a different duration:

☞ **Tap the desired time setting**

☞ **Tap**
  ‹ Display & Brightn

💡 Tip

Change passcode or turn off passcode protection for unlocking the iPad
You can change the four-digit passcode into a six-digit numeric code, a custom alphanumeric or custom numeric code.

☞ **Open the *Settings* app** 6

👉 **Tap**
   🔲 Touch ID & Passco

⌨ **Type your passcode**

👉 **Tap**
   Change Passcode

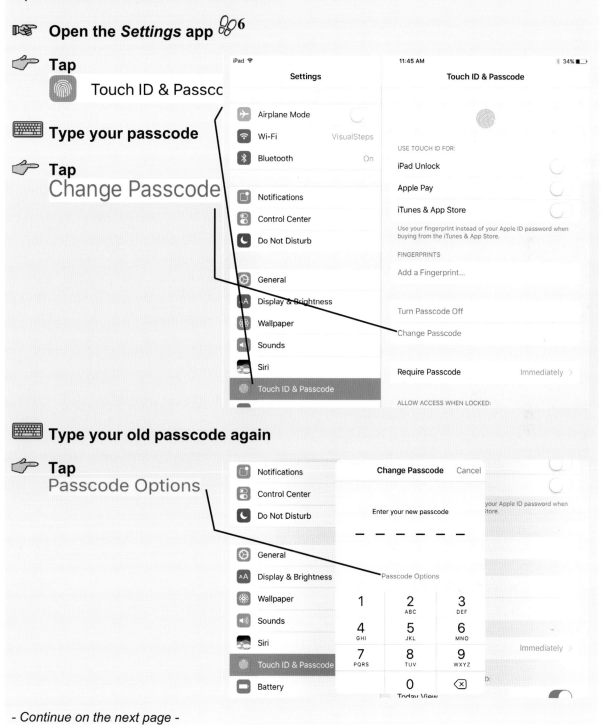

⌨ **Type your old passcode again**

👉 **Tap**
   Passcode Options

- Continue on the next page -

☞ **Tap**
4-Digit Numeric Co

⌨ **Type a new four-digit passcode**

⌨ **Type the four-digit code again**

The passcode has changed. If you are annoyed by having to enter the passcode every time you unlock the iPad, you can turn this option off, like this:

☞ **Tap**
Turn Passcode Of

⌨ **Type your passcode again**

Now you no longer need to enter a code if you want to unlock the device.

💡 **Tip**

Type faster
This is how you can quickly type a period and a blank space at the end of a sentence:

☞ **Double-tap the space bar twice, quickly**

Tip
Enable Caps Lock
If you only want to use capitals:

☞ **Double-tap**

The key will turn into ____. Now you will only see capital letters when you type something.

To return to the normal operation of this key:

☞ **Tap** ____

Tip
Letters with accent marks
You will not find letters with accent marks on the onscreen keyboards. But you can still type them:

☞ **For example, press the** ____ **key**

You will see a small window with various accents marks for the letter e, such as é and è.

☞ **Move your finger from the** ____ **key to the e key with the accent mark you want to use**

Please note: when you release the ____ key first, the window will disappear.

☞ **Release the key**

The e with the accent mark will appear in the text.

💡 Tip

Larger keys

If you disable the rotation lock and position the iPad horizontally, the keys on the onscreen keyboard will become larger:

You can tap to close the menu on the left:

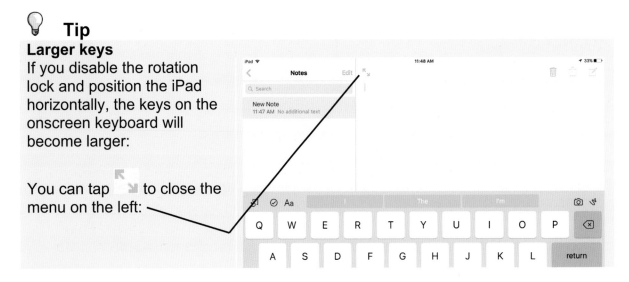

💡 Tip

Backup copy

If you chose not to synchronize your iPad with *iTunes* each time you connect it to your computer, you will not be creating an automatic backup. A backup will contain the iPad's system settings, app data, Camera Roll album, and more. Things that you put on your iPad by way of *iTunes*, such as music, movies, podcasts and more remain in the *iTunes* data folders. It is important that you backup your computer now and then as well. You can make a backup of the iPad by doing the following:

☞ **Connect the iPad to the computer**

⊕ **If necessary, click** ▯

⊕ **Click**

      Back Up Now

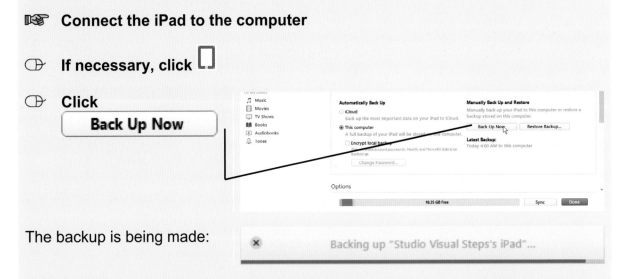

The backup is being made:

      ✕   Backing up "Studio Visual Steps's iPad"...

It is also possible to create a backup through *iCloud*. You can make the settings for that via the app *Settings*. Then tap ☁ iCloud and make sure the 🔄 Backup option is on.

2. Sending Emails with Your iPad

Your iPad contains a standard email app called *Mail.*

With *Mail* you can send, receive and compose email messages, just like on your regular computer. In this chapter you can read how to adjust the settings for your email account. We will explain how to do this for Internet service providers (ISP), such as Charter, Comcast, Cox, AT & T or Verizon and also for web-based email services such as *Outlook.com* or *Hotmail*. If you use multiple email accounts, you can configure each one to work with the *Mail* program.

Composing an email on your iPad is quite easy. You will have lots of opportunity to practice this by working though this chapter. You will learn how to select, copy, cut, and paste items using the iPad screen. You will also become familiar with the autocorrect function that is built into the iPad.

Later on this chapter, we will explain how to send, receive and delete email messages.

In this chapter you will learn how to:

- set up an email account;
- set up an *Outlook.com*, *Hotmail* or *Gmail* account;
- send an email;
- receive an email;
- reply an email;
- move an email to the *Recycle Bin*;
- permanently delete an email.

2.1 Setting Up an Email Account

Before you can start sending emails, you need to adjust the settings on your iPad so that it can work with at least one email account. In this section, you can read how to do this for your own Internet service provider, such as Charter, Comcast, Cox, AT & T, EarthLink or Verizon. To do this, you will need the information about the incoming and outgoing mail server, the user name and password given to you by your provider.

☞ **Wake up the iPad from sleep mode or turn it on** 𝒪𝒪²

☞ **Open the *Settings* app** 𝒪𝒪⁶

☞ **Drag upwards over the settings**

☞ **Tap** ✉ **Mail**

☞ **Tap Accounts**

☞ **Tap Add Account**

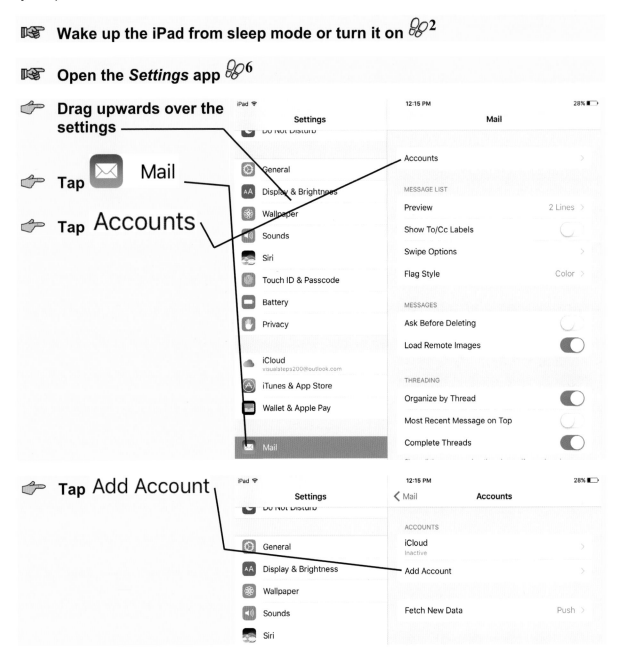

Please note:

If you have a *Hotmail* account, you can skip this section and continue further in *section 2.2 Setting Up an Outlook.com, Hotmail or Gmail Account.*

You can choose from various well-known web-based providers. If you have an account with one of these popular providers, you only need your user name and password. If your provider is not included in this list:

☞ **Tap** Other

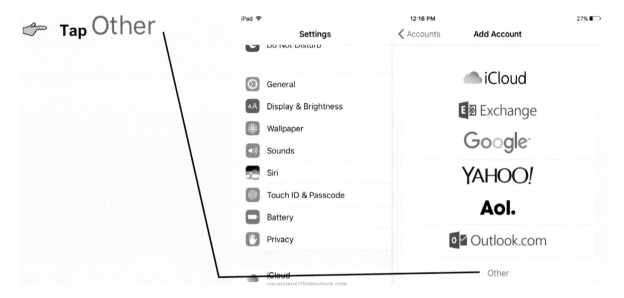

You can now add an email account:

☞ **Tap** Add Mail Accoun

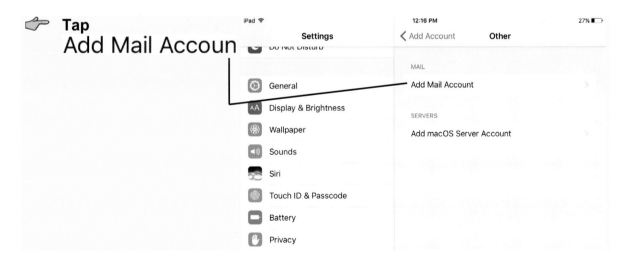

Now you will see a screen where you need to enter some basic information concerning your email account. To do this, you can use the onscreen keyboard from the iPad:

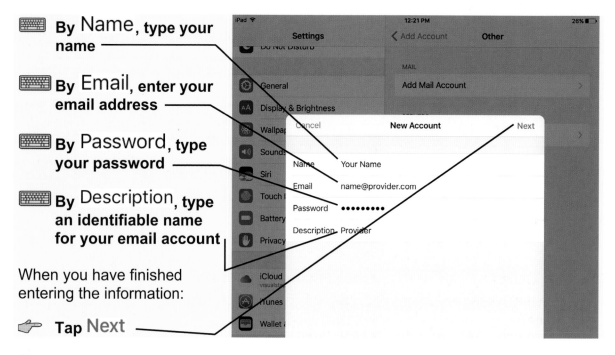

By Name, type your name

By Email, enter your email address

By Password, type your password

By Description, type an identifiable name for your email account

When you have finished entering the information:

☞ Tap Next

   Tip

Onscreen keyboard
Have you forgotten how to use the iPad onscreen keyboard? Go back to *section 1.6 Using the Keyboard*.

Now you can select whether you want to set your email account as an *IMAP* or a *POP* account:

- IMAP stands for *Internet Message Access Protocol*. This means that you will manage your messages on the mail server. Messages that have been read will be stored on the mail server, until you delete them. IMAP is useful if you manage your emails from multiple computers. Your mailbox will look the same on each computer. When you create folders for organizing your email messages, you will see the same folders on the other computers as well as your iPad. If you want to use IMAP, you will need to set your email account as an IMAP account on all the other computers too.
- POP stands for *Post Office Protocol*, the traditional way of managing email. When you retrieve your messages, they will immediately be deleted from the server. Although, on your iPad the default setting for POP accounts is for a copy to be stored on the server, after you have retrieved a message. This means you will still be able to retrieve the message on your other computer(s). In the *Tips* at the back of this chapter you can read how to modify these settings.

By INCOMING MAIL SERVER:

By Host Name type the name of the incoming mail server

By User Name type the user name

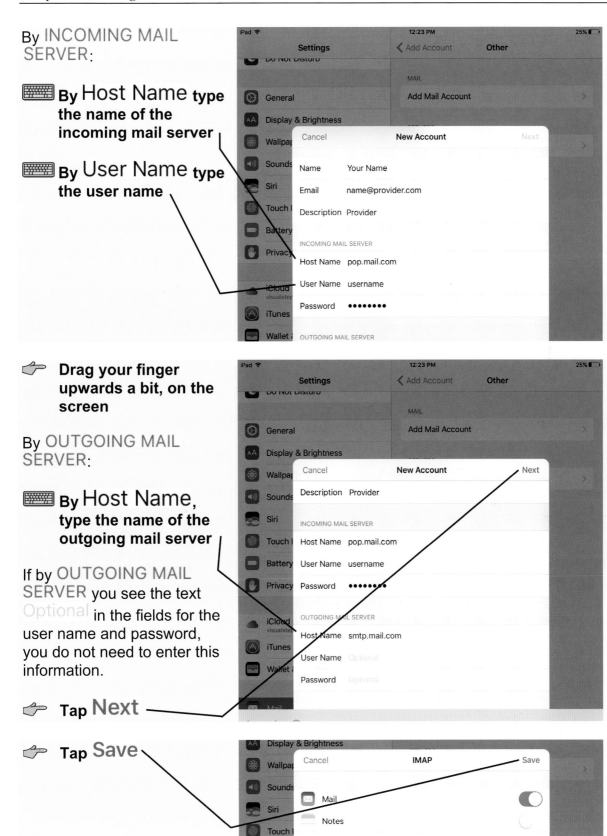

Drag your finger upwards a bit, on the screen

By OUTGOING MAIL SERVER:

By Host Name, type the name of the outgoing mail server

If by OUTGOING MAIL SERVER you see the text Optional in the fields for the user name and password, you do not need to enter this information.

Tap Next

Tap Save

Now your email account has
been added:

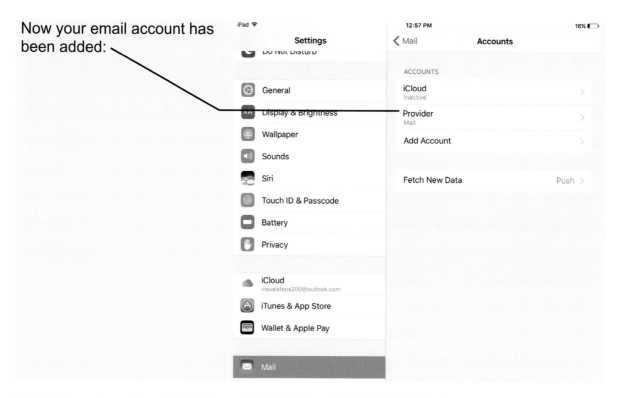

☞ **Go back to the home screen** ᗭᗴ**8**

✚ HELP! It does not work.

Because of the growing popularity of the iPad and the iPhone, many providers such
as AT&T and AOL have put instructions on their websites about setting up an email
account for the iPad. Just look for something like 'email settings iPad' on your
provider's website and follow the instructions listed.

2.2 Setting Up an Outlook.com, Hotmail or Gmail Account

If you have an *Outlook.com* or *Hotmail* account, you can set this up on your iPad too. You can set up a *Gmail* account in a similar way.

☞ **If necessary, open the *Settings* app** 🦶⁶

👉 **Tap** ✉ Mail

👉 **Tap** Accounts

👉 **Tap**
Add Account

👉 **Tap**
O⃞ Outlook.com

If you use *Gmail*, tap
Google™.

In this example we have used an email address that ends with outlook.com.

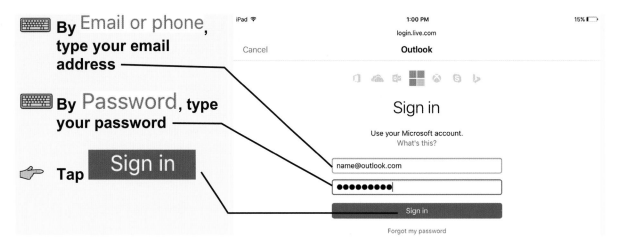

The iPad will recognize the server automatically. On the next page you give permission to some settings:

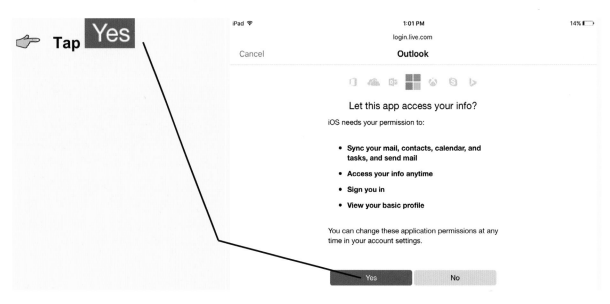

On this page you can select an option to synchronize your contacts and calendars too, besides your email. By default, these options are enabled:

You will see that the account has been added:

☞ **Go back to the home screen** 🐾⁸

2.3 Sending an Email

Just for practice, you are going to write an email message to yourself. First, you need to open the *Mail* app:

At the bottom of the home screen:

👉 **Tap**

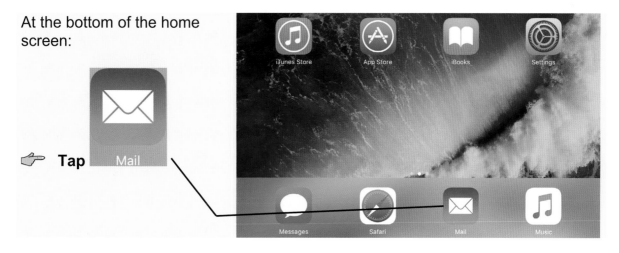

The app will immediately check for new messages. In this example there are not any new messages, but your own *Mail* app may contain some new messages. You are going to open a new, blank email:

👉 **Tap**

A new message will be opened.

🖮 **By** T○:**, type your**
email address

You will see the ⓐ key
appear in the onscreen
keyboard when you start
typing in the T○: field:

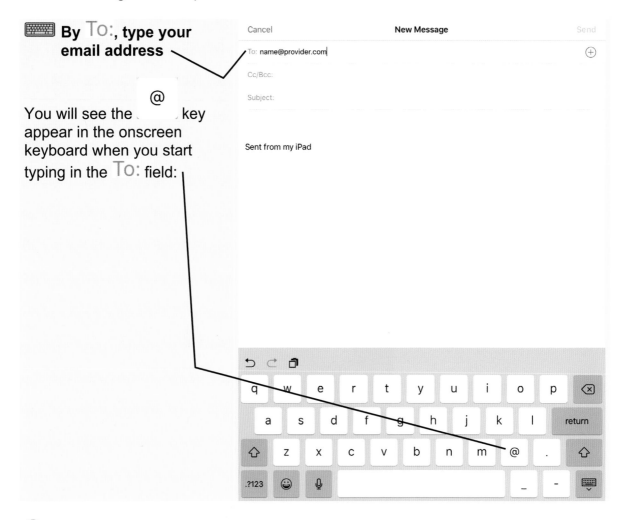

💡 **Tip**
Contacts
You can use the ⊕ button to open the list of contacts. You can select the recipient
from this list by tapping his or her name.
In *Chapter 4 The Standard Apps on Your iPad* you will learn how to enter contacts in
the list with the *Contacts* app.

👉 **Tap** Subject:

⌨ **Type:** Test

👉 **Tap the white area where you want to type your message**

⌨ **Type:** This is a test.

Continue on a new line:

👉 **Tap** return

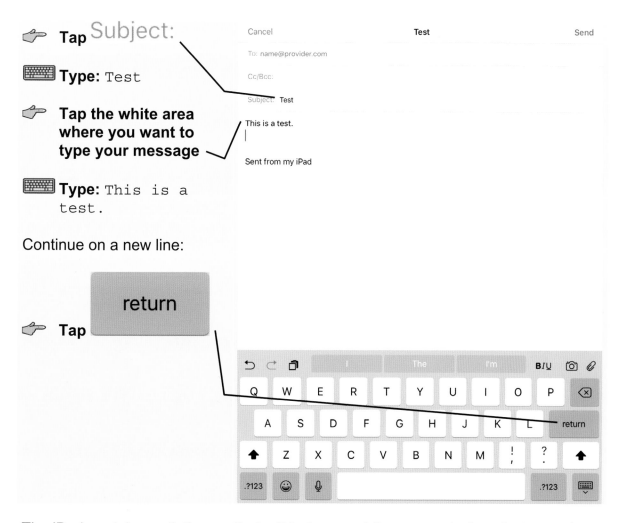

The iPad contains a dictionary that will help you while you are typing. Just see what happens when you intentionally make a spelling mistake:

⌨ **Type:** Type a speling

While you are typing, the bar above the keyboard will display suggestions for the word you are typing:

The correct spelling is shown in the middle:

You can accept the suggested correction without stopping, just continue typing:

 Type a blank space

You will see that the mistake is corrected:

 Type: `mistake`

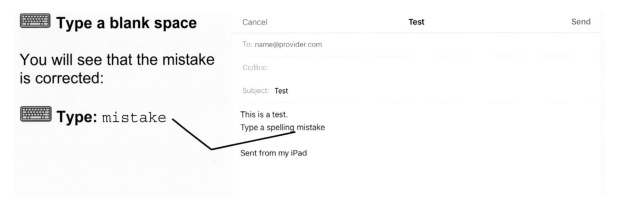

💡 **Tip**

Accept correction
A suggested correction will also be accepted if you type a period, comma or another punctuation symbol.

💡 **Tip**

Refuse correction
You can also refuse to accept a given suggestion. You do that like this:

👉 **Tap the correction that is shown between the double quotes**
"Maria"

You need to do this before you type a blank space, period, comma or other punctuation symbol, otherwise the correction will be accepted.

💡 **Tip**

Turn off Autocorrect
In the *Tips* at the back of this chapter you can read how to disable the auto correction function while typing.

If you are not satisfied with your text, you can erase the text quickly with the Backspace key:

☞ **Press your finger on**

and keep it there until both lines have been deleted ——

You will see that at first, each letter is deleted one by one. When you reach the next line, the words will be deleted one by one.

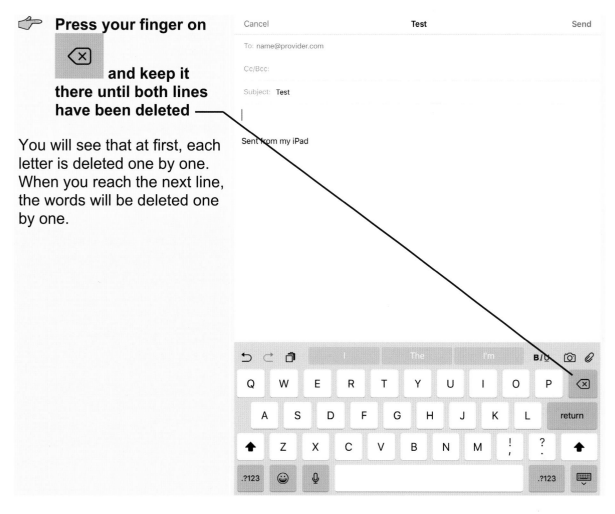

In *Mail* you can also copy, cut and paste. You can do this with an entire word, multiple words or the entire text. Here is how you select a word:

☞ **Press your finger on the word** iPad ——

Now you will see a magnifying glass with the selected word: ——

☞ **Release your finger**

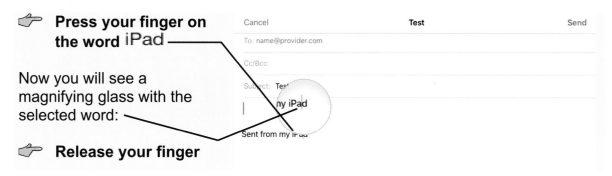

Now you can choose whether you want to select a single word or the entire text. You are going to select the word:

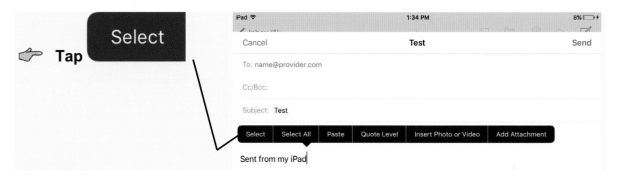

☞ **Tip**

Magnifying glass
With the magnifying glass, you can easily position the cursor on the exact spot inside a word, or between two words. This is helpful when you want to edit or correct text. Move your finger along, until you can see the correct position of the cursor in the magnifying glass, then release your finger. You will not need to use the

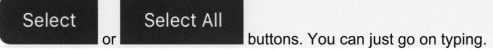 or buttons. You can just go on typing.

The word has been selected. To select multiple words, you can move the pins and

. Now you can cut or copy it, or replace it by a similar word. You are going to copy the word:

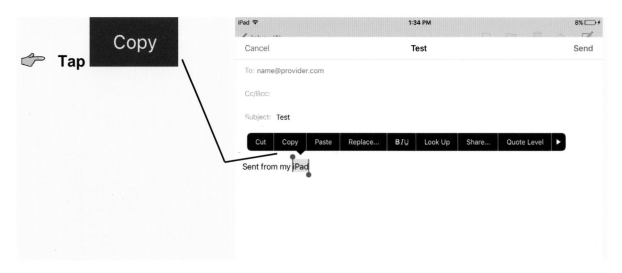

The word has been copied to the clipboard. This is how you paste it in the text:

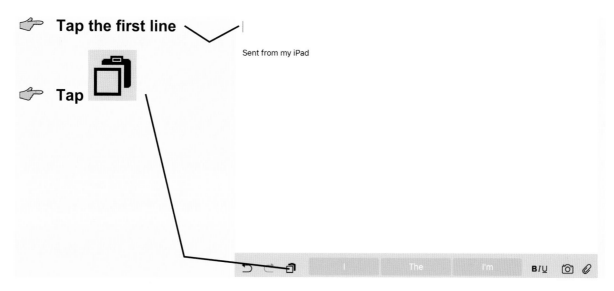

☞ **Tap the first line**

☞ **Tap** [icon]

The copied word is pasted on the first line. It is also possible to format the text in an email message. For example, you can render words in bold or in italics.

🖝 **Select the word 'iPad'**
   ✂ 13

☞ **Tap** B*I*U

By tapping [▶] you can see more options, such as inserting a photo or video. In the *Tips* at the end of this chapter you can read more about this. ——

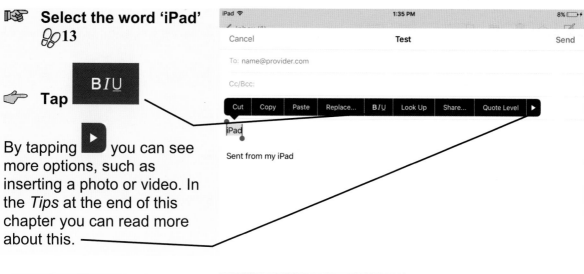

To render the word bold:

☞ **Tap** Bold

In the same way, you can render the text in italics, and underline it.

☞ **Tap next to the word**

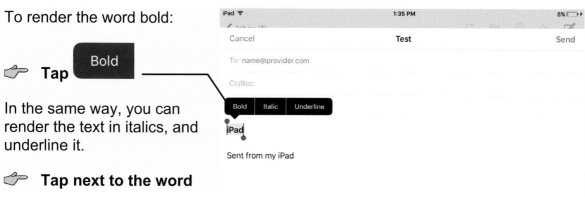

🔅 Tip
Formatting options on the keyboard
You can also use the formatting options on the keyboard. First you will need to select the format option. The text that you will type will have the selected format:

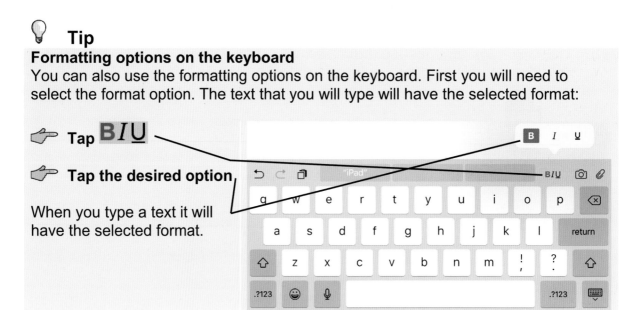

👉 **Tap** B*I*U̲

👉 **Tap the desired option**

When you type a text it will have the selected format.

Now you can send your test email message:

👉 **Tap Send**

Your email message will be sent, and if the sound on your iPad is turned on, you will hear a sound.

2.4 Receiving an Email

Shortly afterwards, your message will be received. You may hear another sound signal. This is how you open the *Inbox* folder, where your incoming messages are stored:

👉 **Tap** ❮ Inbox (1)

The number by < Inbox (1) indicates how many new messages you have received. In this example we have just one new message, but you may have received multiple new messages:

You can recognize an unread message by the blue dot ● :

☞ **Tap the incoming message** ──────

At the bottom of the screen you will see this message: Updated Just Now

1 Unread . This means that the system has recently checked for new email messages.

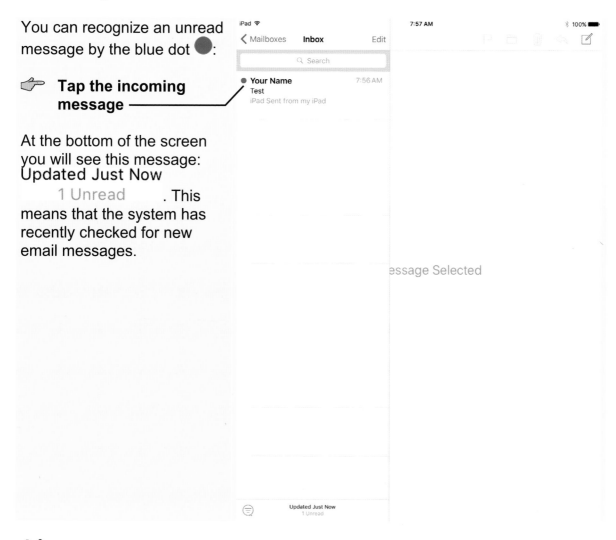

HELP! I do not see a new message.
When you do not see a new email message:

☞ **Tap** < Inbox

☞ **Swipe downwards over the left side of the screen**

You will see the content of the message:

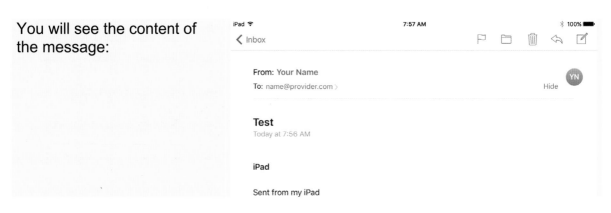

In the toolbar above a message you will find a few buttons. Here are the functions of these buttons:

< Inbox   View the content of the *Inbox* folder.

        Skip to the next or previous message.

        Flag or mark a message as unread.

        Move a message to a different folder. The default folders include the *Inbox*, *Sent* and *Trash* folders.

        Move a message to the *Trash* folder.

        Reply to a message, forward or print a message.

        Write a new message.

2.5 Replying To an Email

This is how you reply to an email:

Tap

Tap Reply

You will see the screen in which you can type your reply:

You can send the message in the usual way. The email address has already been entered:

For now, you do not need to send the message:

☞ **Tap** Cancel

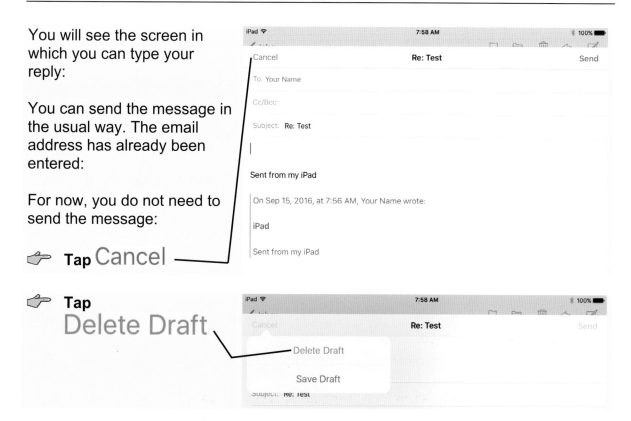

☞ **Tap**
Delete Draft

You will see the screen again with the message you have previously sent to yourself.

2.6 Deleting an Email

You are going to delete your test message:

☞ **Tap** 🗑

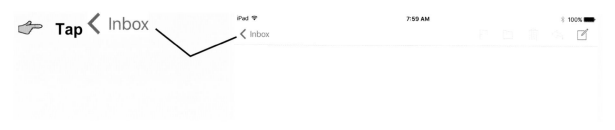

Now the email message has been moved to the *Trash* folder. You can check to make sure:

☞ **Tap** ‹ Inbox

In this example there are no other messages in the *Inbox* folder:

If you have set up a single
email account:

☞ **Tap** ❮ Mailboxes

You will see at least four folders:

☞ **Tap** 🗑 Trash

⤵ Please note:

If you have set up multiple email accounts, you need to tap the name of your
account first before you see the *Trash* folder.

The deleted message is stored in the *Trash* folder:

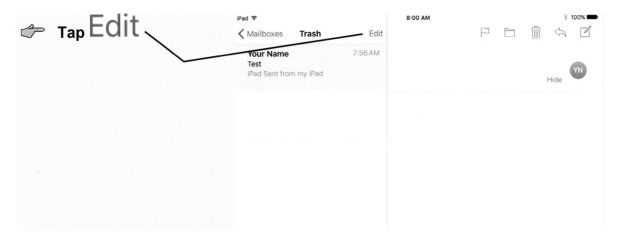

☞ **Tap** Edit

This is how you permanently delete the message:

 Tap the message

You will see a red checkmark  next to the message:

Now you can choose whether you want to delete the message, mark it or move it to another folder. You are going to delete the message:

 **Tap** Delete

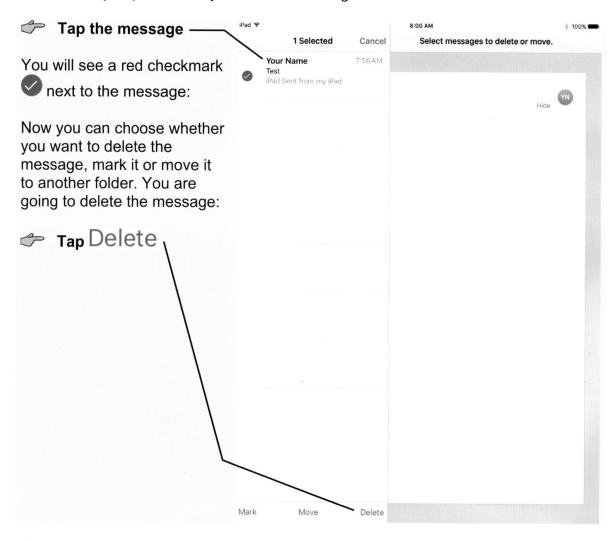

💡 **Tip**

Delete all messages
If you want to delete all messages, you do not need to tap the message. Instead:

👉 **Tap** Delete All

If you are sure:

👉 **Tap** Delete All

This is how you return to the *Inbox*:

 Tap ❮ Mailboxes

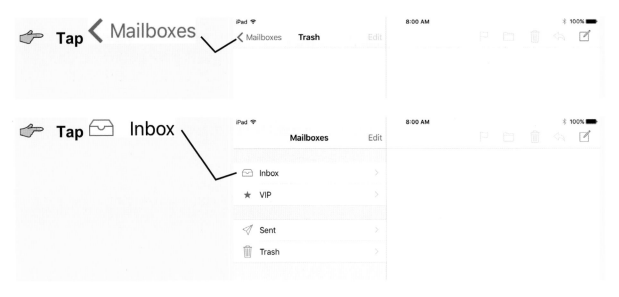

 Tap ✉ Inbox

Now you see your *Inbox* again.

⬇ Please note:

If you have set up multiple email accounts, your *Inbox* looks a bit different. You need to tap the name of your account first before you can tap the *Inbox*.

☞ **Go back to the home screen** &⁸

☞ **If you want, put the iPad into sleep mode, or turn it off** &¹

In this chapter, you have set up an email account on the iPad, sent and received an email message and deleted an email. In the following section you can practice these operations once more.

2.7 Exercises

To be able to quickly apply the things you have learned, you can work through the following exercises. Have you forgotten how to do something? Use the numbers next to the footsteps 🦶**1** to look up the item in the appendix *How Do I Do That Again?*

Exercise 1: Writing and Correcting an Email

In this exercise you will write a new email and practice editing, copying and pasting.

👉 If necessary, wake up the iPad from sleep mode, or turn it on. 🦶**2**

👉 Open the *Mail* app. 🦶**14**

👉 Open a new message. 🦶**15**

👉 By To:, enter your own email address. 🦶**16**

👉 By Subject:, type this text: `Practice` 🦶**17**

👉 Type this text in the email , including the typo: 🦶**18**
`With lots of practice I will become an iPad wizzard`

👉 Do not accept the suggested correction, by tapping the option "wizzard". 🦶**19**

👉 Delete the word `wizzard` with the backspace key. 🦶**20**

👉 Type this text: 🦶**18**
`expert with the keyboard.`

👉 Go to a new line. 🦶**21**

👉 Select the word 'practice'. 🦶**13**

👉 Copy the word 'practice'. 🦶**22**

👉 Paste the word 'practice' on the second line. 🦶**23**

Exercise 2: Sending and Receiving an Email

In this exercise you will send and receive the email message from the previous exercise.

☞ Send the email. $\mathcal{CO}^{24}$

☞ Read the message you have received. $\mathcal{CO}^{25}$

Exercise 3: Permanently Deleting an Email

You do not need to save the practice message. In this exercise you will permanently delete the message.

☞ Delete the message. $\mathcal{CO}^{26}$

☞ View the content of the *Trash*. $\mathcal{CO}^{27}$

☞ Delete the message once and for all. $\mathcal{CO}^{28}$

Exercise 4: Check for New Email Messages

In this exercise you are going to look and see if any new messages have arrived.

☞ Return to the *Inbox* folder. $\mathcal{CO}^{29}$

☞ Manually check if there are any new email messages. $\mathcal{CO}^{30}$

☞ Go back to the home screen. $\mathcal{CO}^{8}$

☞ If you want, put the iPad into sleep mode, or turn it off. $\mathcal{CO}^{1}$

2.8 Background Information

Dictionary

Account	A combination of a user name and password that gives you access to a specific protected service. A subscription with an Internet service provider is also called an account.
AOL	Short for *America Online*, a major American Internet service provider.
Attachment	A file that can be linked to an e-mail message and sent along with it. This can be a document, picture, or another type of file.
Contacts	Standard app on the iPad with which you can view and edit the information about your contacts.
Fetch	Fetching is the traditional method of retrieving new email messages: you open your email program and connect with the mail server. You can set the program to check for emails at regular intervals, when the email program is opened.
Gmail	Free email service provided by the manufacturers of the well-known *Google* search engine.
Hotmail	Free email service of Microsoft.
IMAP	IMAP stands for *Internet Message Access Protocol*. This means that you manage your emails on the mail server. Messages that you have read, will be stored on the mail server until you delete them. IMAP is useful if you want to manage your email from multiple computers. Your mailbox will look the same on all the computers you use. If you create folders to organize your email messages, these same folders will appear on each computer, as well as on your iPad. If you want to use IMAP, you will need to set up your email account as an IMAP account on every computer you use.
Inbox	Folder in *Mail* where you can view the email messages you have received.

- Continue on the next page -

Mail	Standard app on the iPad with which you can send and receive email messages.
Microsoft Exchange	A mail server used by businesses, educational institutions and organizations.
Outlook	Email program that is part of the *Microsoft Office* suite.
Outlook.com	Free email service of Microsoft.
POP	POP stands for *Post Office Protocol*, the traditional method of managing your emails. When you retrieve your email, the messages will be deleted from the server right away. But on your iPad, the default setting for POP accounts is for saving a copy on the mail server, even after you have retrieved the message. This means you will also be able to retrieve the same message on your computer.
Push	When *push* is set and is supported by your provider, new email messages will be sent to your email program right after they are received on the mail server. Even when your email program is not open and your iPad is locked.
Signature	Standard ending that will be inserted at the end of all your outgoing emails.
Synchronize	Literally this means: making things the same. Not only can you synchronize your iPad with the content of your *iTunes Library*, but you can also synchronize the data of an email account.
Trash	Folder in *Mail* where all your deleted messages are stored. Once you have deleted a message from the *Trash*, it will be deleted permanently.
Yahoo!	Search engine that also offers free email services.

Source: User Guide iPad, Wikipedia.

2.9 Tips

 Tip

Email from Apple
When you created your *Apple ID*, Apple sent you one (or multiple) email message(s). In these messages you were asked to verify the email address. This is how you do it:

☞ **Open the *Mail* app** 𝒸𝒸**14**

☞ **Open the most recent message sent by Apple** 𝒸𝒸**25**

☞ **Tap** Verify now >

A web page will be opened. Here you need to sign in with your *Apple ID* and your password, in order to verify your email address:

⌨ **Type your email address** ——

⌨ **Type your password**

☞ **Tap** Continue

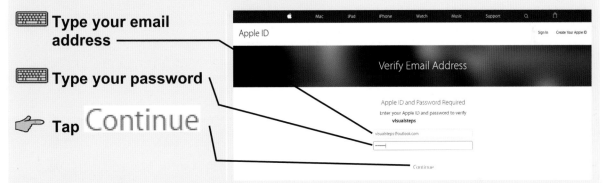

You may be asked if you want to save your password:

☞ **If necessary, tap** Not Now

You will see a confirmation message:

☞ **Go back to the home screen** 𝒸𝒸**8**

 Tip

Choosing a sender
If you have multiple email accounts setup on your iPad, you can decide from which sender an email message is sent.

☞ **Tap** Cc/Bcc:

☞ **Tap** From:

☞ **Tap the desired email address**

Tip

Disable Auto-Correction

Sometimes, the autocorrect function on the iPad will insert unwanted corrections. The dictionary will not recognize every single word you type, but will try to suggest a correction, nevertheless. This may result in strange corrections, which you might accept without knowing it, whenever you type a period, comma or blank space. This is how to disable the autocorrect function:

☞ **Open the *Settings* app** 🦶⁶

👉 **If necessary, tap** ⚙ General

👉 **Tap** Keyboards

👉 **By** Auto-Correction, **tap the** ⬤ **button**

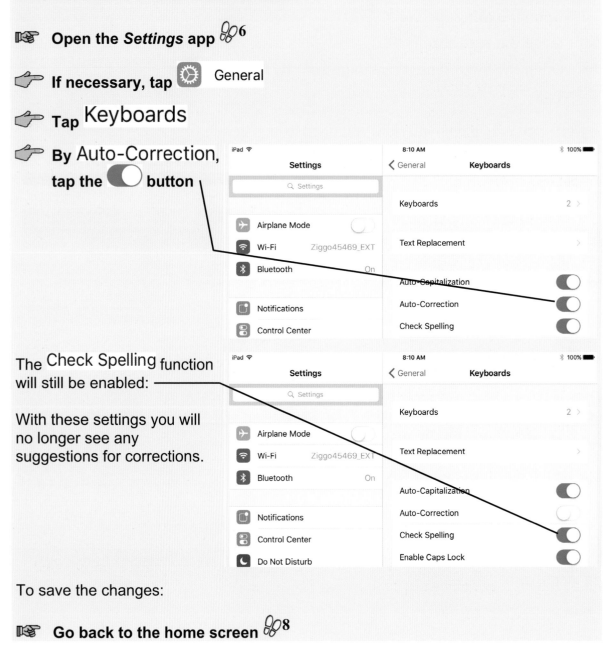

The Check Spelling function will still be enabled:

With these settings you will no longer see any suggestions for corrections.

To save the changes:

☞ **Go back to the home screen** 🦶⁸

Tip

Signature

By default, each email you send will end with the text *Sent from my iPad.* This text is called your *signature*. You can replace this text by a standard ending for your messages or by your name and address. This is how to change your email signature:

☞ **Open the *Settings* app** ✄⁶

👉 **Tap** Mail

👉 **Tap Signature**

You will see this signature appear in the text box:

To delete the signature:

👉 **Tap next to** iPad

👉 **Tap** ⌫ **until the text is deleted**

⌨ **Type the desired signature**

If you do not want to use a signature, do not enter anything.

👉 **Tap** ‹ Mail

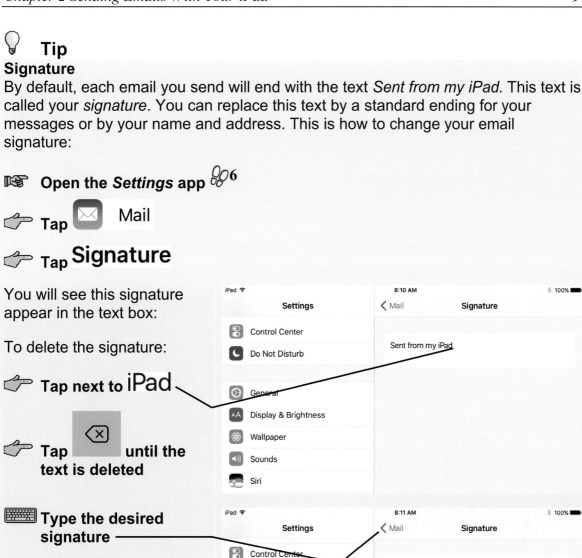

Please note: if you have set up multiple email accounts, this signature will be used for all the messages that are sent from these accounts.

Tip
CC/BCC
The screen in which you can type a new email message also contains the Cc/Bcc: field. With CC (*Carbon Copy*) and BCC (*Blind Carbon Copy*) you can send others a copy of your message. The recipients in the BCC field will not be visible to the other recipients of this message. But if you use the CC field, every recipient can view the other recipients.

☞ **Tap** Cc/Bcc:

Now you will see both
options apart from each
other:

⌨ **Type the email
address in the desired
field** ——————

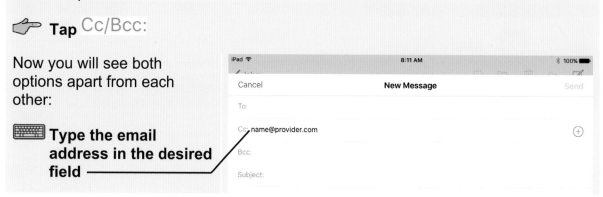

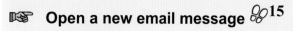

Tip
Adding an attachment
You can send an attachment such as a photo or short video with your email message. In this example a photo is being sent. In *Chapter 6 Photos and Video* you can learn more about working with photos and video.

☞ **Open a new email message** ℗₀15

☞ **Tap** 📷

- Continue on the next page -

👉 **Tap the desired folder containing the photo you want to send**

👉 **Tap the desired photo**

👉 **Tap Use**

The photo will be added to the email message.

You can also send a photo using the Photos app. See section *6.11 Sending a Photo by Email* for more information.

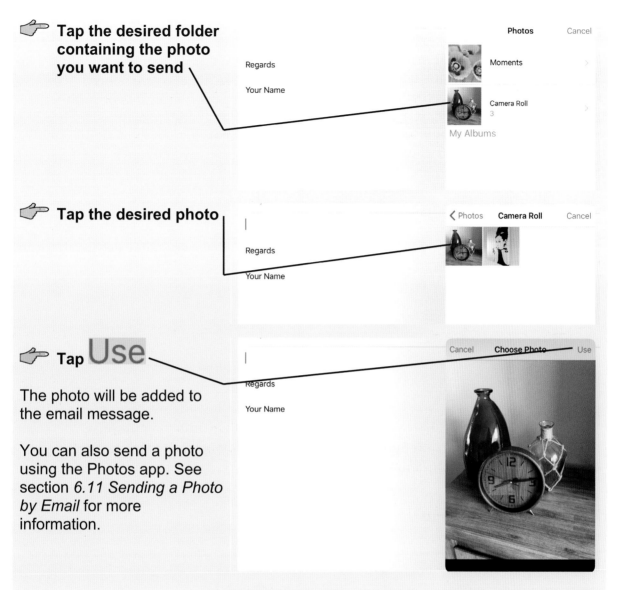

If you have other types of documents such as a text file or a PDF file stored on your iPad, you can send these as attachments as well. You do this using a slightly different method. Instead of using the *Mail* app, you open the document with the app you normally use to view or edit the document. For PDFs this can be *iBooks* for

example. Once the document is opened, tap ⬆️ and Mail.

Tip

Opening an attachment received in an email

Once you have used email on your iPad for a little while, you will eventually receive a message with an attachment. This can be in the form of a photo, video or other type of document such as a PDF file. Most of these types of files can be opened directly on your iPad. In this tip we will show you how to open a *Word* document that has been received as an attachment to an email. For other types of files, the procedure is pretty much the same.

☞ **Open the email message with the attachment** 𝒫𝒫²⁵

The attachment icon is shown underneath the message.

☞ **Tap the icon**

The Word document opens and you can start to read it.

When you have finished, you can close the document. You will return to the *Mail* app once more:

☞ **Tap the screen**

☞ **Tap Done**

- Continue on the next page -

If desired, you can use this document with other apps or even print it. To do this, you

click ⬆️ and select one of the options shown.

If you have received a document that you want to open in a specific app, such as *iBooks* for a PDF file, then you need to select the app from the list of available options shown.

☞ **Hold your finger on the icon for a moment until a small window appears**

☞ **Tap the desired app**

The document will be opened in the selected app. You can also save it to *iCloud Drive* if this is activated on your iPad.

In the case of a photo, you also have the option of saving it to your iPad:

☞ **Tap the photo and hold your finger on it until a small window appears**

☞ **Tap Save Image**

Tip

Moving email messages to folders

You can also move your emails to different folders. If you have not yet created any folders you can do this in the *Mailboxes* window:

Note: creating new folders is only possible in an IMAP account. In an POP account this is not possible.

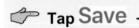 **Tap** Edit

 **At the bottom, tap** New Mailbox

⌨ **Type the desired name**

By MAILBOX LOCATION you can choose a location, if you wish:

When you are done:

👉 **Tap** Save

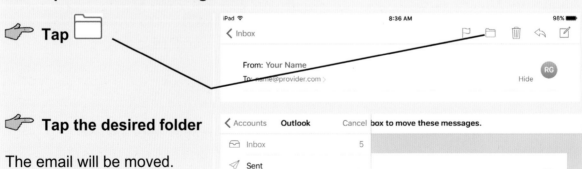

In the next screen, you will see the new folder:

👉 **Tap** Done

This is how you move an email:

☞ **Open an email message** 👣**25**

👉 **Tap** 📁

👉 **Tap the desired folder**

The email will be moved.

Tip

iPad horizontal

If you hold the iPad in a horizontal position, by default, you will see your mailbox with email messages on your screen:

The mailbox with the messages:

The email message:

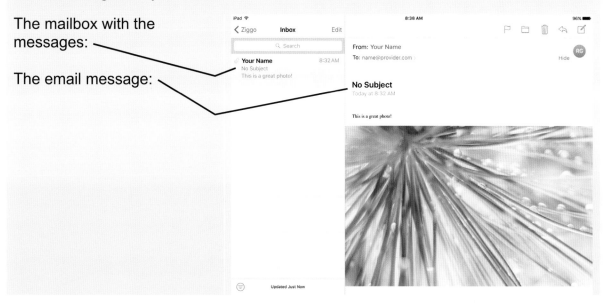

 Tip

Push or fetch

If you also retrieve your email on a regular computer, you will be used to retrieving your email through *fetch*: you open your email program and it will connect to the mail server to retrieve your new messages. You can modify the program settings to check for new messages at regular intervals, while your email program is open.

With the *push* function, new email messages will be immediately sent to your email program by the mail server, right after the mail server has received the messages. Even if your email program has not been opened, and your iPad is locked.

The email accounts from providers such as *Microsoft Exchange* and *Yahoo!* support push, but for other email accounts, fetch is used.

Please note: if you connect to the Internet through the mobile data network and you do not have a contract for unlimited data transfer, it is recommended to turn off the push function. That is because you will be paying for the amount of data you use. If any email messages with large attachments are pushed to your iPad, you might be facing higher data transfer fees. In this case, it is better to retrieve your email manually, as soon as you have connected to the Internet through Wi-Fi.

- Continue on the next page -

This is how you can view the settings for push or fetch:

☞ **Open the *Settings* app** ✂️**6**

👉 **Tap** ✉️ **Mail**

👉 **Tap** **Accounts**

By default, Push is set for all email accounts:

👉 **Tap Fetch New Data**

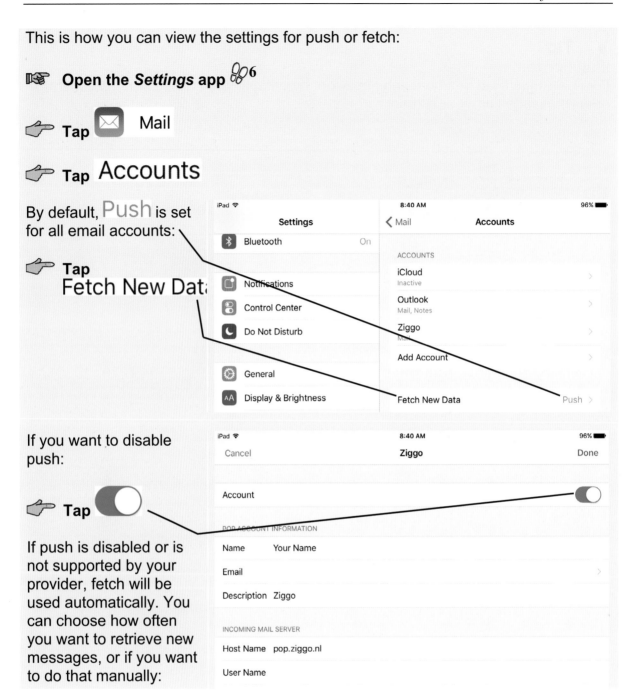

If you want to disable push:

👉 **Tap** ⬜

If push is disabled or is not supported by your provider, fetch will be used automatically. You can choose how often you want to retrieve new messages, or if you want to do that manually:

💡 Tip

Should I save my emails on the server or not?

For POP email accounts you can modify the settings yourself and choose to save a copy of the received emails on the mail server. If a copy is stored, you will also be able to retrieve the email messages on your computer, even after you have retrieved them on your iPad. Here is how to modify the settings to suit your own preferences:

☞ **Open the *Settings* app** 👣6

👉 **Tap ✉ Mail**

👉 **Tap Accounts**

👉 **Tap your POP email account**

You will see the page with the account information.

👉 **Swipe upwards the screen**

👉 **Tap Advanced**

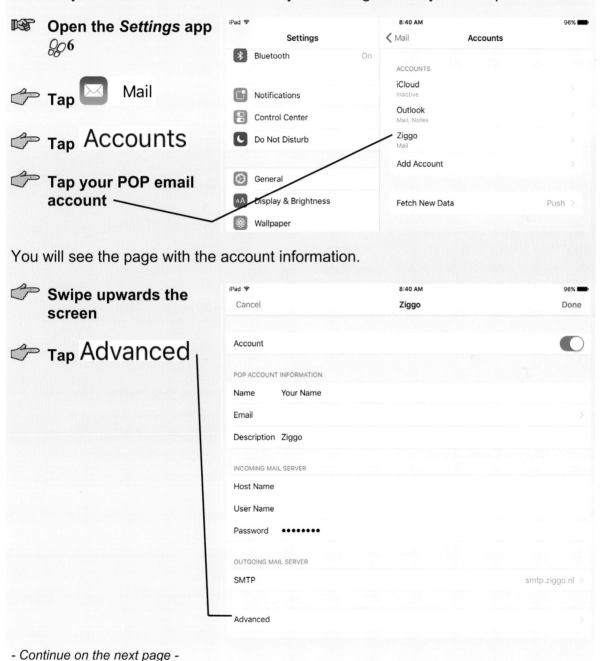

- Continue on the next page -

By default, the setting is for new emails never to be deleted from the server. This means that the messages will only be deleted from the server if you retrieve them in an email program where the setting is adjusted in such a way that the messages from the server will be deleted.

☞ **Tap**
Delete from serve

You can set the program never to delete messages from the mail server, delete them after seven days, or only after they have been deleted from the *Inbox* folder:

☞ **Tap the desired option** √

iPad 🛜	8:40 AM	96% 🔋
❮ Ziggo	**Advanced**	

MOVE DISCARDED MESSAGES INTO:

Deleted Mailbox	✓
Archive Mailbox	

DELETED MESSAGES

Remove	After one week ❯

INCOMING SETTINGS

Use SSL	🔘
Authentication	Password ❯
Delete from server	Never ❯
Server Port 995	

iPad 🛜	8:40 AM	96% 🔋
❮ Advanced	**Delete from server**	

Never	✓
Seven days	
When removed from Inbox	

 Tip

VIP

With the new feature VIP you can automatically route mail from persons you designate as 'VIPs' into the special folder ★ VIP in the *Mail* app. Even if you have more than one email account set up for you iPad, all mail from your VIPs will automatically appear in the ★ VIP folder. Here is how you add someone to the VIP list.

🖙 **Open the *Mail* app** 👣14

☞ **If necessary, tap** ❮ Inbox

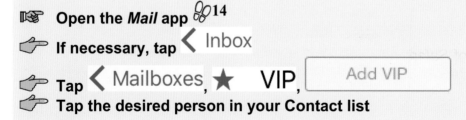
☞ **Tap** ❮ Mailboxes, ★ VIP, [Add VIP]
☞ **Tap the desired person in your Contact list**

In *Chapter 4 The Standard Apps on Your iPad* you will learn how to add new people to the list in the *Contacts* app.

3. Surfing with Your iPad

In this chapter you are going to get acquainted with *Safari*, the web browser used by all Apple devices. With this web browser you can surf the Internet using your iPad. If you are familiar with using the Internet on your computer, you will see that surfing on the iPad is just as easy. The big difference is that you do not need a mouse, or keyboard to navigate. You surf by using the touchscreen on your iPad.

You will learn how to open a web page, zoom in and out and how to scroll by touching the screen in a specific way. We will also discuss how to open a link (or hyperlink) and work with web pages that you have saved, also called bookmarks.

In *Safari* you can open multiple web pages at a time. In this chapter you will learn how to switch back and forth between these open pages.

While you are surfing, you may want to do something else, such as listening to some music or modifying a particular setting. Your iPad can perform multiple tasks simultaneously, so this is not a problem. You can switch from one app to another app easily. In this chapter you will learn how to do this.

In this chapter you will learn how to:

- open a web page;
- zoom in and zoom out;
- scroll;
- open a link on a web page and on a new tab;
- switch between multiple open page tabs;
- go to the previous or next page;
- add a bookmark;
- search;
- switch between recently used apps;
- view the settings of *Safari*;
- use a different search engine.

3.1 Opening a Web Page

This is how you open *Safari*, the app that allows you to surf the Internet:

☞ **If necessary, wake up the iPad from sleep mode or turn it on** 🦶²

👉 **Tap**   Safari

This is to how to display the onscreen keyboard, in order to enter the web address:

👉 **Tap the address bar**

🩹 **HELP! A web address is already entered.**
If another web address is shown in the address bar, you can delete it like this:

👉 **Tap**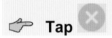

To practice, you can take a look at the Visual Steps website:

Type:
www.visualsteps
.com

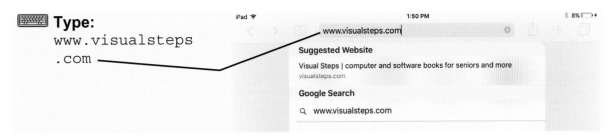

When you have finished typing:

☞ **Tap** Go

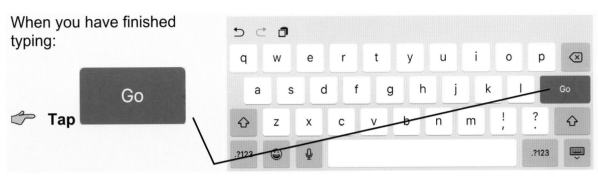

Now you will see the Visual Steps website:

3.2 Zoom In and Zoom Out

If you think that the letters and images on a website are too small, you can zoom in. This is done by double-tapping. Tap the desired spot twice, in rapid succession:

☞ **Double-tap the menu on the left-hand side**

🩹 **HELP! A new web page is opened.**

If you do not double-tap in the right way, a new tab might be opened. If that is the case, just tap 〈 on the screen at the top left and try again. You can also practice double-tapping in a blank area of your screen.

You will see that the web page is rendered in a larger size:

☞ **Double-tap the menu once more**

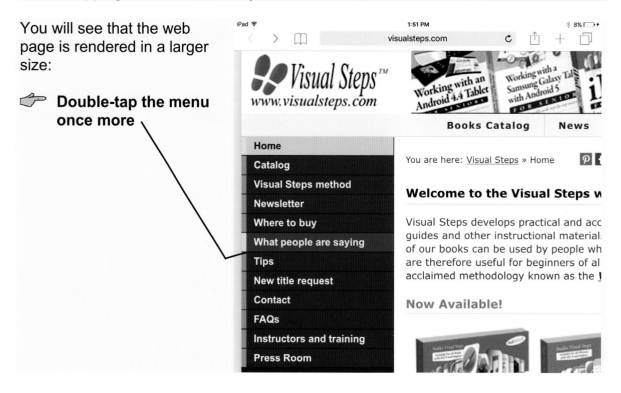

Now the screen will zoom out to the standard view again. There is also another way to zoom in and out; sort of like pinching. You use your thumb and index finger. Set them on the spot that you want to enlarge:

☞ **Slowly spread your thumb and index finger away from each other on the screen**

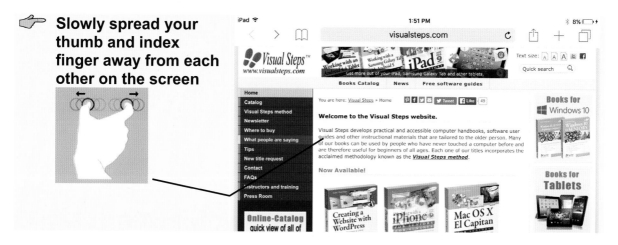

You will see that you can zoom in even further. It will take a moment for the screen to focus. You can zoom out by reversing the movement of your fingers:

☞ **Move your thumb and index finger towards each other on the screen**

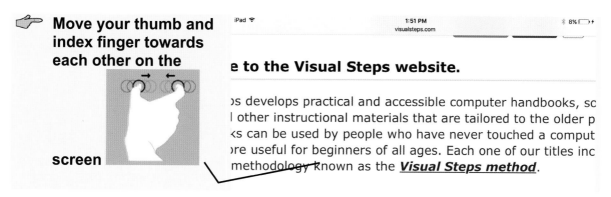

Now you are going to return to the view you had when you zoomed in for the first time:

☞ **Double-tap the page**

You will see the view after zooming in once:

3.3 Scrolling

Scrolling allows you to view the entire content of the web page. You scroll up or down to see more of the page. On your iPad, you do this with your fingers:

☞ **Drag your finger upwards a bit, on the** ⬆ **screen**

You will see that the page scrolls downwards:

☞ **Drag your finger downwards a bit, on the screen** ⬇

You will see that the page scrolls upwards:

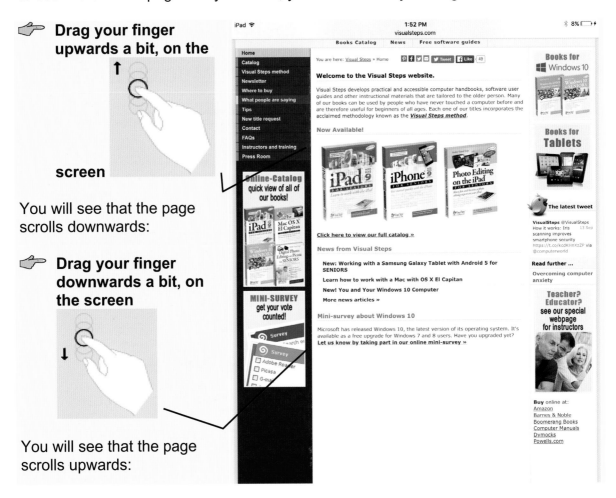

Tip

Scrolling sideways
You can scroll sideways by moving your finger from right to left, or from left to right.

If you want to quickly scroll a longer page, you can swipe your finger over the screen:

☞ **Move your finger upwards in a swiping gesture, over the screen** ———

You will see that you will quickly scroll down to the bottom of the page:

 Tip

Moving in different directions
You can also quickly scroll upwards, to the left, or to the right, if you swipe the screen in that direction.

This is how you quickly return to the top of the web page:

☞ **Tap the status bar twice**

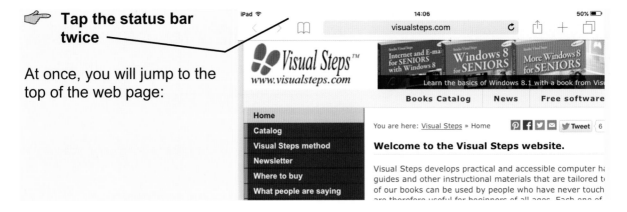

At once, you will jump to the top of the web page:

3.4 Opening a Link on a Web Page

If a page contains a (hyper) link, you can follow this link by tapping it. Just try this:

☞ **If necessary, move your finger from left to right until you see the menu**

☞ **Tap** **Catalog**

✂ **HELP! Tapping the link does not work.**
If you find it difficult to tap the right link, you can zoom in more. This way, the links will be displayed in a much larger format, and tapping the link will be easier.

Now the catalog will be opened, where you can view the Visual Steps books:

Here you see that the new
page is displayed in the
regular size:

3.5 Opening a Link in a New Tab

You can also open a link in a new tab:

☞ **Put your finger on**
Where to buy

 HELP! Tapping the link does not work.
If you find it difficult to tap the right link, you can zoom in first. This way, the links will
be displayed in a much larger format, and tapping the link will be easier.

In a few seconds, you will see a menu:

☞ **Tap**
   Open in New Tab

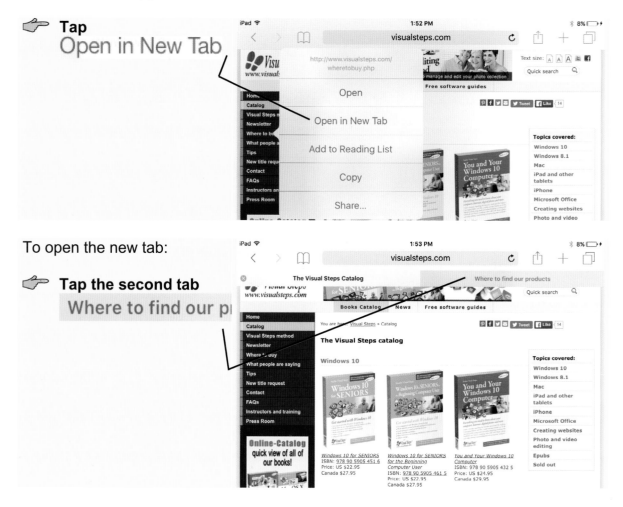

To open the new tab:

☞ **Tap the second tab**
   Where to find our pr

Now you will see the information on where to find the Visual Steps products:

You can sign up for our *Notify me* email service. Then you will be notified by email when each new book is released. You can open this page on a new tab:

☞ **Put your finger on**
   Notify me email

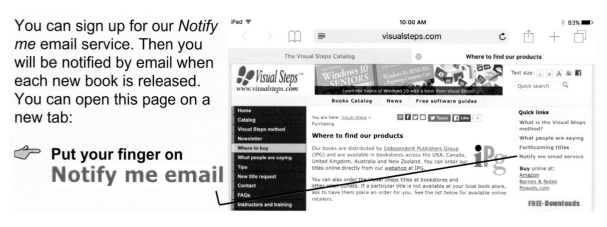

In a few seconds, you will see a menu:

☞ **Tap**
Open in New Tab

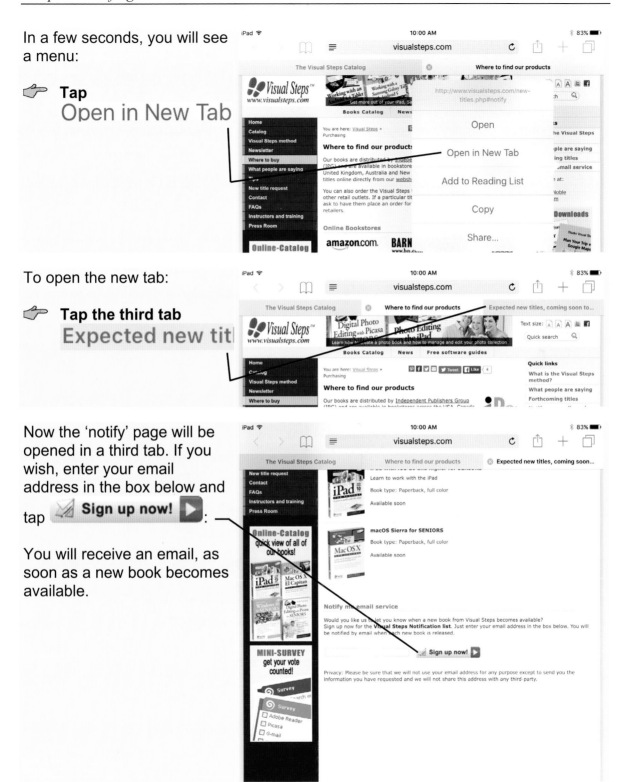

To open the new tab:

☞ **Tap the third tab**
Expected new tit

Now the 'notify' page will be opened in a third tab. If you wish, enter your email address in the box below and tap **Sign up now!** :

You will receive an email, as soon as a new book becomes available.

3.6 Switching Between Multiple Tabs

A very useful option in *Safari* is being able to switch between multiple tabs with open web pages.

At the top of the page you will see three tabs:

This means that at the moment, three web pages are opened. This is how you return to the second page:

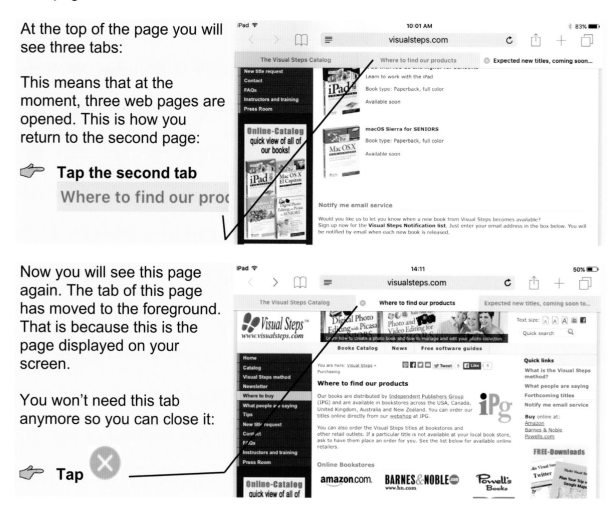

☞ **Tap the second tab**

Where to find our proc

Now you will see this page again. The tab of this page has moved to the foreground. That is because this is the page displayed on your screen.

You won't need this tab anymore so you can close it:

☞ **Tap** ⊗

You can also close the third tab.

☞ **Close the** Expected new titles, coming soon to... **tab** ⫘⁣³¹

In this example the first tab **The Visual Steps Catalog** will be left open.

Tip
Enter a new web address in the address bar
If you want to type a new address in the address bar, you can remove the web address of the open web page in the following way:

 Tap the address bar

☞ **Tap**

 Tip
Open a new, blank page in a new tab
This is how you open a new, blank page in *Safari*:

☞ **Tap**

You will see a new tab:

☞ **Tap the address bar**

The onscreen keyboard will be opened. Now you can enter a web address.

When you have accidently closed a tab you can open it again by using ┼ . Tap ┼ and hold your finger on it for a moment until you see the *Recently Closed Tabs* window. You can open the tab again by tapping one of the items shown.

3.7 Go to Previous or to Next Page

You can return to the web page you have previously visited. Here is how to do that:

☞ **Tap** ⟨

You will again see the Visual Steps home page. You can also skip to the next page.

To do this, you use the ⟩ button, but right now this will not be necessary.

3.8 Adding a Bookmark

If you want to visit a page more often, you can make a bookmark for this page. A bookmark is a favorite website which you want to visit again, later on. In this way, you do not need to type the full web address every time you want to visit the site.
A bookmark will be saved in *Safari* even after you have viewed the web page. This is how you add a bookmark:

☞ **Tap** ⬆️

A menu appears:

☞ **Tap** Add Bookmark

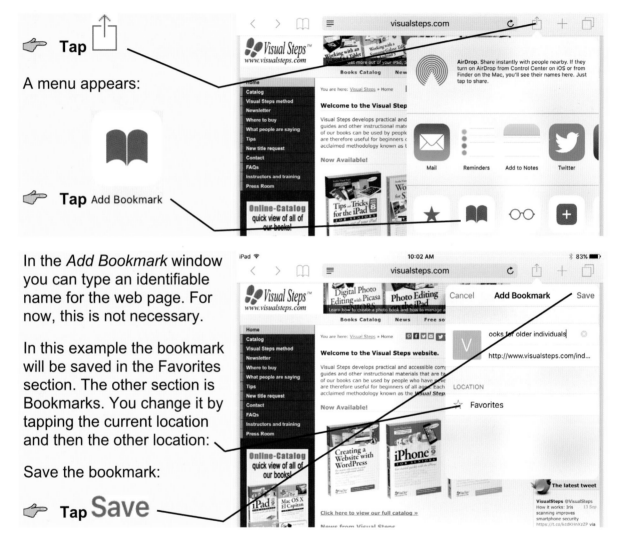

In the *Add Bookmark* window you can type an identifiable name for the web page. For now, this is not necessary.

In this example the bookmark will be saved in the Favorites section. The other section is Bookmarks. You change it by tapping the current location and then the other location:

Save the bookmark:

☞ **Tap** Save

The web page has been added to your bookmarks. You can check this yourself:

☞ **Tap** 📖

☞ **Tap** ☆ Favorites

You will see the new
bookmark in the list:

Apple has added a number of
useful bookmarks to this list,
such as the Apple website:

This is how you open the
Visual Steps bookmark:

☞ **Tap**
　📖 **Visual Steps, user**

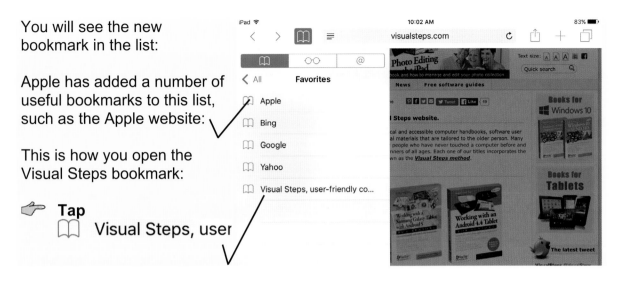

Now the Visual Steps web page will be opened.

3.9 Searching

In *Safari*, *Google* is set as the default search engine. You can use the address bar to
start a search:

☞ **Tap the address bar**
　visualsteps.com

The onscreen keyboard is displayed. Now you can type your keyword(s):

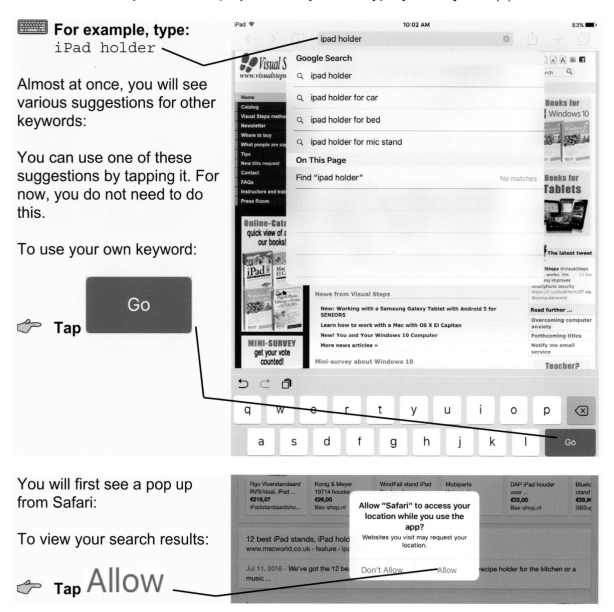

⌨️ **For example, type:**
   iPad holder

Almost at once, you will see various suggestions for other keywords:

You can use one of these suggestions by tapping it. For now, you do not need to do this.

To use your own keyword:

☞ **Tap** Go

You will first see a pop up from Safari:

To view your search results:

☞ **Tap** Allow

You will see the search results:

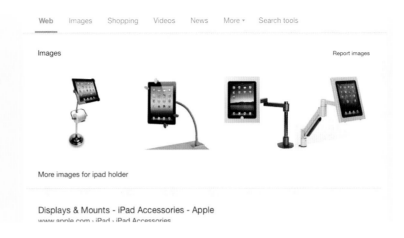

Tap the link to view a result. For now, this is not necessary.

3.10 Switching Between Recently Used Apps

By using the Home button, you can quickly switch between the apps you have recently used. Just try it:

☞ **Press the Home button twice quickly**

You will see the recently used apps:

You will switch to the *Settings* app:

☞ **If necessary, swipe across the screen from right to left**

☞ **Tap the screen below**

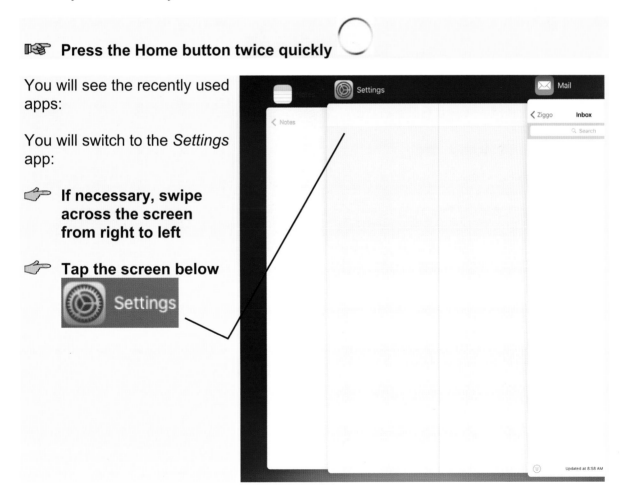

Tip

Multiple open apps
If you have opened more than three apps you will not see them on your screen all at once. You can swipe across the screen from right to left or in the opposite direction to see the other opened apps.

You will again see the *Settings* app. For instance, on the *Safari* settings page you can set the search engine you want to use:

☞ **Drag upwards across the left column**

At the bottom left-hand side of the screen:

☞ **Tap** Safari

☞ **Tap** Search Engine

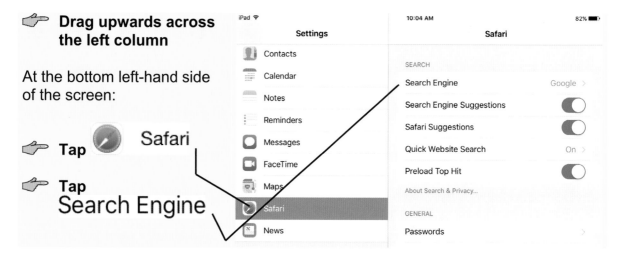

You can choose between *Google, Yahoo!*, *Bing* and *DuckDuckGo*:

☞ **Tap the desired search engine**

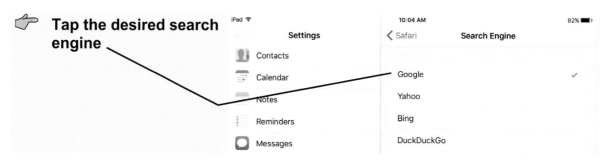

After you have selected a search engine, you can save your selection:

☞ **Press the Home button**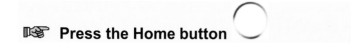

You will see the home screen once again.

☞ **If you want, put the iPad into sleep mode or turn it off** 👣[1]

3.11 Exercises

To be able to quickly apply the things you have learned, you can work through these exercises. Have you forgotten how to do something? Use the numbers next to the footsteps $\%^1$ to look up the item in the appendix *How Do I Do That Again?*

Exercise 1: View a Web Page

In this exercise you are going to view a web page in *Safari*.

☞ If necessary, wake the iPad up or turn it on. $\%^2$

☞ Open *Safari*. $\%^{32}$

☞ Open the website www.nyt.com $\%^{33}$

☞ Scroll downwards a little. $\%^{34}$

☞ Quickly scroll all the way to the bottom of the page. $\%^{35}$

☞ Return to the top of the web page. $\%^{36}$

☞ Zoom in on the web page. $\%^{37}$

☞ Zoom out again. $\%^{38}$

Exercise 2: Add a Bookmark

In this exercise you are going to add a bookmark.

☞ Add a bookmark for the current web page. $\%^{39}$

Exercise 3: Open a Link

In this exercise you are going to use different methods for following a link to an interesting article on a new page.

☞ Open a link to an interesting article. $\mathcal{QQ}$**40**

☞ If possible, scroll downwards to the end of the article. $\mathcal{QQ}$**34**

☞ Open a link to another article in a new tab. $\mathcal{QQ}$**41**

Exercise 4: Recently Used Apps

In this exercise you are going to switch between recently used apps.

☞ Take a look at the recently used apps. $\mathcal{QQ}$**42**

☞ Switch to the *Settings* app. $\mathcal{QQ}$**43**

☞ Take a look at the recently used apps. $\mathcal{QQ}$**42**

☞ Open the *Safari* app. $\mathcal{QQ}$**43**

☞ Go back to the home screen. $\mathcal{QQ}$**8**

☞ If you want, put the iPad into sleep mode or turn it off. $\mathcal{QQ}$**1**

3.12 Background Information

Dictionary

Bing	Search engine manufactured by *Microsoft*.
Bookmark	A link to a web address that has been stored in a list, so you can easily find the web page later on.
DuckDuckGo	Search engine.
Google	Search engine.
Hyperlink	A hyperlink is a navigation tool on a web page, which will automatically lead the user to the information when it is tapped. A hyperlink can be displayed in text or in an image, such as a photo, a button or an icon. Also called link.
Link	A different name for a hyperlink.
Safari	Web browser manufactured by Apple.
Scroll	Moving a web page on the screen upwards, downwards, to the left, or to the right. To do this on the iPad you need to touch the screen in a certain way.
Yahoo!	Search engine.
Zoom in	Take a closer look at an item; the letters and images will become larger.
Zoom out	Look at an item from a distance; the letters and images will become smaller.

Source: iPad User Guide, Wikipedia

Flash
The fact that your iPad cannot display *Flash* content is a bit of a limitation. *Flash* is a technique that is used for interactive websites and animations on websites. As a result of this, some elements of a web page may not be correctly rendered on the iPad.

3.13 Tips

💡 Tip
Delete a bookmark
If you no longer want to use a bookmark, you can delete it. Here is how to do that:

👉 **Tap** 📖

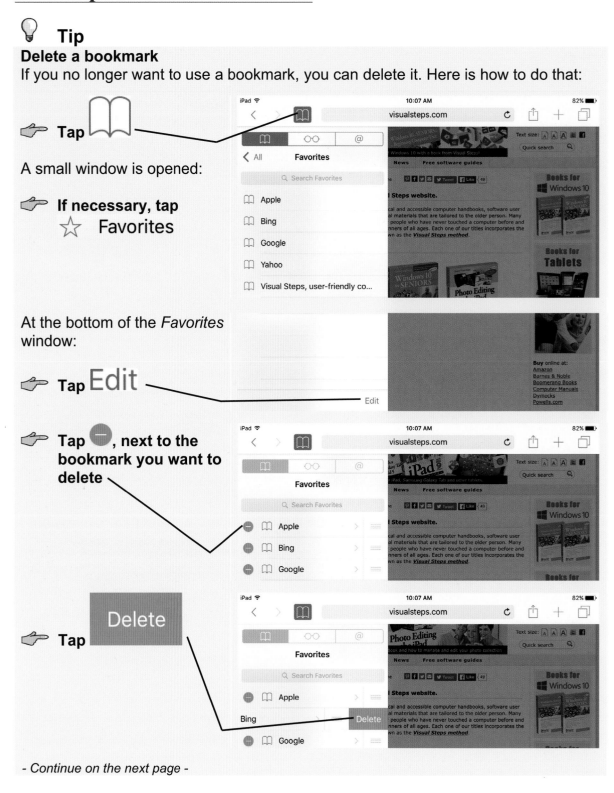

A small window is opened:

👉 **If necessary, tap**
   ☆ **Favorites**

At the bottom of the *Favorites* window:

👉 **Tap Edit**

👉 **Tap ➖, next to the bookmark you want to delete**

👉 **Tap** Delete

- Continue on the next page -

Please note: you can also drag your finger horizontally across the bookmark and then tap Delete .

The bookmark has been deleted:

You can close the window:

At the bottom of the *Favorites* window:

☞ Tap Done

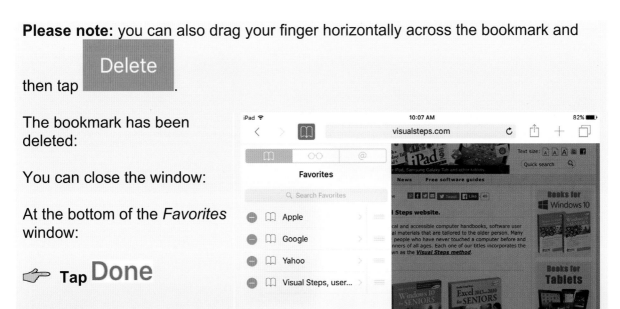

💡 **Tip**

View and delete history
In the history, all recently visited websites are stored. This is how you can view the history:

☞ Tap 📖

☞ If necessary, tap ❮ All

☞ Tap 🕐 History

- Continue on the next page -

You can also delete the history:

At the bottom of the *History* window:

☞ Tap Clear

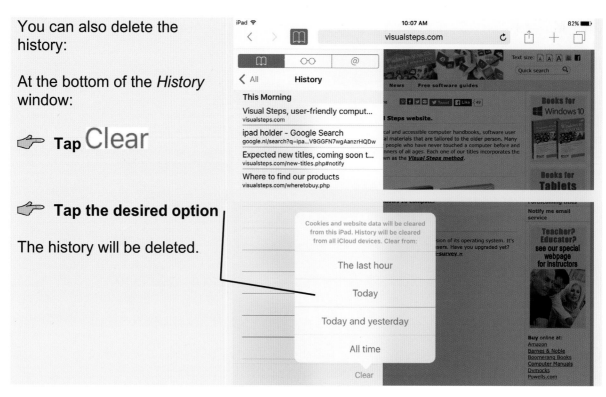

☞ **Tap the desired option**

The history will be deleted.

💡 **Tip**

Synchronize bookmarks with Internet Explorer

If you have stored lots of favorites (bookmarks) on your computer, in *Internet Explorer*, you can synchronize these with your iPad.

☞ **Connect your iPad to the computer**

☞ **If necessary, open *iTunes* ⚹12**

⊕ **If necessary, click** ☐

⊕ **Click ⓘ Info**

⊕ **Drag the scroll bar downwards**

⊕ **By Other, check the box ☑ at Sync bookmarks with**

By default, **Internet Explorer ⌄** is selected.

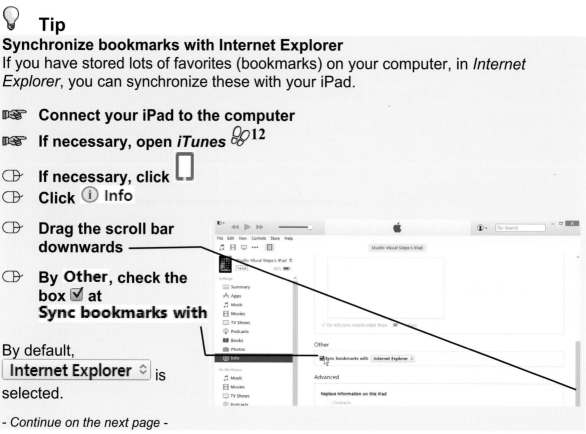

- Continue on the next page -

☞ **Make sure no other options are checked in this window**

If that is the case:

☞ **Uncheck** 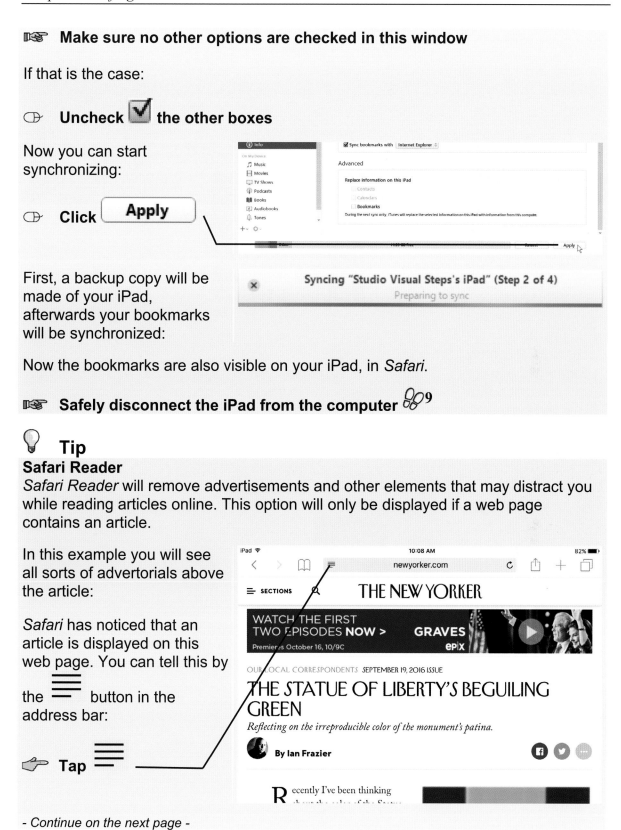 **the other boxes**

Now you can start
synchronizing:

☞ **Click** **Apply**

First, a backup copy will be
made of your iPad,
afterwards your bookmarks
will be synchronized:

Syncing "Studio Visual Steps's iPad" (Step 2 of 4)
Preparing to sync

Now the bookmarks are also visible on your iPad, in *Safari*.

☞ **Safely disconnect the iPad from the computer** ᙅᙆ**9**

💡 **Tip**
Safari Reader
Safari Reader will remove advertisements and other elements that may distract you
while reading articles online. This option will only be displayed if a web page
contains an article.

In this example you will see
all sorts of advertorials above
the article:

Safari has noticed that an
article is displayed on this
web page. You can tell this by

the ≡ button in the
address bar:

☞ **Tap** ≡

THE NEW YORKER

OUR LOCAL CORRESPONDENTS   SEPTEMBER 19, 2016 ISSUE

THE STATUE OF LIBERTY'S BEGUILING
GREEN

Reflecting on the irreproducible color of the monument's patina.

By Ian Frazier

- Continue on the next page -

Now the article will be opened in a new window. You can read the article without being distracted.

The ☰ button has now turned black ☰. You can close the *Safari Reader* screen by clicking ☰:

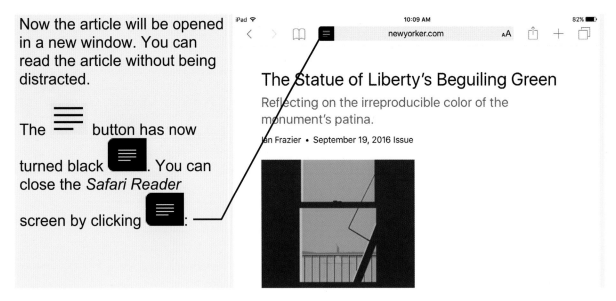

🔆 Tip
Creating a Reading List
In *Safari* you can create a reading list. A reading list contains links to web pages you want to visit at a later time. For that, you do not need an Internet connection.
This is how you add the current page to a reading list:

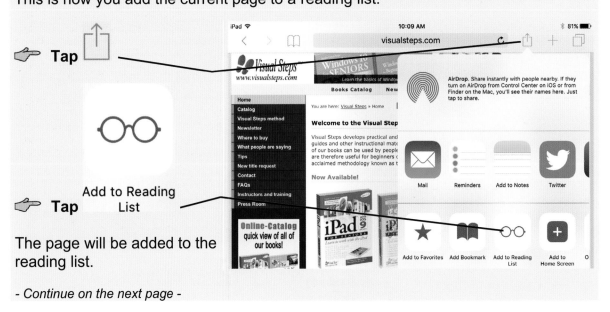

☞ Tap 📤

☞ Tap **Add to Reading List**

The page will be added to the reading list.

- Continue on the next page -

You can also add a link to the reading list like this:

☞ **Put your finger on**
Catalog

Wait a moment for the menu to appear:

☞ **Tap**
Add to Reading Li

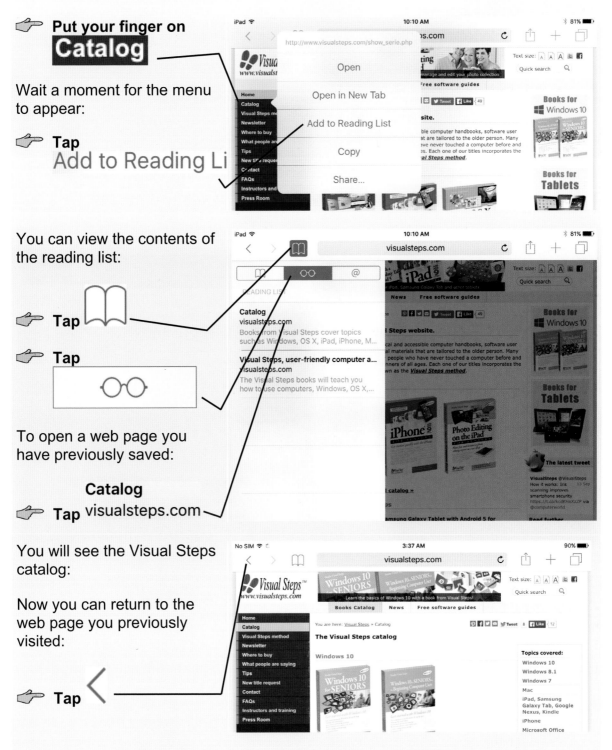

You can view the contents of the reading list:

☞ **Tap** 📖

☞ **Tap** 👓

To open a web page you have previously saved:

Catalog
☞ **Tap** visualsteps.com

You will see the Visual Steps catalog:

Now you can return to the web page you previously visited:

☞ **Tap** ‹

The page has been read and will be removed from the reading list.

Tip

Multitasking gestures
The iPad will also react to gestures made with four or five fingers at once. These are called *multitasking gestures*. First, you need to check if the multitasking gestures have been enabled on your iPad:

☞ **Open the *Settings* app** ✿✿6

👉 **If necessary, tap** ⚙ General

👉 **If necessary, tap** Multitasking

👉 **If necessary, drag the slider** ⬭ **by** Gestures **to the right**

There are three different multitasking gestures:

👉 **Swipe upwards across the screen, with four or five fingers**

The multitasking bar is displayed. This is how you make it disappear:

☞ **Press the Home button**

You can also quickly switch between opened apps without using the multitasking bar:

👉 **Swipe across the screen from right to left, with four or five fingers**

You will see the next opened app.

👉 **Swipe across the screen from left to right, with four or five fingers**

You will see the previous opened app.

The last multitasking gesture will quickly take you back to the home screen, without using the Home button:

👉 **Use your thumb and three or four finger to make a pinching gesture on the screen**

Now you will see the home screen.

4. The Standard Apps on Your iPad

Along with *Mail* and *Safari*, there are other useful apps already installed on your iPad. The *Contacts* app allows you to manage your contacts. You can synchronize your contacts with your computer and edit, delete or add new contacts with the iPad.

The *Calendar* app lets you keep track of your appointments and daily activities. If you already have a calendar in *Outlook.com, Hotmail* or *Google Calendar*, you can show it with your iPad. You can add new events and edit or delete activities already made.
Next to the *Calendar* app, the *Reminders* app will help you save important appointments and tasks.

In the *Maps* app you can look up addresses and well-known places. You can view these locations on a regular map or on a satellite photo. Once you have found the desired location, you can also get directions on how to get there.

Spotlight is the iPad's search utility. With this app you can search through the apps, files, activities and contacts stored on your iPad. Another helpful function is *Siri*. *Siri* lets you give verbal instructions for the iPad to execute, and lets you ask the iPad for information.

There is also a central option with which you can neatly arrange and display all the messages you have received on your iPad, such as new email messages and the notifications you have set up on your iPad. This is called the *Notification Center*.

In this chapter you will learn how to:

- add and edit contacts in the *Contacts* app;
- add an activity in the *Calendar* app;
- set a reminder;
- establish your current location in the *Maps* app;
- change the view;
- search for a location and get directions;
- search with *Spotlight*;
- ask *Siri* for help;
- view notifications;
- disable apps.

4.1 Adding a Contact

You can open the *Contacts* app on the home screen of your iPad.

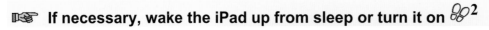 **If necessary, wake the iPad up from sleep or turn it on** 👣²

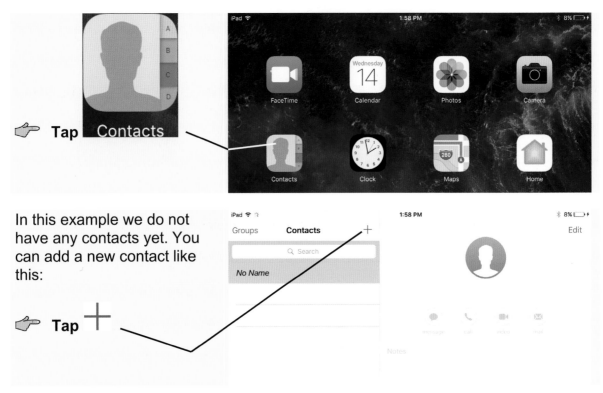

☞ **Tap** Contacts

In this example we do not have any contacts yet. You can add a new contact like this:

☞ **Tap** +

You can practice with a fictitious contact or if you like, use a real person that you know. You will be using the onscreen keyboard:

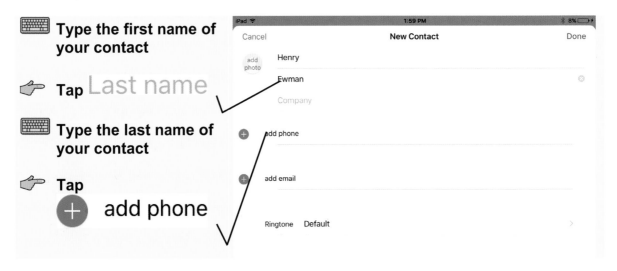

⌨ **Type the first name of your contact**

☞ **Tap** Last name

⌨ **Type the last name of your contact**

☞ **Tap**

⊕ **add phone**

Type the phone number of your contact

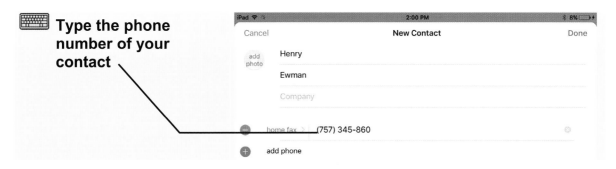

Please note:

When you enter a phone number, the digits will automatically be grouped in the right order, including parentheses, dashes or no dashes as needed. The format used depends on the region format settings in the *Settings* app.

As soon as you start entering a phone number in a field, a new line will appear where you add another phone number. This will also happen when you enter data in other fields. The default label for the first phone number field is home fax. You can change the name of this label and other labels as well. In this example the field will be changed in mobile:

Tap home fax

You will see a list from which you can select a label:

Tap mobile

You can enter a lot of other information about your contact. It is up to you to fill in all the fields, or leave them blank.

☞ **Add your contact's email address. If he has a homepage (web address) you can enter that as well** 👣**44**

Tip

Change the label

You can change the label for the email address. You can select home for a personal email address and work for a work-related one, for example.

At the bottom of the page you will find even more fields:

☞ **Drag the page upwards**

☞ **Tap**

⊕   add addr

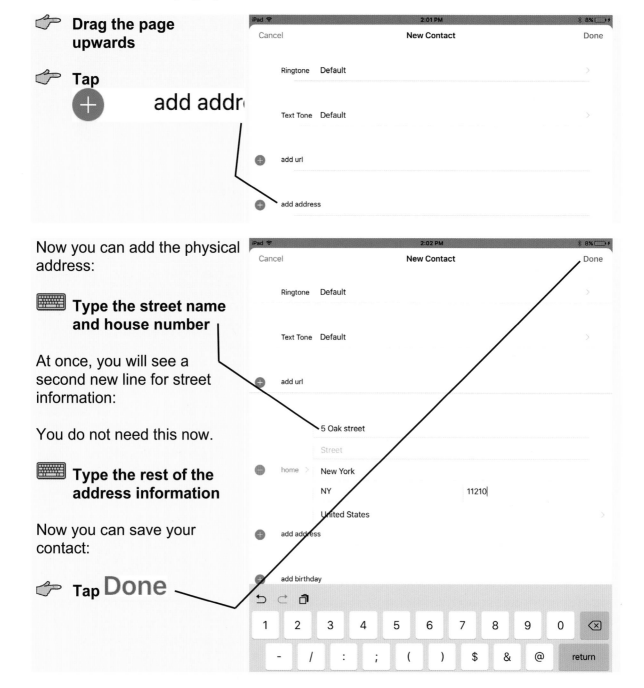

Now you can add the physical address:

⌨ **Type the street name and house number**

At once, you will see a second new line for street information:

You do not need this now.

⌨ **Type the rest of the address information**

Now you can save your contact:

☞ **Tap Done**

Now your contact will appear in the **Contacts** list:

The contact information is shown on the right-side:

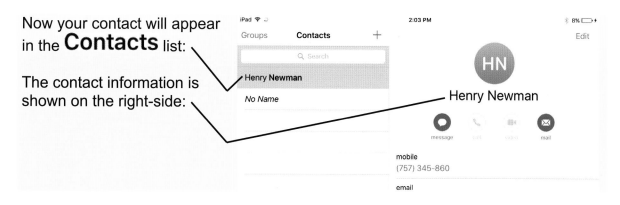

☞ **Add another four contacts** ⁴⁵

💡 **Tip**

Add a field for a middle name
A contact called De Vere will be listed under the letter D in the All Contacts list. If you prefer to classify this name under the letter V, you can add a field for the middle name:

☞ **Drag the page all the way upwards**

☞ **Tap** add field

You will see a list of fields you can add:

☞ **Tap** Middle name

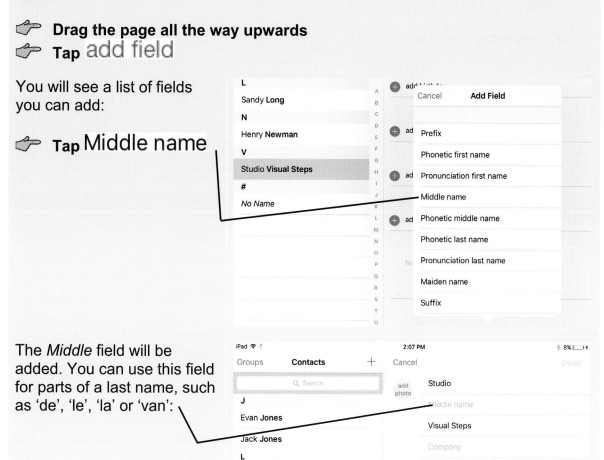

The *Middle* field will be added. You can use this field for parts of a last name, such as 'de', 'le', 'la' or 'van':

4.2 Editing a Contact

After you have entered all your contacts, you might want to edit them. Perhaps, a contact has moved and has a new address or a new phone number. This is how you open a contact for editing:

👉 **Tap the desired contact**

👉 **Tap** Edit

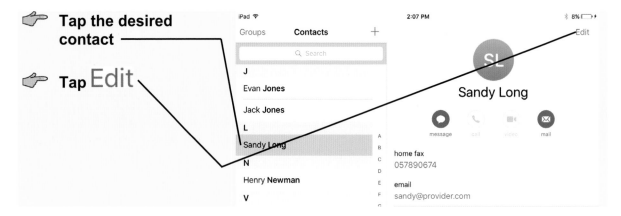

If you need to change the phone number:

👉 **Tap the phone number**

👉 **Tap** ⊗

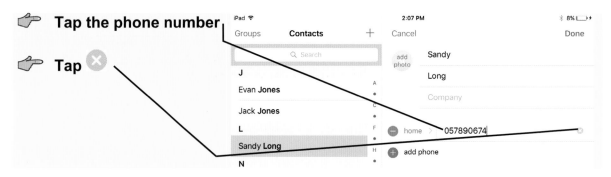

The phone number will be deleted:

⌨ **Type the new phone number**

👉 **Tap** Done

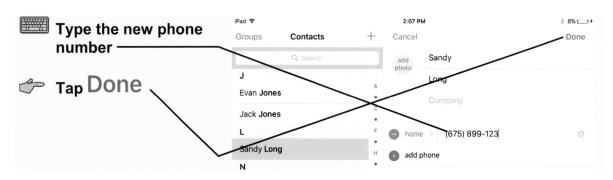

You can do the same thing for any other field that needs editing.

👉 **Go back to the home screen** 👣**8**

4.3 Calendar app

With the *Calendar* app you can keep track of your appointments, upcoming activities, birthdays and more. You open the *Calendar* app like this:

☞ **Tap** Calendar

When you open the *Calendar* app for the first time, you might see a window with the new options. You can close that window:

☞ **Tap** Continue

You might see this message:

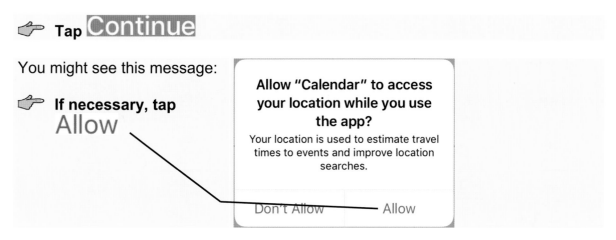

☞ **If necessary, tap** Allow

Allow "Calendar" to access your location while you use the app?

Your location is used to estimate travel times to events and improve location searches.

Don't Allow   Allow

The calendar opens showing the current date and time.

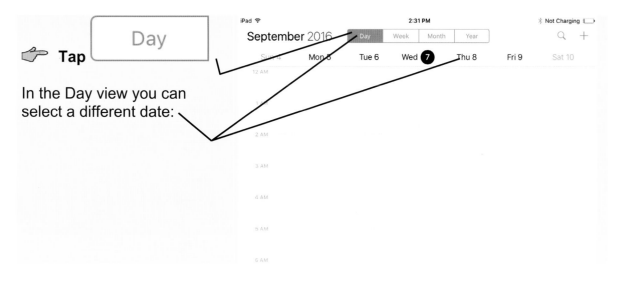

☞ **Tap** Day

In the Day view you can select a different date:

If you have selected a different date from the current date, you can use the Today button to quickly return to your current appointments:

First, you check if the calendar is displayed on the iPad:

☞ **Tap** Calendars

If there is no checkmark on the left side of ● Calendar:

☞ **By** ON MY IPAD, **tap** ● Calendar

☞ **Tap** Done

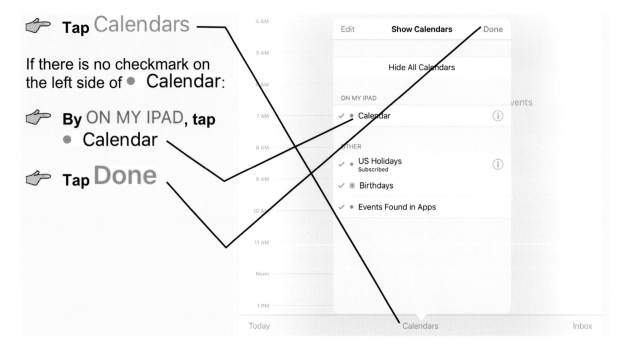

You can change the view to display the full week, month or year. This is how to view the full week:

☞ **Tap** Week

You will see the week view for the current week. You can quickly scroll to the next week like this:

☞ **Swipe from right to left over the screen**

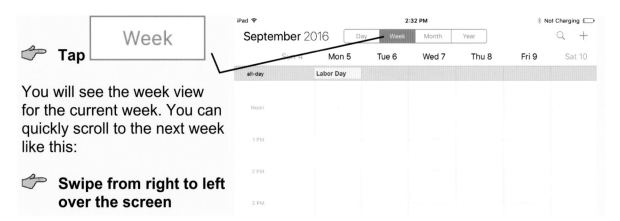

Now you will see the following week on your screen.

4.4 Adding an Event

In the *Calendar* app, an appointment is called an *event*. It is easy to add a new event to your calendar. Give it a try:

☞ **Tap** ✛

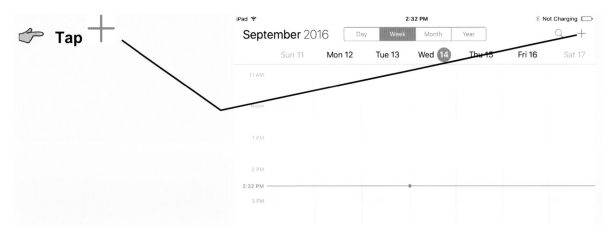

Now you can add a name and location for the event:

⌨ **Type a name, for example:** Tennis lessons

☞ **Tap** Location

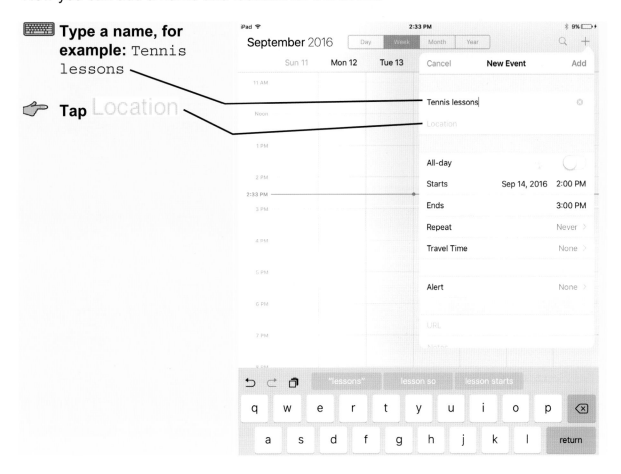

Type a location, for instance: `Tennis court`

A search is made for locations and several options are shown:

In this example, we will be using the general option, which is the text that you typed:

☞ **Tap** Tennis court

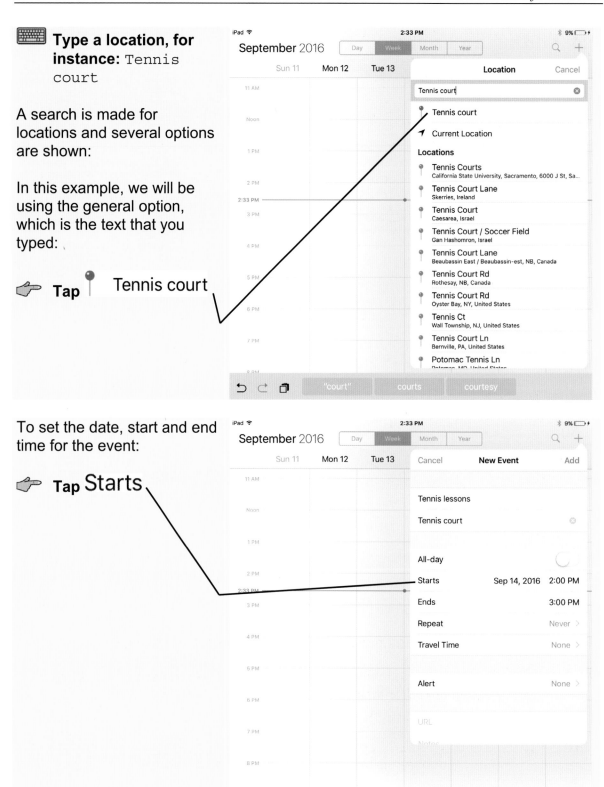

To set the date, start and end time for the event:

☞ **Tap** Starts

The date and time are displayed as three revolving wheels, a bit like a slot machine. You can change the time by turning the wheels. You need to touch the screen in a certain way:

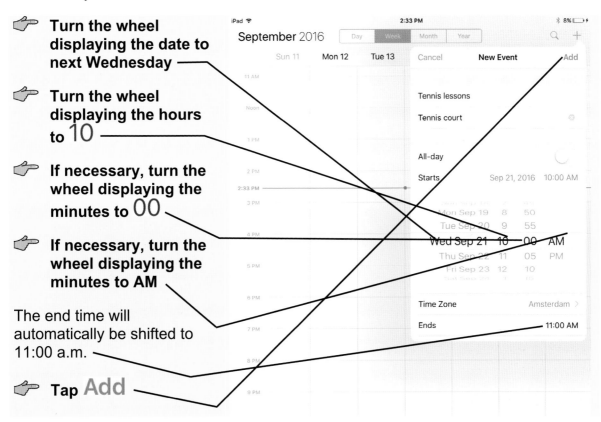

☞ **Turn the wheel displaying the date to next Wednesday** —

☞ **Turn the wheel displaying the hours to** 10 —

☞ **If necessary, turn the wheel displaying the minutes to** 00

☞ **If necessary, turn the wheel displaying the minutes to AM**

The end time will automatically be shifted to 11:00 a.m.

☞ **Tap** Add —

💡 **Tip**
All day
If the event takes all day:

☞ **By** All-day**, tap**

On the screen where you add an event, you will see three more options:

Repeat | Here you can set whether the event has to be repeated, and what the frequency is. For instance, every week or every month. By default, the Never option is selected.

Travel Time | Here you can add the travel time you need to get to the location for an event. Event alerts will take this time into account.

Alert | Here you can set up an alert, a sort of reminder, for a specific event. You can set a time for this alert: several minutes, hours, or days before the event. By default, the None option is selected.

☞ **Swipe from right to left over the screen**

You will see the event in the calendar:

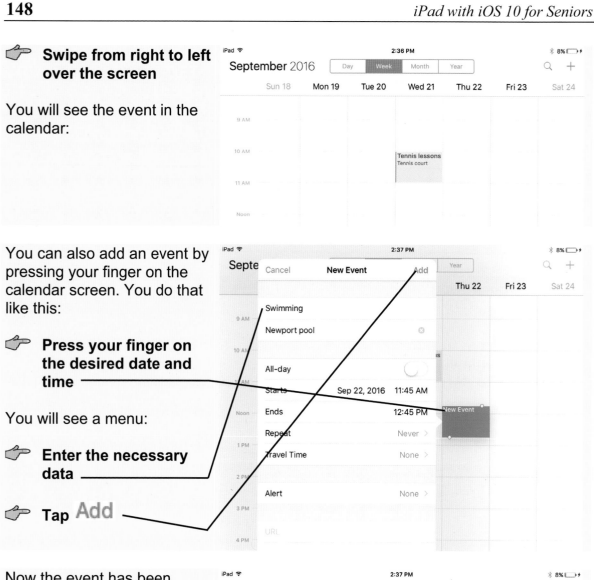

You can also add an event by pressing your finger on the calendar screen. You do that like this:

☞ **Press your finger on the desired date and time**

You will see a menu:

☞ **Enter the necessary data**

☞ **Tap** Add

Now the event has been added to the calendar:

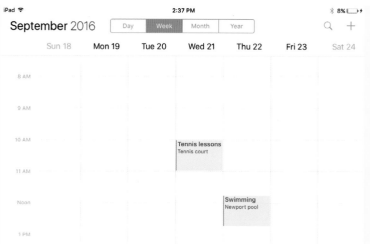

☞ **Go back to the home screen** ✌8

4.5 Reminders app

The *Reminders* app will help you save important appointments and tasks. You can create lists of tasks yourself, including dates and locations.

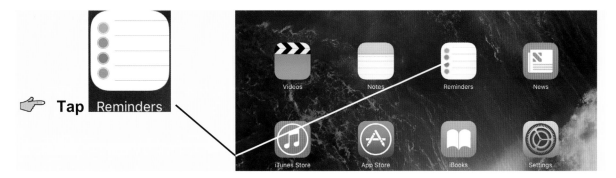

☞ **Tap** Reminders

You will see an overview to which you can add a new task:

☞ **Tap the first line**

⌨ **Type a reminder**

☞ **Tap** return

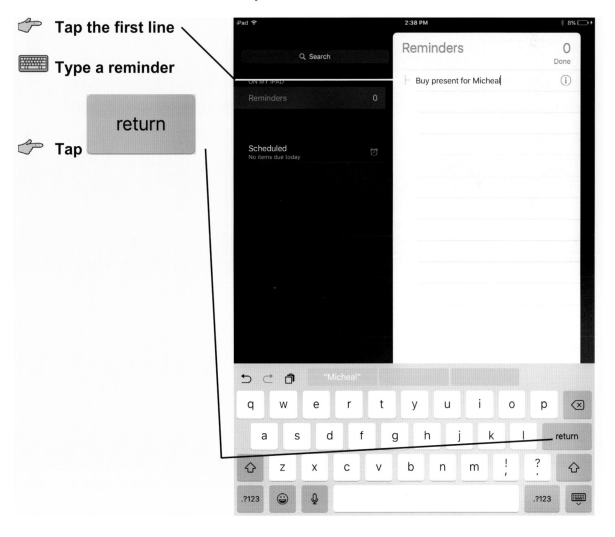

After you have added a reminder, you can add additional information:

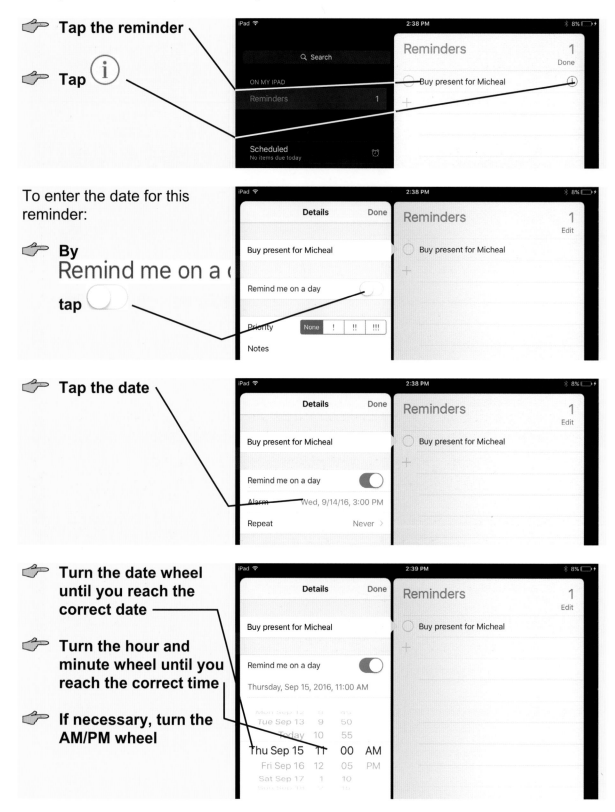

☞ **Tap the reminder**

☞ **Tap** (i)

To enter the date for this reminder:

☞ **By**
Remind me on a
tap ⬭

☞ **Tap the date**

☞ **Turn the date wheel**
until you reach the
correct date

☞ **Turn the hour and**
minute wheel until you
reach the correct time

☞ **If necessary, turn the**
AM/PM wheel

You can add even more information, like a note, for example:

 Tap below Notes

⌨ **Type a note**

After you have finished typing:

☞ **Tap** Done

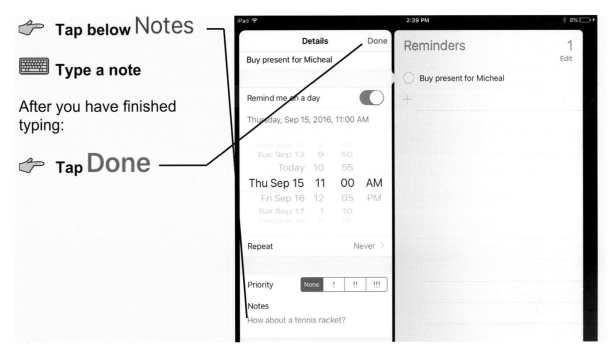

💡 **Tip**

Sound the alarm
When the date and time of your reminder occurs, an alarm goes off and a small window pops up on your screen. If the iPad is in sleep mode:

If you want to turn off the reminder:

☞ **Swipe over the screen**

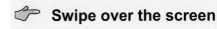

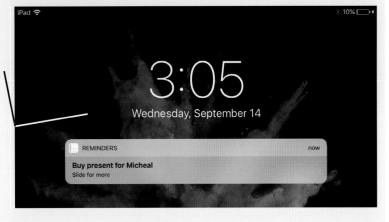

- Continue on the next page -

If the iPad is not in sleep mode you will see a message:

You can use the Later button to show the reminder again at a later moment.

To close it and mark as completed:

☞ **Tap** Mark as Completed

If you have stored a lot of reminders in this app, you can order them into lists. In this way, you can separate personal chores from work-related tasks, for instance. This is how you create a list:

At the bottom of the screen:

☞ **Tap** Edit

At the bottom of the screen:

☞ **Tap** Add List

⌨ **Type a name for the list**

☞ **Tap** Done

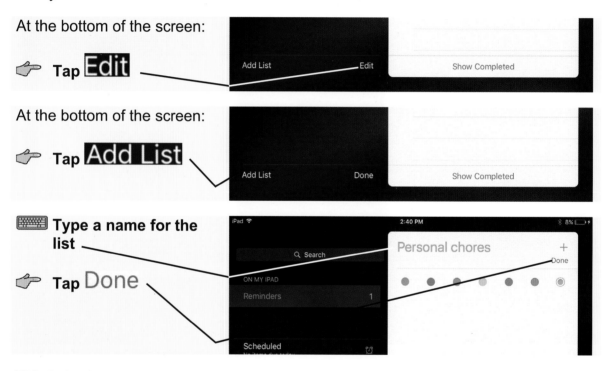

This is how you add a reminder to a list:

☞ **If necessary, tap** Reminders

☞ **Tap the reminder**

☞ **Tap** ⓘ

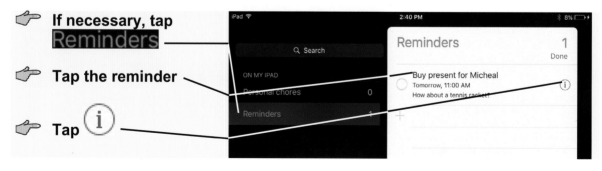

☞ **Tap** List

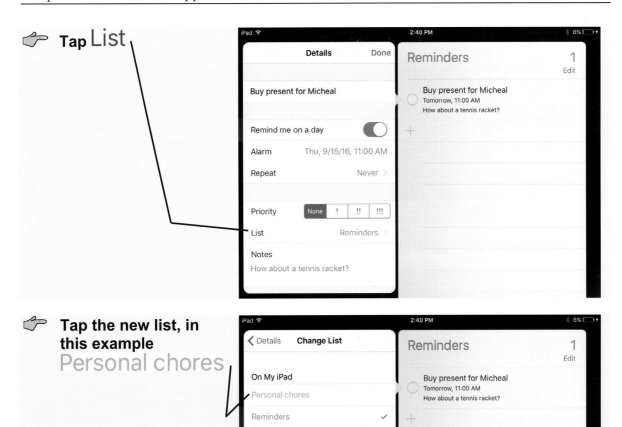

☞ **Tap the new list, in this example** Personal chores

☞ **Tap** Done

☞ **Tap** Personal chore

You see the reminder in the Personal chores list:

To delete the reminder:

☞ **Tap** Edit

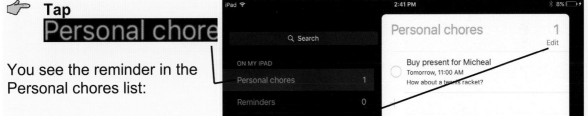

☞ **By the reminder, tap**

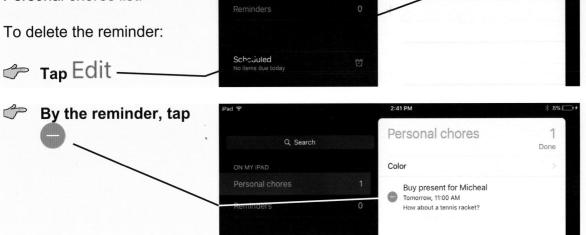

👉 **Go back to the home screen** 👣**8**

4.6 Maps app

With the *Maps* app you can search for a specific location and get directions for how to get there. To do this, you need to be connected to the Internet.

This is how you open the *Maps* app:

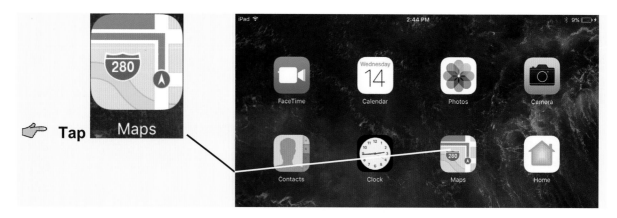

You will see the map of the country where you are located. You will be asked for permission to use your current location:

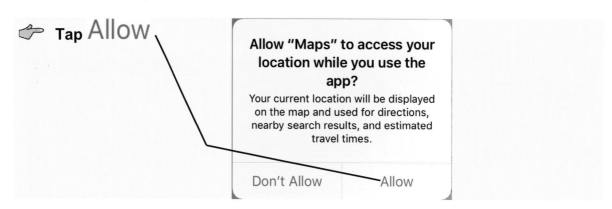

You might also see a window about helping to improve *Maps*. In this example, we will not choose to allow that:

☞ **Tap** Don't Allow

Now you can determine your current location:

☞ **At the top right corner of the screen, tap**

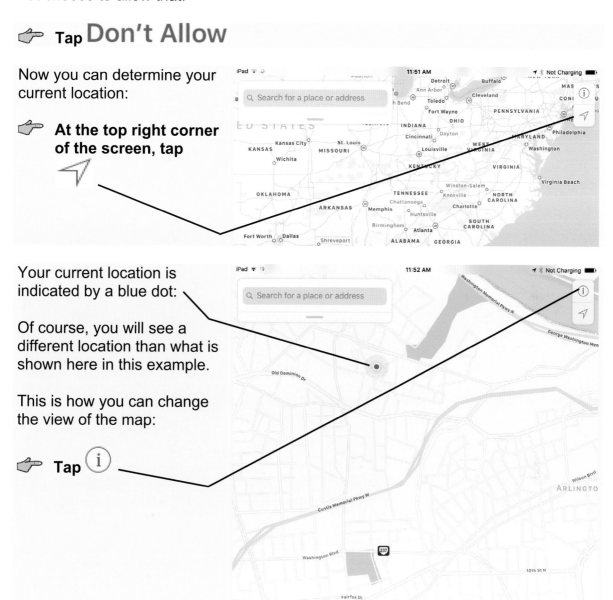

Your current location is indicated by a blue dot:

Of course, you will see a different location than what is shown here in this example.

This is how you can change the view of the map:

☞ **Tap** (i)

You can select a view:

Map: regular view.

Satellite: satellite photo.

☞ **Tap** Satellite

To hide the window:

☞ **Tap** ⊗

You will see a combination of a map and a satellite photo of your current location:

Tip

Zooming in and out

Move two fingers apart from each other (spread), or move them towards each other (pinch) to zoom in or out.

4.7 Find a Location

You can use *Maps* to look for a specific location. You can search for a house or business address as well as a famous public place:

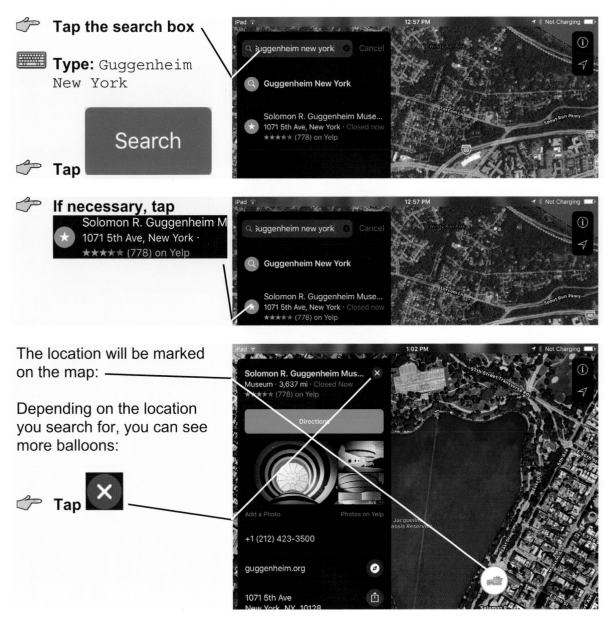

☞ **Tap the search box**

⌨ **Type:** Guggenheim New York

☞ **Tap** Search

☞ **If necessary, tap**
Solomon R. Guggenheim M
1071 5th Ave, New York ·
★★★★★ (778) on Yelp

The location will be marked on the map:

Depending on the location you search for, you can see more balloons:

☞ **Tap** ✕

4.8 Map Out your Trip

Once you have found the desired location, you can plot a course for how to get there. This is how you do it:

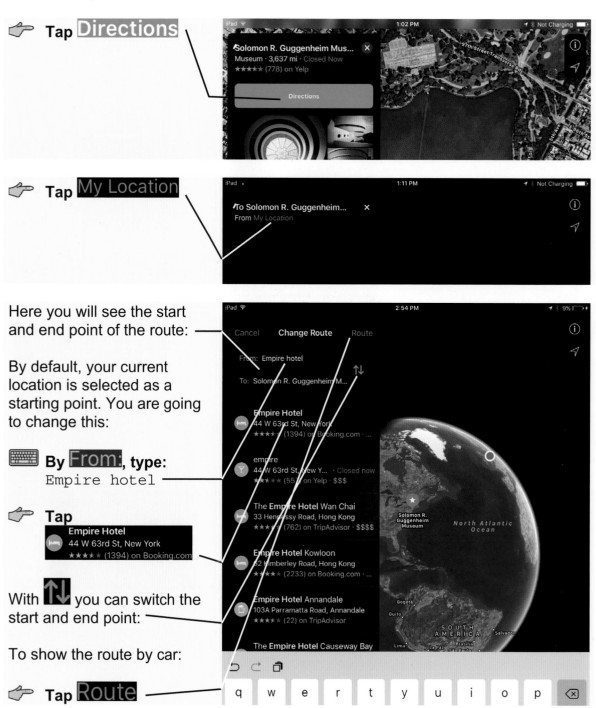

☞ Tap Directions

☞ Tap My Location

Here you will see the start and end point of the route:

By default, your current location is selected as a starting point. You are going to change this:

⌨ By From:, type:
Empire hotel

☞ Tap

Empire Hotel
44 W 63rd St, New York
★★★★★ (1394) on Booking.com

With ⇅ you can switch the start and end point:

To show the route by car:

☞ Tap Route

You may see a safety warning:

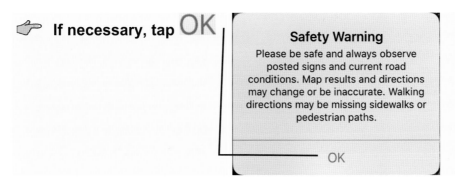

If necessary, tap OK

The car route will be shown starting from the starting point. The route is indicated by a blue line: —————

Here you can see the directions, the amount of time and mileage needed to take this route: —————

In this example an alternative

route is also given,

With 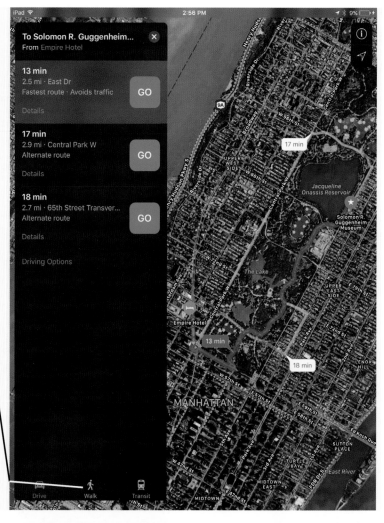 you can view the route, the distance and the amount of time needed to walk to the destination:

You can display the route step by step:

Next to the shortest route:

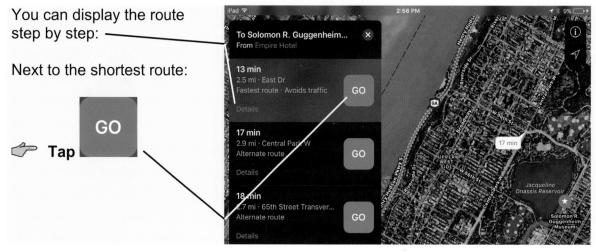

☞ **Tap**

You will see the first step of the route. You will also see the instruction in the box at the top:

In order to display the next step you need to swipe to the adjacent box:

👉 **Swipe from right to left**

Now you can follow the route step by step by tapping the next box every time. For now this will not be necessary.

👉 **Tap** **End**

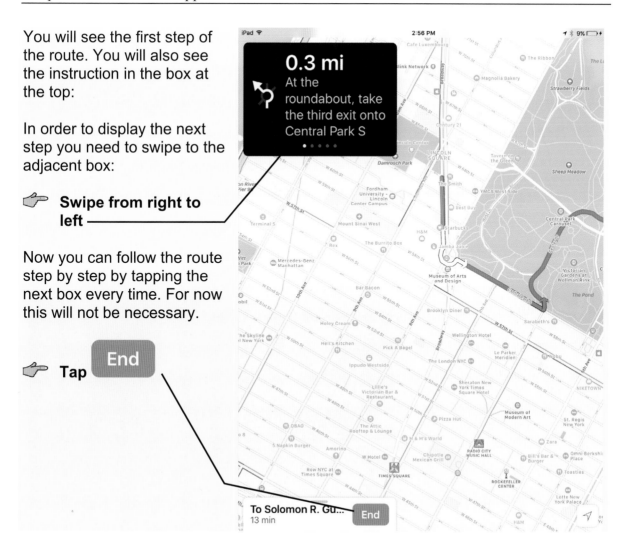

Tip

iPad with 3G/4G

If you are using an iPad with Wi-Fi + 3G/4G and your own location has been entered at Start:, the screen will look different. Because an iPad with 3G/4G is equipped with a built-in GPS receiver you can use it as a navigational device.

You will hear the spoken instructions and you will see your current location marked on the screen:

As soon as you move, the icon for your current location moves also and you will hear the next instruction.

You can close the route:

 Tap End

Note: your window might look a bit different.

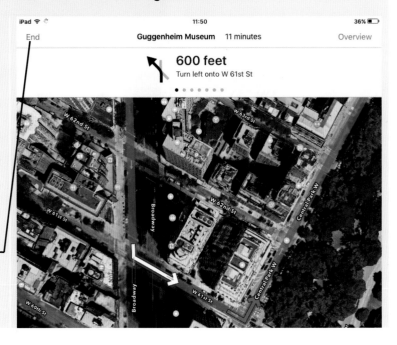

You will see your current location again.

☞ **Go back to the home screen** 🐾⁸

4.9 Spotlight

Spotlight is your iPad's search utility. This is how you open *Spotlight*:

👉 **Swipe downwards across the screen a bit, halfway the screen**

Spotlight will be opened:

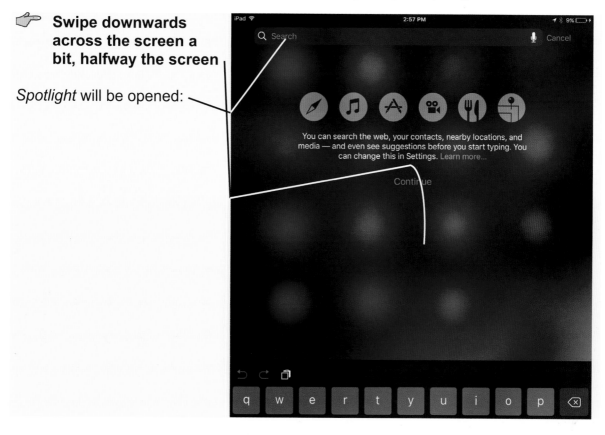

You can type your query right away. In this example we are searching for an event that has been previously entered in the *Calendar* app:

⌨ **Type:** Tennis lessons

You will also see the appointment:

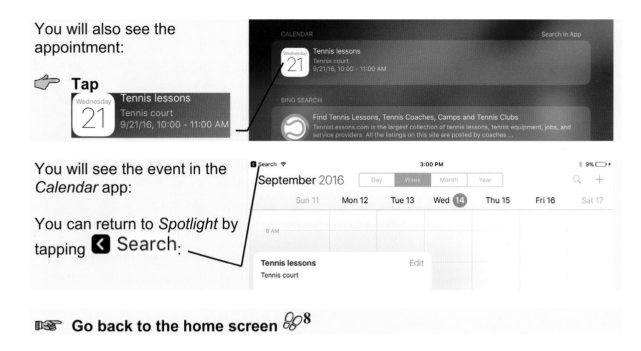

☞ **Tap**

You will see the event in the *Calendar* app:

You can return to *Spotlight* by tapping ◀ **Search**.

☞ **Go back to the home screen** 🦶8

4.10 Siri

The iPad has a useful function with which you can give verbal instructions for the iPad to execute, and you can also use it to ask for information. This is how you open *Siri*:

☞ **Press and hold the Home button**

Siri opens and you can ask a question out loud:

☞ **Speak loudly and clearly and ask: What's the weather in New York?**

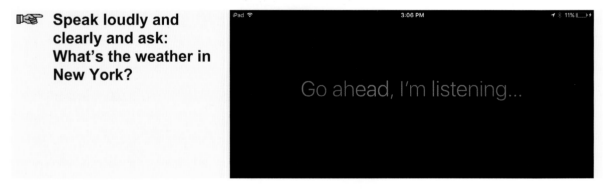

You will both see and hear the answer:

If you wish, you can tap the screen to open the weather forecast in the *Weather* app. For now this will not be necessary.

Pose another question:

☞ **Tap**

☞ **Speak loudly and clearly and ask: Do I have any appointments today?**

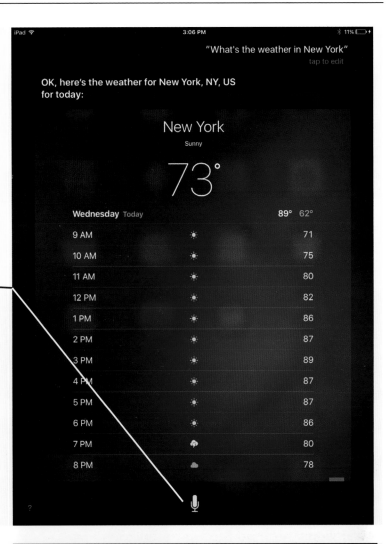

You will both see and hear the answer:

You can ask many more questions in the same way.

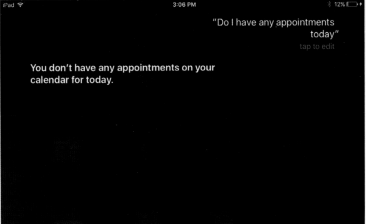

☞ **Go back to the home screen** 🦶🦶8

4.11 Notification Center

The messages you receive on your iPad, such as new email messages or other messages set to be displayed on your iPad, can all be viewed in the *Notification Center* in a neatly arranged list. This way, you can quickly see which messages you have recently received. This is how you open the *Notification Center*:

☞ **Swipe your finger across the screen, from top to bottom**

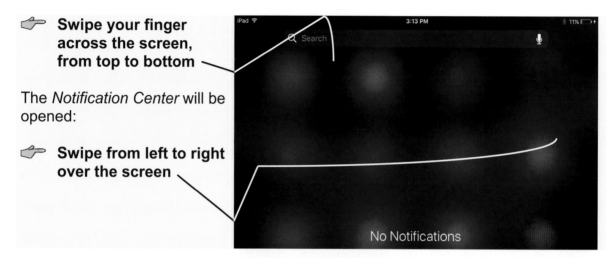

The *Notification Center* will be opened:

☞ **Swipe from left to right over the screen**

In this example, you can see the notification about the tennis lesson:

You can also view all notifications or the missed notifications:

This is how you open a message:

☞ **Tap a message, for example, the event**

The *Calendar* app will be opened and you will see the event:

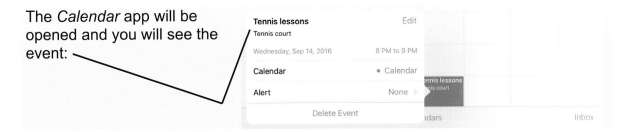

In this way you can view lots of things that are important for today.

☞ **Go back to the home screen** 𝒬ℓ⁸

Email messages will not be displayed in the *Notification Center* by default. You need to change the settings in the *Settings* app:

☞ **Open the *Settings* app** 𝒬ℓ⁶

☞ **Tap**

Notifications

In this screen you can see all the settings for the *Notification Center*:

To display email messages:

☞ **Tap** ✉ **Mail**

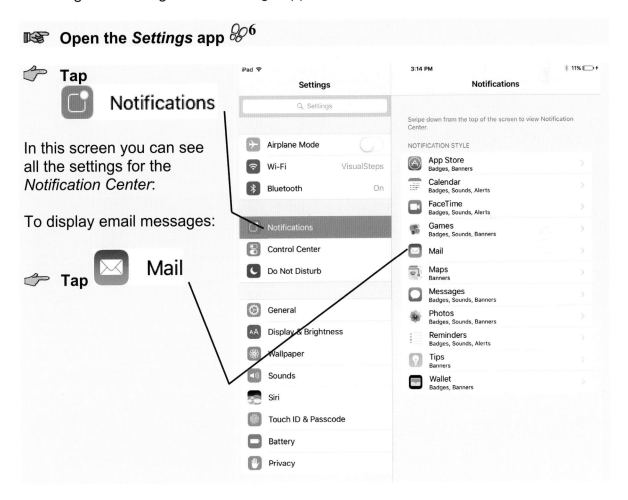

☞ **By**
Show in Notificat
tap

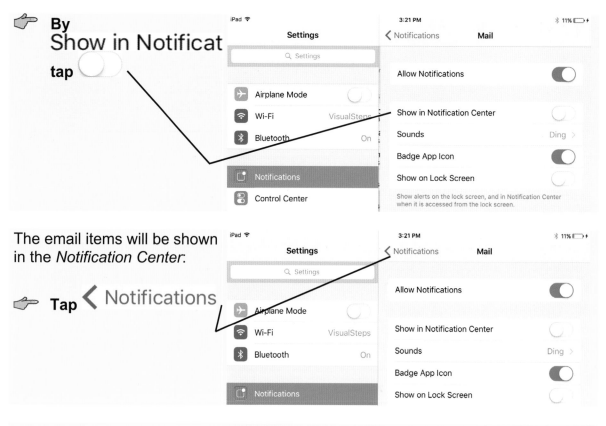

The email items will be shown in the *Notification Center*:

☞ **Tap** ❮ Notifications

☞ **Go back to the home screen** 🐾 **8**

☞ **Swipe your finger across the screen, from top to bottom**

In this example you will see a new email message has been received:

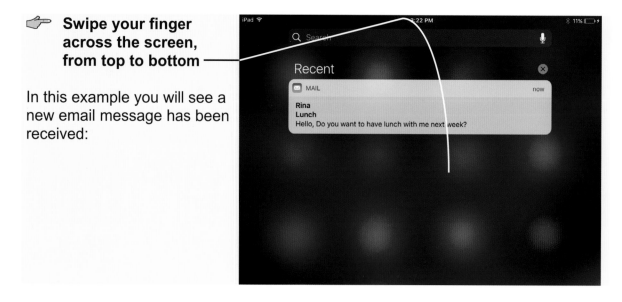

4.12 Disabling Apps

By now, you have used a number of different apps on the iPad. Each time after using an app, you have returned to the home screen. But the apps have not been disabled by this action. Actually, this is not really necessary, because the iPad uses very little power in sleep mode, and you have the advantage of being able to continue at the same spot, once you start working again.

Nevertheless, it is possible to close the apps, if you want. This is how you do it:

☞ **Press the Home button twice**

☞ **Drag the app window upwards**

The app will be closed.

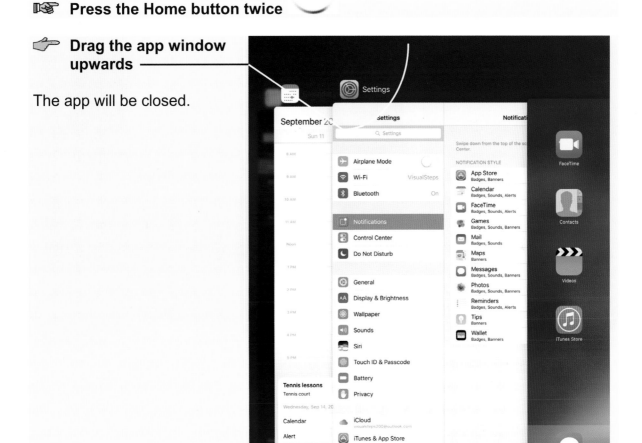

You will see the screen for
the next app:

You can close the other apps
in the same way:

☞ **Close the other apps
too**

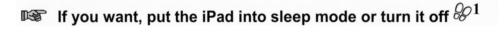

☞ **Press the Home button**

☞ **If you want, put the iPad into sleep mode or turn it off** ✌¹

In this chapter you have learned more about some of the standard apps that are
installed on your iPad. The following exercises will let you practice using these apps.

4.13 Exercises

To be able to quickly apply the things you have learned, you can work through these exercises. Have you forgotten how to do something? Use the numbers next to the footsteps $\mathscr{CO}^1$ to look up the item in the appendix *How Do I Do That Again?*

Exercise 1: Contacts

In this exercise you will practice adding and editing contacts.

☞ If necessary, wake the iPad up from sleep or turn it on. $\mathscr{CO}^2$

☞ Open the *Contacts* app. $\mathscr{CO}^{46}$

☞ Add a new contact. $\mathscr{CO}^{45}$

☞ Open the information about the contact to edit it. $\mathscr{CO}^{47}$

☞ Change the *home* label to *mobile*. $\mathscr{CO}^{48}$

☞ Save the changes. $\mathscr{CO}^{49}$

☞ Go back to the home screen. $\mathscr{CO}^8$

Exercise 2: Calendar

In this exercise you will practice adding a new event to the *Calendar* app.

☞ Open the *Calendar* app. $\mathscr{CO}^{50}$

☞ Select the *Day* view. $\mathscr{CO}^{51}$

☞ Go to Today. $\mathscr{CO}^{52}$

☞ Skip to the day after tomorrow. $\mathscr{CO}^{53}$

☞ Open a new event. $\mathscr{CO}^{54}$

☞ Enter these items: $\mathscr{O}\!\!\mathscr{O}^{55}$
name: lunch, location: Lunchroom The Jolly Joker.

☞ Change the times: starts: 12:00 PM, ends 1:00 PM. $\mathscr{O}\!\!\mathscr{O}^{56}$

☞ Save the changes. $\mathscr{O}\!\!\mathscr{O}^{49}$

☞ Go back to the home screen. $\mathscr{O}\!\!\mathscr{O}^{8}$

Exercise 3: Maps

In this exercise you are going to look for a location.

☞ Open the *Maps* app. $\mathscr{O}\!\!\mathscr{O}^{57}$

☞ Find your current location. $\mathscr{O}\!\!\mathscr{O}^{58}$

☞ Change the view to *Satellite*. $\mathscr{O}\!\!\mathscr{O}^{59}$

☞ Search for this location: Arc de Triomphe Paris. $\mathscr{O}\!\!\mathscr{O}^{60}$

☞ Map out a trip from Rue de Rivoli to the Arc de Triomphe. $\mathscr{O}\!\!\mathscr{O}^{61}$

☞ Display a full set of directions for walking the route. $\mathscr{O}\!\!\mathscr{O}^{62}$

☞ Go back to the home screen. $\mathscr{O}\!\!\mathscr{O}^{8}$

Exercise 4: Spotlight

In this exercise you are going to practice searching with *Spotlight*.

☞ Open *Spotlight*. $\mathscr{O}\!\!\mathscr{O}^{63}$

☞ Search for one of your contacts. $\mathscr{O}\!\!\mathscr{O}^{64}$

☞ Tap the desired search result.

☞ Go back to the home screen. $\mathscr{O}\!\!\mathscr{O}^{8}$

☞ If you want, put the iPad into sleep mode or turn it off. $\mathscr{O}\!\!\mathscr{O}^{1}$

4.14 Background Information

Dictionary

Calendar	An app that lets you keep track of your appointments and activities.
Contacts	An app that you can use to manage your contacts.
Event	An appointment in the *Calendar* app.
Field	Part of the information you can enter about a contact. For example, *First name* and *Postal code* are fields.
Google Calendar	A *Google* service that lets you keep a calendar or agenda.
Google Contacts	A *Google* service that allows you to store and manage contacts.
Maps	An app where you can look for locations and addresses, view satellite photos and plan routes.
Microsoft Outlook	An email program that is part of the *Microsoft Office* suite.
Notification Center	A central option with which you can neatly arrange and display all the messages you have received on your iPad, such as new e-mail messages and the notifications you have set up on your iPad. You can open this option by dragging across the screen from top to bottom.
Siri	A function that lets you give verbal instructions for the iPad to execute, and lets you ask the iPad for information too.
Slide over	With this option you can open and look at two apps at the same time.
Split View	With this option you can use two apps at the same time.
Spotlight	The search utility on the iPad.
Synchronize	Literally: make even. Not only can you synchronize your iPad with the content of your *iTunes Library*, but also the information about your contacts or calendar events.
Windows Contacts	*Windows* service that lets you store and manage contacts.
Yahoo!	Email, calendar and contacts service that lets you store and manage these data.

Source: User Guide iPad, Wikipedia

4.15 Tips

 Tip

Add a photo

If you have a nice picture of your contact stored on your iPad, you can add this photo to his contact information. In *Chapter 6 Photos and Video* you can read how to take a picture with the iPad, and how to transfer photos to your iPad. This is to add an existing photo to your contact:

☞ **Tap the desired contact**

☞ **Tap** Edit

☞ **Tap** add photo

☞ **Tap** Choose Photo

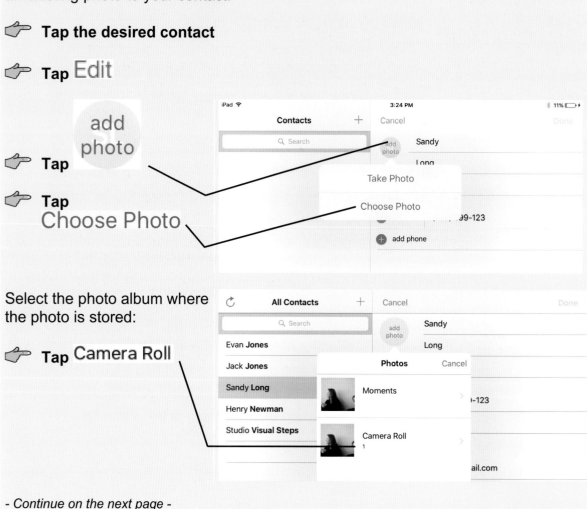

Select the photo album where the photo is stored:

☞ **Tap** Camera Roll

- Continue on the next page -

☞ **Tap the photo you want to use**

If you want, you can move the photo and adjust the scale by zooming in or out:

When you are ready:

☞ **Tap Choose**

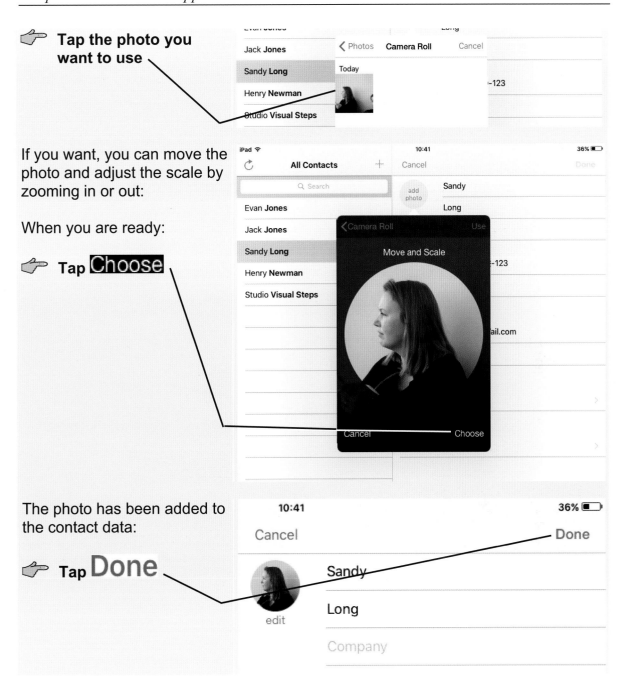

The photo has been added to the contact data:

☞ **Tap Done**

Tip

Delete a contact
This is how to delete someone from your contact list:

☞ **Tap the desired contact**

☞ **Tap** Edit

☞ **Drag the page upwards**

☞ **Tap** Delete Contact

☞ **Tap** Delete Contact

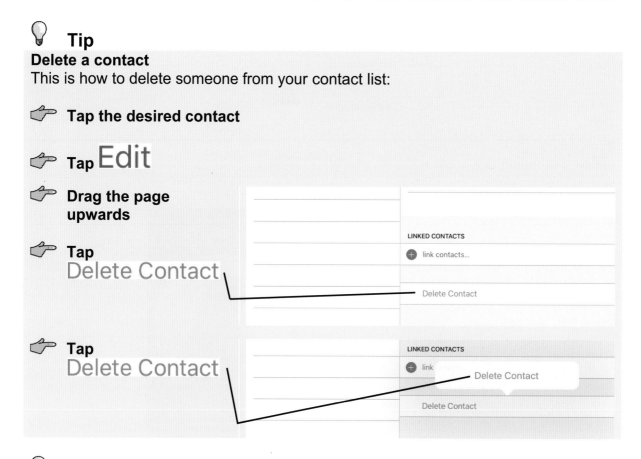

 **Tip**

Edit or delete an event
When a certain event changes or is canceled, you can edit it or delete it:

☞ **Tap the event**

☞ **Tap** Edit

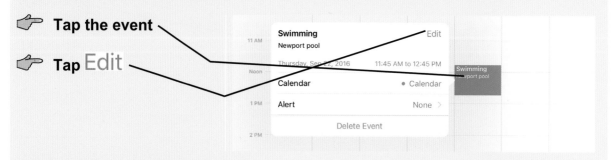

In this screen you can change the description, location, date, or time of the event. When you have finished:

☞ **Tap** Done

- Continue on the next page -

If you want to delete the
event:

☞ **Tap** Delete Event

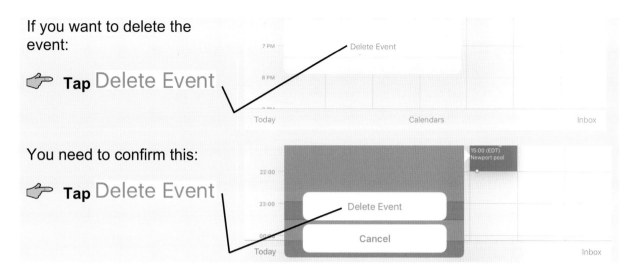

You need to confirm this:

☞ **Tap** Delete Event

💡 **Tip**

Add an event from an email message

Mail recognizes dates in email messages and can insert them into your calendar.
After a date has been recognized, you can quickly add an event to your calendar:

☞ **Tap the date** ———

☞ **Tap** Create Event

- Continue on the next page -

You will see the window in which you can enter the details of the event:

The subject of the email message is used as a name for the event: ————

After you have modified the data, you can add the event to your calendar:

 Tap Add

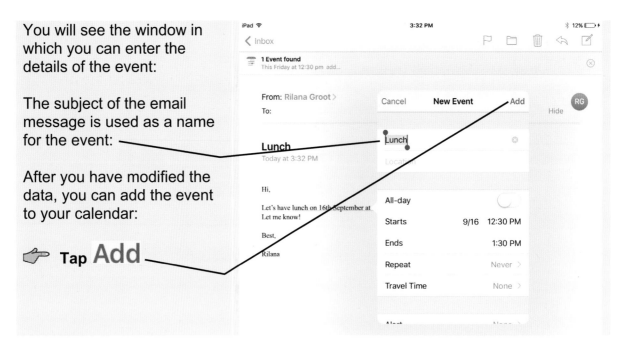

Tip
Detailed information
Many locations offer additional information such as address information, the phone number and the website, if there is one:

You will see the information in the left side of the screen:

If you wish to share the information, tap :

If you swipe upwards over the window, you will see more options, like adding the location to your contacts.

To close the window:

Tap

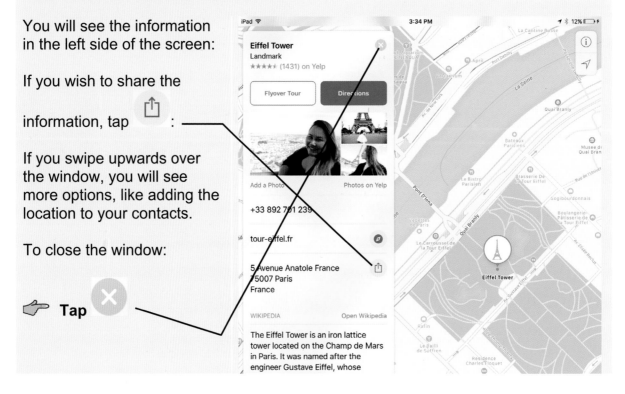

💡 Tip

Display traffic information

You can display the traffic conditions on the main roads and highways on the map:

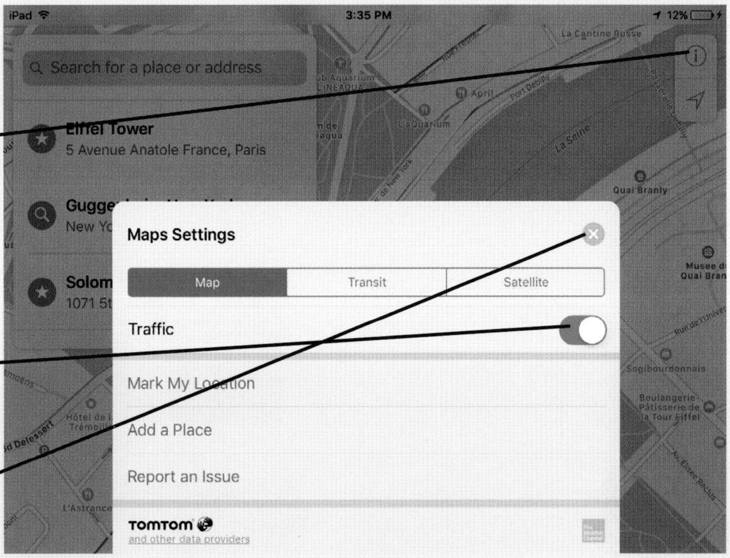

👉 **Tap** ⓘ

If necessary:

👉 **By** Traffic**, tap**

👉 **Tap** ⊗

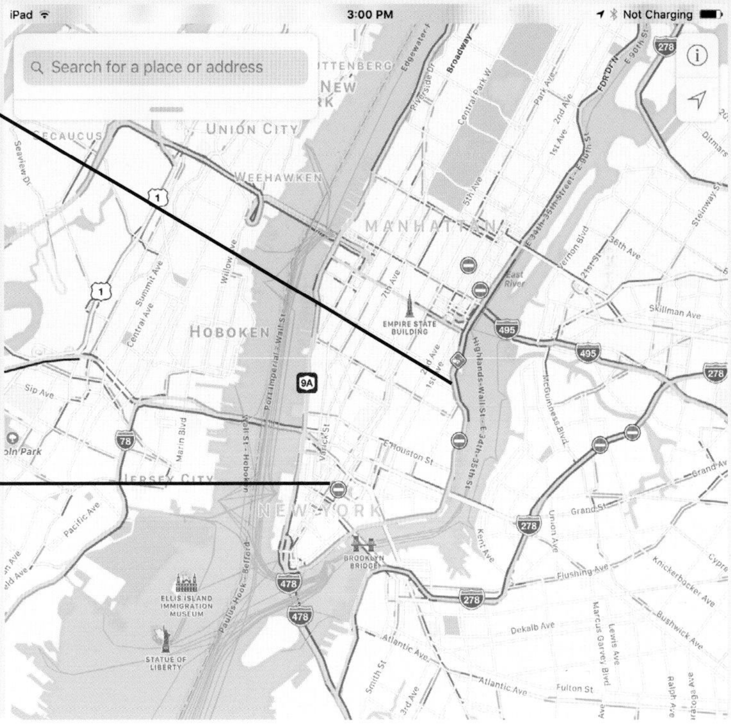

You will see the traffic information marked by the red and orange lines:

To see information about the traffic conditions, you can tap
🚫:

Maps Settings

| Map | Transit | Satellite |

Traffic

Mark My Location

Add a Place

Report an Issue

TOMTOM
and other data providers

Tip

Flyover

In the *Maps* app you can view many urban areas and famous landmarks in 3D. This function is called *Flyover*.

Please note: This function is not available for some cities and well-known places. In this example, you will be viewing the Golden Gate Bridge in San Francisco.

When you have found the location:

 Tap

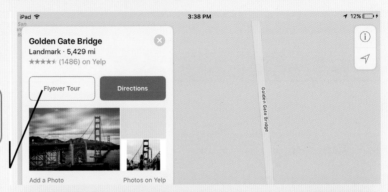

You will see the Golden Gate Bridge in 3D. You can zoom in on the bridge and move the map around by dragging with your fingers. You can even rotate the image. It will appear as if you are flying right alongside the bridge.

 Press gently with your thumb and index finger and make a turning motion

In this way you can see an interesting object up close from all sides and discover new things about it.

To disable or turn off the 3D mode, tap **End**.

Tip

Display Google, Hotmail, Outlook.com or Yahoo! calendar and contacts
Do you use *Google*, *Hotmail, Outlook.com* or *Yahoo! Calendar* to keep track of appointments and activities? Or do you manage your contacts in one of these accounts? If you have set up your *Gmail, Hotmail, Outlook.com* or *Yahoo!* account on the iPad, you can set your account to display your calendar or contacts on the iPad too.

☞ **Open the *Settings* app** 🦶[6]

☞ **Tap** ✉ Mail

☞ **Tap Accounts**

In this example a *Gmail* account is chosen to display the calendar:

To open the account settings:

Gmail
☞ **Tap** Mail, Contacts

By ▦ Calendars:

☞ **Tap** ⬭

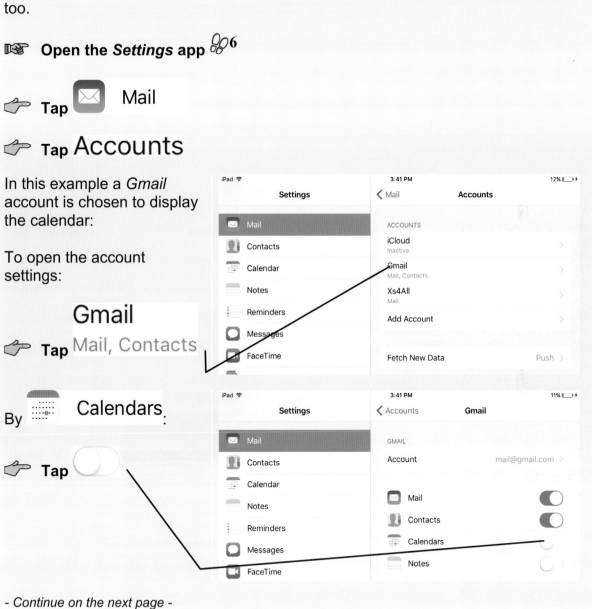

- Continue on the next page -

You may see this message:

👉 **Tap** Keep on My iPad

👉 **Tap** Keep

Now the events from the calendar will be displayed in the *Calendar* app on your iPad.

 Tip
Slide over
An option on the latest type of iPads is *Slide Over*, with which you can open and look at two apps at the same time. This is handy when you read something in an app and want to create a reminder. However you can't use both apps. To use both apps you can read the following Tip. To get the best view you can hold the iPad in horizontal position:

☞ **Turn the iPad to the right or left towards a horizontal position**

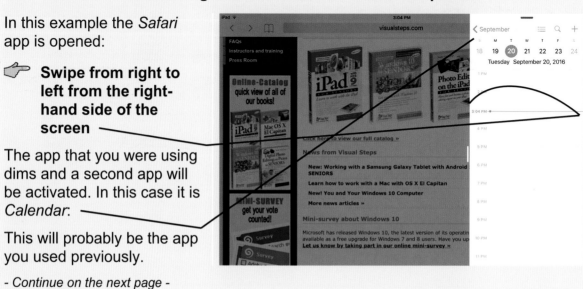

In this example the *Safari* app is opened:

👉 **Swipe from right to left from the right-hand side of the screen**

The app that you were using dims and a second app will be activated. In this case it is *Calendar*:

This will probably be the app you used previously.

- Continue on the next page -

You can also open a different app in the Slide Over modus.

At the top by the activated app:

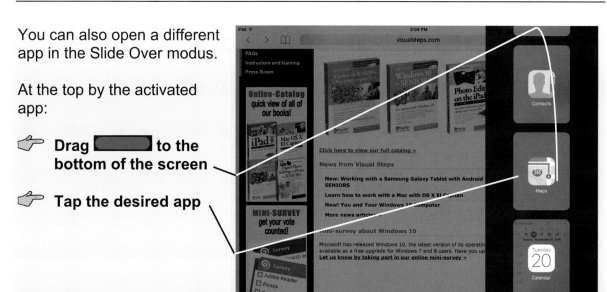

 Drag ▭ **to the bottom of the screen**

 Tap the desired app

To go back to the first app you have used, in this example the *Safari* app:

☞ **Tap the app at the left-hand side**

💡 **Tip**
Split View
On the latest type of iPads you can also use the new option Split View. With this option you can use two apps at the same time. You can use it like this:

☞ **Turn the iPad to the right or left towards a horizontal position**

In this example the *Safari* app is opened. You can open a new app:

☞ **Swipe from right to left from the right-hand side of the screen**

- Continue on the next page -

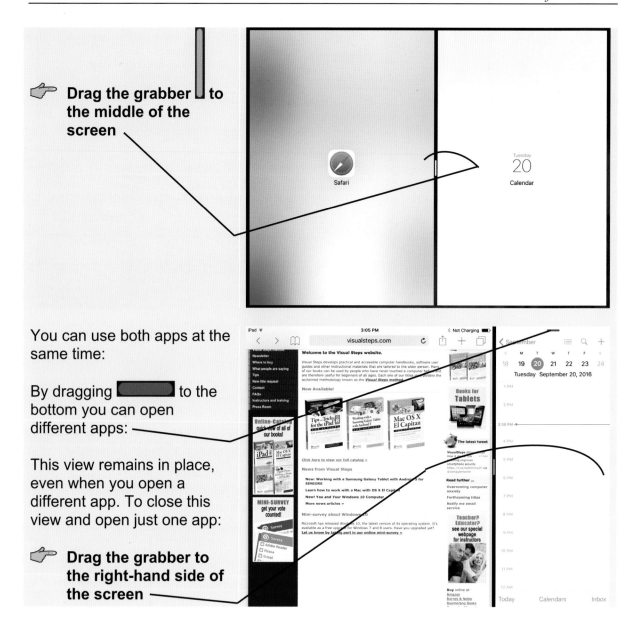

👉 **Drag the grabber ▯ to the middle of the screen**

You can use both apps at the same time:

By dragging ▭ to the bottom you can open different apps:

This view remains in place, even when you open a different app. To close this view and open just one app:

👉 **Drag the grabber to the right-hand side of the screen**

 Tip

Synchronize contacts
Do you manage your contacts already on your computer? Then you might be able to synchronize these contacts with your iPad. You can synchronize with contacts from *Microsoft Outlook* and *Windows Contacts*.
You can synchronize your contacts in the same way as your bookmarks in *Internet Explorer* or *Safari*, as explained in the *Tip* at the back of *Chapter 3 Surfing with Your iPad*.

5. Downloading Apps

In the previous chapters you have become acquainted with the standard apps installed on the iPad. But there is so much more for you to discover! In the *App Store* you will find thousands of apps, free of charge or for a small fee, which you can download and install.

There are so many apps, it is impossible to list them all. Apps for news, magazines, the weather, games, recipes, sports results: you name it, there is bound to be an app available that interests you!

In this chapter you will learn how download apps. If you want to download apps that charge a fee, you can pay for them safely with an *iTunes Gift Card*. This is a prepaid card available in a variety of different venues. You can also link a credit card to your *Apple ID*.

Once you have purchased apps, you can arrange them on your iPad in any order you want. You can also create folders that can hold multiple apps in the same folder. If you are no longer happy with a particular app, you can delete it.

In this chapter you will learn how to:

- download and install a free app;
- use an *iTunes Gift Card*;
- buy and install an app;
- sign out from the *App Store*;
- move apps;
- save apps in a folder;
- delete apps.

Please note:

To follow the examples in this chapter you will need to have an *Apple ID*. If you have not created an *Apple ID* when you started using the iPad, you can learn how to do that in the *Bonus Chapter Creating an Apple ID*. In *Appendix C Opening a Bonus Chapter* you can read how to open a bonus chapter.

5.1 Downloading and Installing a Free App

In the *App Store* you will find thousands of apps that can be used on your iPad. This is how you open the *App Store*:

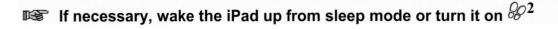 **If necessary, wake the iPad up from sleep mode or turn it on** $\mathcal{B}^2$

☞ **Tap** App Store

The first time you log in to the *App Store*, you will see this window.

To give access:

☞ **Tap** Allow

Allow "App Store" to access your location while you use the app?

This information will be used to suggest Apps that are more relevant to you.

Don't Allow   Allow

You may see this window about Family Sharing:

☞ **If necessary, tap** Not Now

Set Up Family Sharing

Share music, movies, apps, photos, and more with members of your family.

Not Now   Set Up

★

You will see the Featured page, where attention is paid to a number of new and popular apps.

You will open the Top Charts page:

At the bottom of the screen:

☞ **Tap** Top Charts

The most popular apps are shown:

You can also show the Top Charts per category:

☞ **Tap** Categories

☞ **Swipe upwards over the menu**

☞ **Tap** Weather

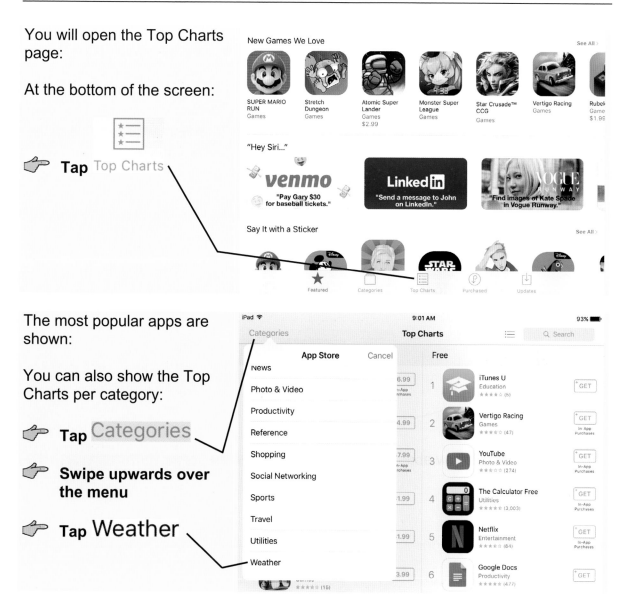

You will see several popular apps about the weather. This is how you download an app:

☞ **Tap**

 HELP! I do not see the app.

If you cannot find the *The Weather Channel* app in the list, you can look for it through the search box. This is how you do it:

👉 **Tap the search box**

⌨ **Type:** `Weather channel`

👉 **Tap** the weather channel®

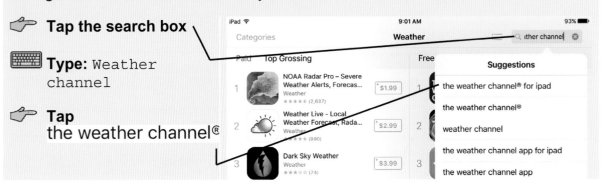

More information about the app is shown. This is how you download an app:

👉 **Tap** `GET`

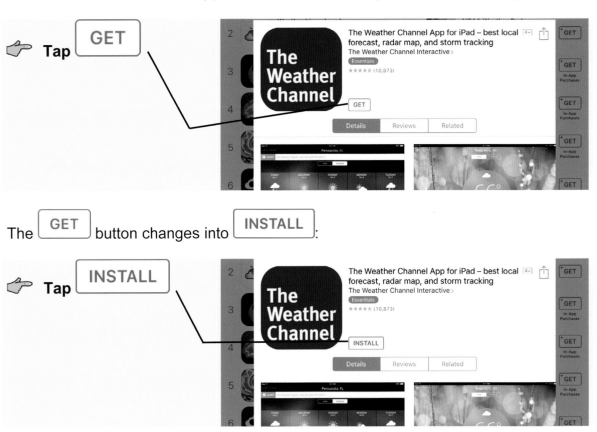

The `GET` button changes into `INSTALL`:

👉 **Tap** `INSTALL`

You need to sign in with your *Apple ID* in order to install the app:

If you have not yet downloaded an app in the *App Store* previously, you might see the message below. If you have already used the *App Store* you can continue at the middle of page 191.

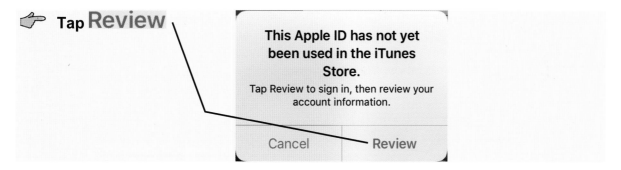

Your *Apple ID* needs to be completed with extra information, such as your country and your home address:

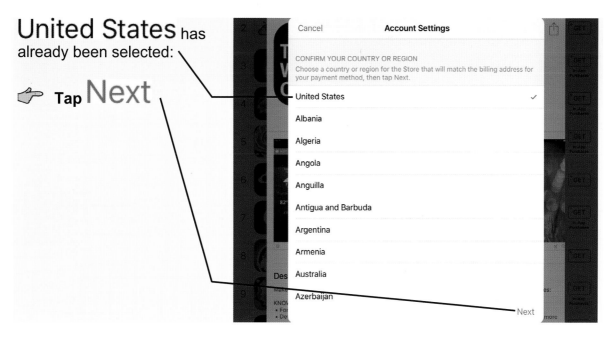

You see the *Account Settings* window:

☞ **Swipe upwards over the text**

☞ **Tap** Agree

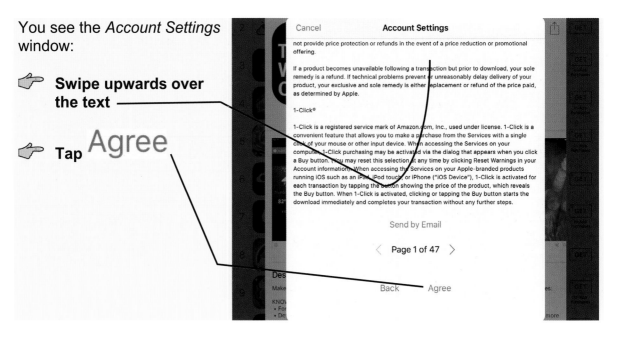

Once more, you need to confirm that you agree to the general terms and conditions:

☞ **Tap** Agree

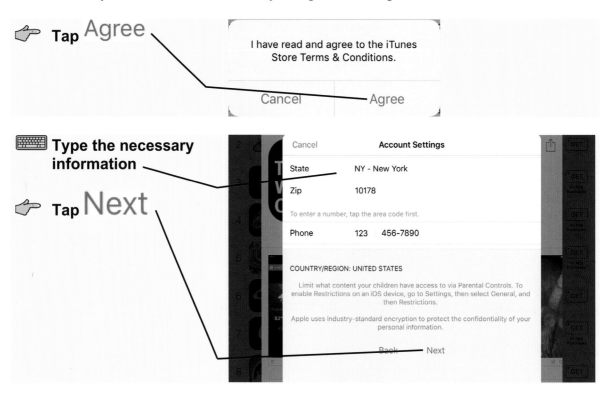

⌨ **Type the necessary information**

☞ **Tap** Next

HELP! I am asked to enter payment information and I do not want to do that.

Apple would like you to link your payment method to your *Apple ID*. If you do not want to this, you can select **None** at the top of the window, by **Payment Method**. If you cannot select this option and you do not want to enter any credit card information, you can link an *iTunes Gift Card* to your *Apple ID*. You can fill in the gift card code by **iTunes Gift Cards and iTunes Gifts**. We will tell you more about this subject in the next section.

Your *Apple ID* is ready:

 Tap Done

Now you can download and install the free *The Weather Channel* app:

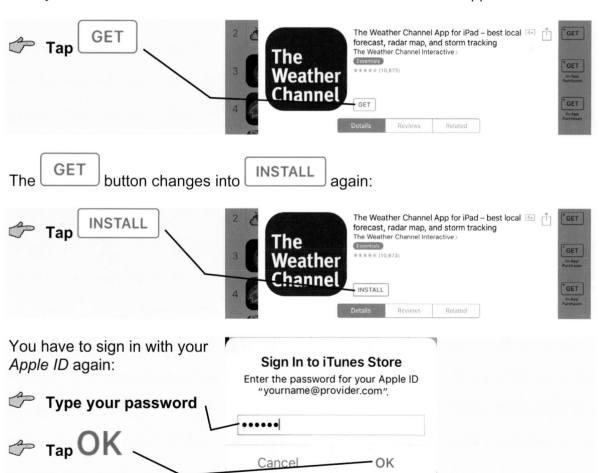

 Tap GET

The GET button changes into INSTALL again:

 Tap INSTALL

You have to sign in with your *Apple ID* again:

Sign In to iTunes Store
Enter the password for your Apple ID
"yourname@provider.com".

••••••

Cancel   OK

 Type your password

 Tap OK

☞ **Tap**
Require After 15 Min

You will see the *App Store* again. The app is installed when you see the ⃞ OPEN button. For now you do not need to open the app, you can take a look at it later on, in your own time.

☞ **Tap next to the window**

You will see the *App Store* again.

☞ **Go back to the home screen** 👣8

You will see the app at the second page: ——

To go back to the home screen:

☞ **Swipe from left to right over the screen**

💡 **Tip**

Manage apps
In *section 5.5 Managing Apps* you can read how to move apps on a page, and between pages.

In the next couple of sections you will learn how to use an *iTunes Gift Card* to purchase a paid app.

5.2 The iTunes Gift Card

The *iTunes Gift Card* is a prepaid card that you can use to purchase items in the *App Store.* By using an *iTunes Gift Card*, you can avoid using a credit card.

 Tip

iTunes Gift Card

The *iTunes Gift Card* comes in different denominations. You can purchase these cards from the *Apple Online Store*, at your *Apple* retailer and at thousands of other retailers across the USA, the UK and Australia.

You can also get the *iTunes Gift Card* at www.instantitunescodes.com.

This web store allows you to pay online and you will receive the code for the card by email, right away. *iTunes Gift Cards* purchased at this store are only valid in the United States.

 Please note:

To be able to follow the examples in the next section, you need to have an *iTunes Gift Card* available. If you do not (yet) have such a card, you can just read the text.

☞ **Open the** *App Store* ✂[65]

At the bottom of the page, you will find the link to redeem an *iTunes Gift Card*:

👉 **Tap** Featured

👉 **Swipe from the bottom to the top of the screen**

👉 **Tap**

Redeem

Now you will see a window where you can enter the code for your *iTunes Gift Card*.

You will find the code under the scratch layer on the back of the card: —————

☞ **Carefully remove the scratch layer**

You may need to sign in with your *Apple ID*:

⌨ **Type your password**

☞ Tap **OK**

Now you will see a code composed of 16 digits and letters that you need to enter:

☞ **Tap**
You can also enter

Although the code on the *iTunes Gift Card* contains capital letters, you can just type lower-case letters.

⌨ **Type the code** ————

☞ Tap **Redeem**

When the code is approved, you will see a confirmation and the balance of your credit.

5.3 Buying and Installing an App

Now that you have purchased a prepaid credit for your *Apple ID*, you will be able to buy apps in the *App Store*. Previously, you used the Top Charts page to look for an app. In this example we will purchase the *Weather+* app. First we will search for this app:

You can still see the text 'the weather channel' in the search box:

☞ **Tap the search box**

⌨ **Type:** weather

☞ **Tap weather**

The window with the search results will be opened:

☞ **If necessary, drag your finger upwards**

☞ **Tap** with the price button **$1.99** next to it

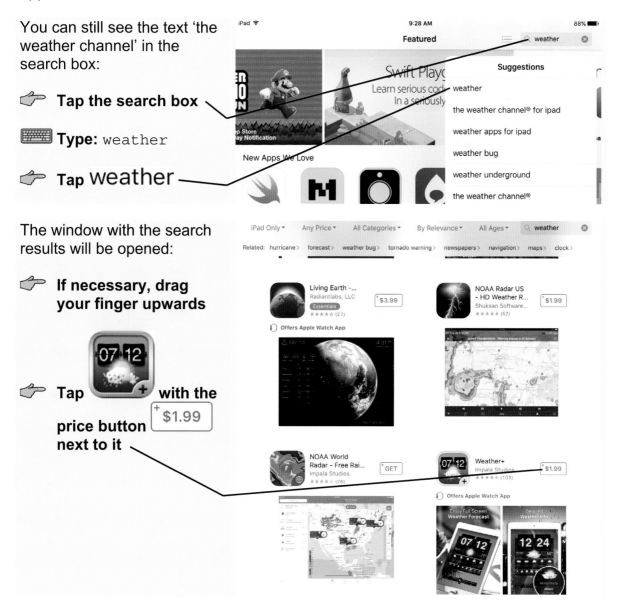

🐟 Please note:

In the example below we will be purchasing an app. You can decide whether you want to follow the steps and buy an app. Of course, you do not need to buy exactly the same app as in this example.

Please note:

You will only be able to follow the steps below if you have redeemed an *iTunes Gift Card* or if you have linked your credit card to your *Apple ID*. If you have not (yet) done this, you can just read through the rest of this section.

You will see additional information about this app:

If you want to buy the app:

 Tap $\boxed{^+\text{\$1.99}}$

The $\boxed{^+\text{\$1.99}}$ button will turn into $\boxed{\text{BUY}}$.

♀ **Tip**

iPhone and iPad

The plus sign ✚ on the $\boxed{^+\text{\$1.99}}$ button indicates that the app is suitable for the iPhone, as well as for the iPad. In the *Tips* at the end of this chapter you can read how to transfer the items you have purchased to *iTunes* on the computer.

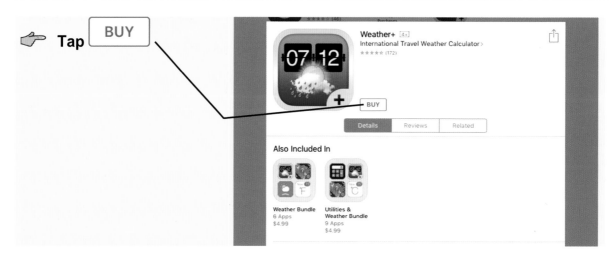

☞ **Tap** $\boxed{\text{BUY}}$

Before you can buy the app, you may have to sign in again with your *Apple ID* and answer your security questions. This is a security measure, to prevent someone else from using your *iTunes* credit or credit card to buy things, for instance if you lend your iPad to someone else.

Type your password

☞ **Tap OK**

Sign In to iTunes Store
Enter the password for your Apple ID
"yourname@provider.com".

Cancel ——— OK

You may see this window:

☞ **If necessary, tap the desired option, for example**
Require After 15 Minutes

iTunes and App Store in the Settings app.

Always Require

Require After 15 Minutes

If you see a couple more windows:

☞ **Follow the instructions in the windows**

↘ **Please note:**
When logged in with another account than you used before, you will probably see a couple more windows. If so, follow the instructions in the windows.

After that, the download will start. You can follow the progress by checking this icon

⬛. If you decide not to buy the app after all, you can still stop the download

operation by tapping ⬛.

When the app is downloaded and installed, you see OPEN :

You do not need to open the app right now:

☞ **Tap next to the window**

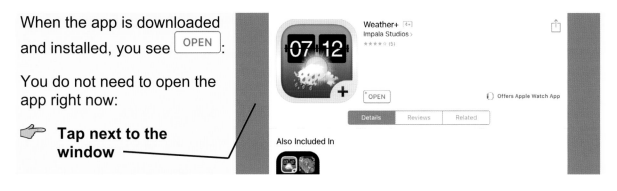

Weather+ Impala Studios

Details Reviews Related

Also Included In

☞ **Go back to the home screen** 🦶8

Just like the free app that you installed previously, this app will be put on the second page of your iPad:

To go back to the home screen:

 Swipe from left to right over the screen

5.4 Sign Out From the App Store

After you have signed in with your *Apple ID*, you will stay logged on for 15 minutes. During that period you can purchase items without having to enter your password again.

 Please note:

In some game apps, such as the popular game *Smurfs Village*, you can buy fake money or credits during the game and use it for bargaining. These *smurfberries* are paid with the money from your remaining *iTunes* credit or from your credit card. If you let your (grand) children play such a game, they can purchase items in these first 15 minutes without having to enter your password. So, it is better to sign out first.

☞ **Open the *App Store*** ✂[65]

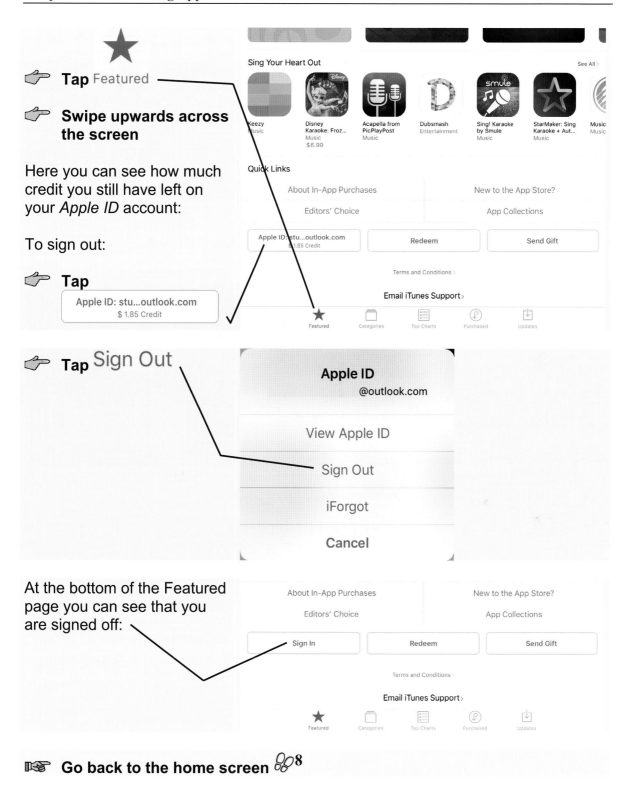

👉 **Tap** Featured

👉 **Swipe upwards across the screen**

Here you can see how much credit you still have left on your *Apple ID* account:

To sign out:

👉 **Tap**

> Apple ID: stu...outlook.com
> $ 1,85 Credit

👉 **Tap** Sign Out

Apple ID
@outlook.com

View Apple ID

Sign Out

iForgot

Cancel

At the bottom of the Featured page you can see that you are signed off:

👉 **Go back to the home screen** 👣**8**

5.5 Managing Apps

You can completely adjust the order of the apps on your iPad to your own taste, by moving the apps around.

 Please note:

In order to carry out the next few steps, you need to have installed at least two apps. If you have not purchased an app, you can download another free app that interests you, as described in *section 5.1 Downloading and Installing a Free App*. Or you can use other apps to perform the steps in this section.

This is how you scroll to the second page with the apps you just bought:

☞ **Swipe across the screen from right to left**

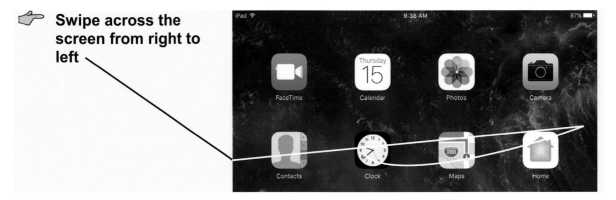

Now you will see the page with the apps you have purchased:

☞ **Press your finger on one of the apps**

The apps will start to jiggle, a little cross ⊗ will appear, and now you can move them:

☞ **Drag** to the right side of the other app

Now the apps have changed place.

You can also move an app to a different page. This is how you move an app to the home screen:

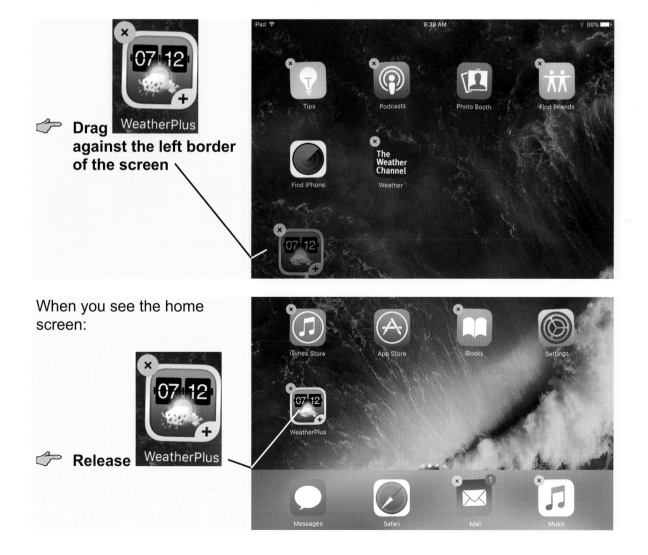

☞ **Drag against the left border of the screen**

When you see the home screen:

☞ **Release**

Now the app has been placed between the other apps on the home screen:

Of course, you can also change the order of the apps on this page. For now, this will not be necessary.

☞ **Flip to the second page** ✇⁶⁶

☞ **Move the other app to the home screen** ✇⁶⁷

You can also store related apps in a separate folder. Here is how to do that:

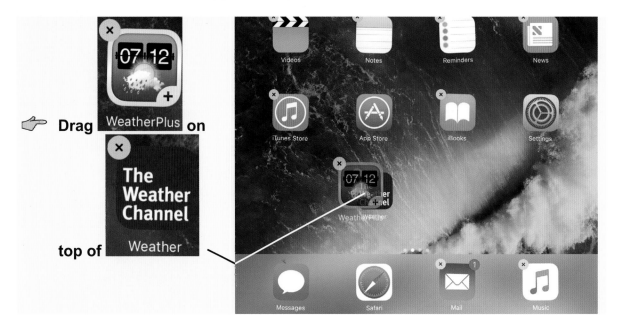

☞ **Drag** WeatherPlus **on top of** Weather

A suitable name will be
suggested for the new folder:

If you want you can also
change this name:

 Tap the name

 Type the desired name

If you are satisfied with the
name:

 Tap next to the folder

Now you will see this folder
on the home screen:

This is how to stop the apps from jiggling:

 **Press the Home button**

Now the apps have stopped moving. To view the contents of the folder:

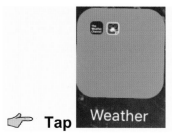

 Tap

You will see both the apps in
this folder:

You can store many apps in
the same folder.

This is how you remove the app from the folder again:

☞ **Make the apps jiggle** 𝒪𝒪**68**

☞ **Tap the folder**

☞ **Drag the app from the
folder**

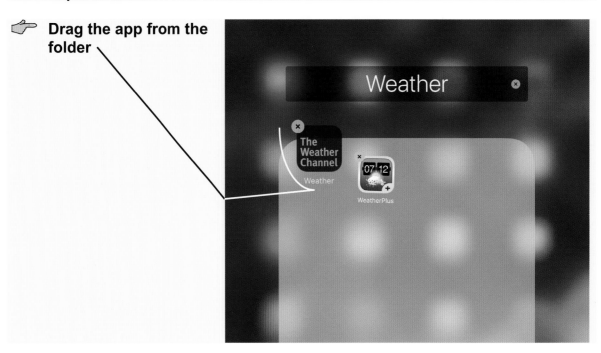

Now the app has returned to the home screen:

If you remove the other app from the folder too, the folder will disappear.

☞ **Drag the other app from the folder** 👣**69**

Stop the apps from jiggling again:

☞ **Press the Home button**

5.6 Deleting an App

Have you downloaded an app that turns out to be a bit disappointing? You can easily delete such an app.

☞ **Make the apps jiggle** 👣**68**

By the app you want to delete:

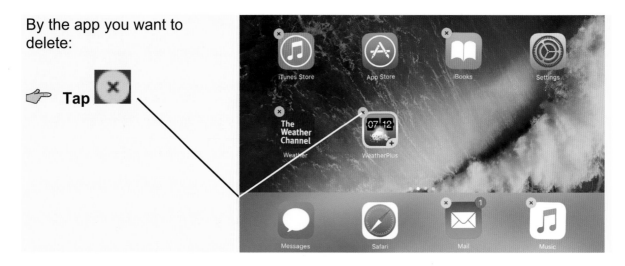

☞ **Tap** ⊗

If you really want to delete the app:

☞ **Tap** Delete

Delete "WeatherPlus"?

Deleting this app will also delete its data.

Cancel　　　　Delete

The app will be deleted.

🖙 **If necessary, move** Weather **to the second screen** ✂️ **67**

🖙 **Press the Home button** ◯

🖙 **If you want, put the iPad into sleep mode or turn it off** ✂️ **1**

In this chapter you have learned how to download free and paid apps from the *App Store*.

5.7 Exercises

To be able to quickly apply the things you have learned, you can work through these exercises. Have you forgotten how to do something? Use the numbers next to the footsteps $\ell\ell^1$ to look up the item in the appendix *How Do I Do That Again?*

Exercise 1: Download Free Apps

In this exercise you are going to download two free apps from the *App Store*.

☞ If necessary, wake the iPad up from sleep or turn it on. $\ell\ell^2$

☞ Open the *App Store*. $\ell\ell^{65}$

☞ Search for the app called *ABC News for iPad*. $\ell\ell^{70}$

☞ Download the free app . $\ell\ell^{71}$

☞ If necessary, sign in with your *Apple ID*. $\ell\ell^{72}$

☞ Press the Home button .

☞ Scroll to the home screen. $\ell\ell^{73}$

☞ Open the *App Store*. $\ell\ell^{65}$

☞ Search for the app called *Fox News for iPad*. $\ell\ell^{70}$

☞ Download the free app . $\ell\ell^{71}$

☞ If necessary, sign in with your *Apple ID*. $\ell\ell^{72}$

Exercise 2: Manage Apps

In this exercise you are going to change the order of the apps on your iPad.

☞ Make the apps jiggle. ℘**68**

☞ Put [abc NEWS] to the right of [FOX NEWS]. ℘**74**

☞ Move [abc NEWS] to the home screen. ℘**67**

☞ Scroll to the second page. ℘**66**

☞ Move [FOX NEWS] to the home screen. ℘**67**

☞ Move [abc NEWS] and [FOX NEWS] to a separate folder ℘**75** and close the folder. ℘**76**

☞ Stop the apps from jiggling. ℘**77**

☞ Make the apps jiggle. ℘**68**

☞ Open the *News* folder. ℘**78**

☞ Delete [FOX NEWS] from the folder. ℘**69**

☞ Delete [FOX NEWS] from the iPad. ℘**79**

☞ Stop the apps from jiggling. ℘**77**

☞ If you want, put the iPad to sleep or turn it off. ℘**1**

5.8 Background Information

Dictionary

App	Short for *application*, a program for the iPad.
App Store	Online store where you can buy and download apps. You can also download many apps for free.
Apple ID	Combination of an email address and a password, also called *iTunes App Store Account*. You need to have an *Apple ID* in order to download apps from the *App Store*.
Authorize	Make sure that a computer can store apps or play music purchased from the *App Store* and *iTunes Store*. You can authorize up to a maximum of five computers per *Apple ID*.
iTunes App Store Account	Another name for an *Apple ID*.
iTunes Gift Card	A prepaid card that can be used to purchase items in the *App Store*.

Source: User Guide iPad

5.9 Tips

 Tip

Update apps

After a while, the apps you have installed on your iPad will be updated for free. These updates may be necessary in order to solve existing problems. But an update may also add new functionalities, such as a new game level. This is how you can check for updates:

☞ **Open the *App Store*** ⚇⁶⁵

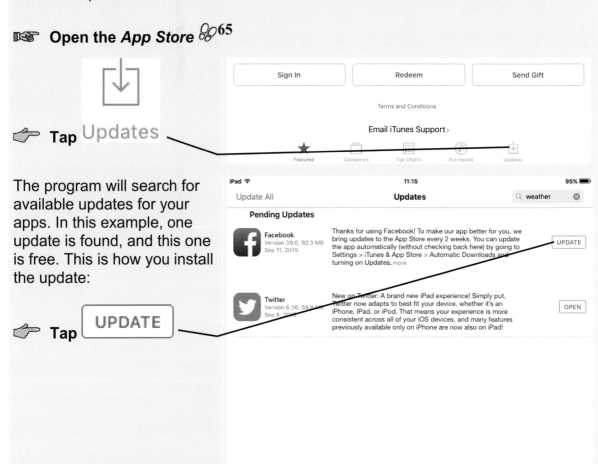

☞ **Tap** Updates

The program will search for available updates for your apps. In this example, one update is found, and this one is free. This is how you install the update:

☞ **Tap** UPDATE

☞ **If necessary, sign in with your *Apple ID*** ⚇⁷²

The app will be updated. Below the relevant app you will see a progress bar.

Tip

Download a paid app once again

If you have deleted a paid app, you will be able to download it again, free of charge. Although you need to use the same *Apple ID* as the first time.

You will see the ⬇ icon that indicates you have already downloaded the app earlier on:

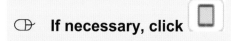 Tap ⬇

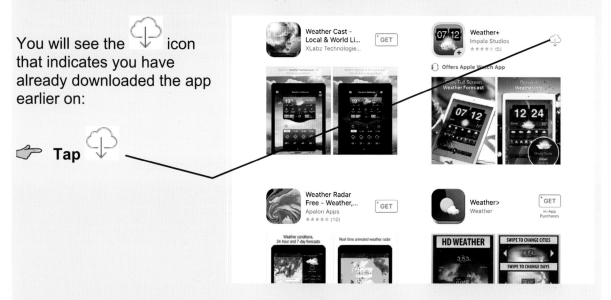

Now the app will be downloaded and installed. You will not be charged for downloading the app.

 Tip

Transfer purchases to iTunes

In *iTunes* you can transfer your purchases to your computer. This way, you will have a backup copy of the apps you purchased and you will also be able to synchronize them with other devices, such as an iPhone. You can do this the same way for music and eBooks you have bought (see *Chapter 7 Entertainment*). This is how you transfer your purchases:

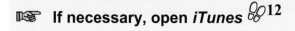 **Connect your iPad to the computer**

☞ **If necessary, open *iTunes* 🐾¹²**

First, you need to authorize your computer to use the content you have downloaded with your iPad:

☞ **If necessary, click** 🔲

- Continue on the next page -

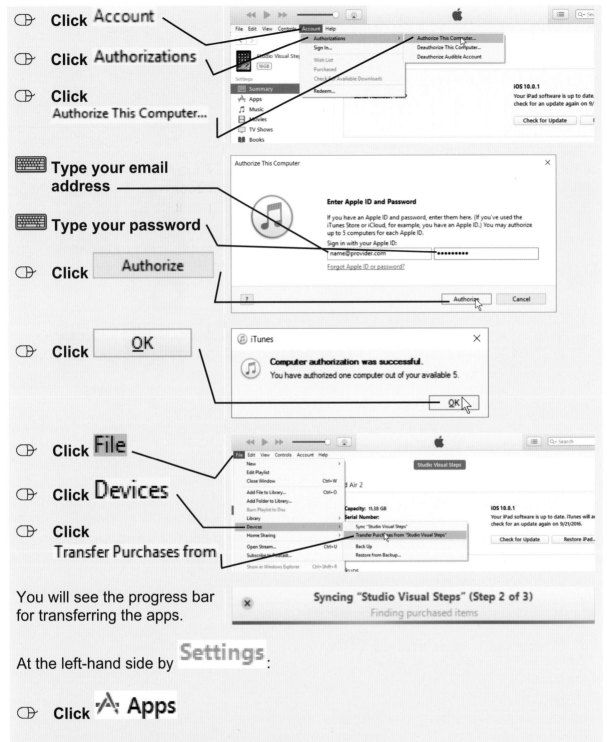

Click **Account**

Click **Authorizations**

Click
Authorize This Computer...

⌨ **Type your email address**

⌨ **Type your password**

Click **Authorize**

Click **OK**

Click **File**

Click **Devices**

Click
Transfer Purchases from

You will see the progress bar for transferring the apps.

At the left-hand side by **Settings**:

Click **Apps**

You will see your iPad apps in the *Library*.
It is also possible to synchronize your apps and purchases by using the same *Apple ID* on different devices. In that way, you can download the apps and purchases on all your devices.

6. Photos and Video

The iPad is equipped with two cameras that will give you plenty of opportunity for taking pictures or shooting videos. The *Camera* app lets you use the built-in back camera of the iPad, so you can take a picture or make a video of an interesting object. While taking a picture, you can focus, zoom in and zoom out. If you switch to the front camera of the iPad, you can also take your own picture.

To view the pictures and videos on your iPad, you can use the *Photos* app. You can view them one by one or view them as a slideshow. You can also edit the pictures in several ways.

You do not need to limit yourself and only use the photos you have made with the iPad. In this chapter you can read how to transfer photos from your computer to the iPad. Of course, you can also do it the other way round and transfer the photos you have made with the iPad to your computer.

In this chapter you will learn how to:

- take pictures with your iPad;
- focus on an object;
- zoom in and zoom out;
- shoot a video with your iPad;
- view photos;
- zoom in and zoom out while viewing pictures;
- view a slideshow;
- play a video recording;
- copy photos and video to the computer;
- copy photos and video to your iPad;
- automatically enhance photos;
- correct contrast and exposure;
- crop a photo;
- use filters;
- send a photo by email;
- print photos.

6.1 Taking Pictures

You can use the *Camera* app to take pictures. This is how to open the app:

☞ **If necessary, wake the iPad up from sleep or turn it on** $\mathscr{O}^2$

☞ **Tap** Camera

When the app is opened, you might see a message asking you if the current location can be used. This information is used to indicate the location of where the picture will be taken:

You can change the settings and turn on the Location Services for the camera.

☞ **Tap** Allow

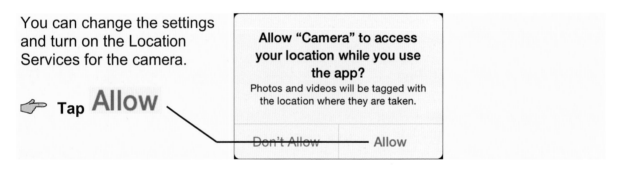

Allow "Camera" to access your location while you use the app?

Photos and videos will be tagged with the location where they are taken.

Don't Allow   Allow

Now you will see the image that is recorded by the camera on the back of the iPad.

☞ **Point the camera towards the object you want to photograph**

➥ **Please note:**

Make sure there is enough light. Your iPad is not equipped with flash photography. If you take a picture in poor lighting conditions, the photo will look grainy and out of focus.

This is how you take a picture:

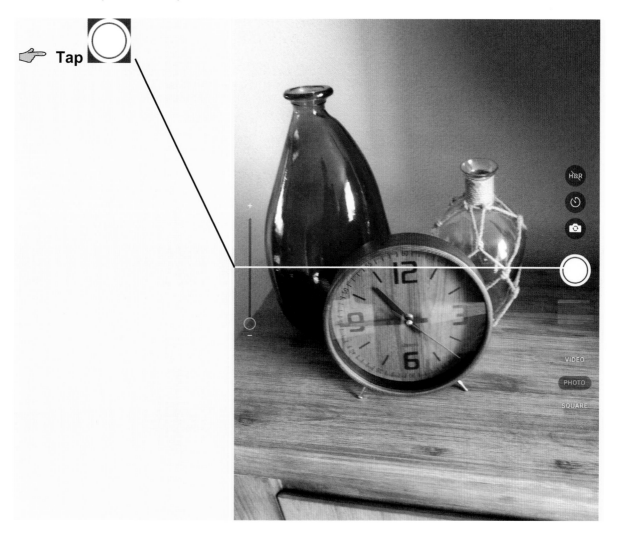

The photo will be stored on your iPad.

 Tip

Taking square pictures
You can also take square pictures. This is how you do it:

👉 **Swipe**  **upwards**

The text is now yellow. This means that this option is active. Now you see a square image and you can take the picture, as you have just learned previously.

Before you take a picture, you can focus on a specific area:

 Tap the part of the object you want to focus on ————

The exposure will be adjusted to the selected object. If you tap a dark part of the object, you will see the image become lighter.

Is the image too light? Then you need to tap a lighter part of the object.

Take another picture:

 Tap ————

Tip
Time-lapse
When the option Time-lapse is activated, the iPad will take photos at selected

intervals. The camera takes pictures until you press the ▬▬▬ button. Once you are done, you will have a video showing the photos in succession.

With the digital zoom you can zoom in on an object, up to five times. You can only do this by using the camera on the back of the iPad. This is how you zoom in:

☞ **Move your thumb and index finger apart, on the screen**

You will zoom in on the object. Take another picture:

☞ **Tap**

This is how you zoom out again:

☞ **Drag the slider to the left**

Or:

☞ **Move your thumb and index finger towards each other, on the screen**

6.2 Shooting Videos

You can also use the back camera of the iPad for shooting videos:

 If desired, turn your iPad a quarter turn, so it is in the horizontal position

♀ **Tip**
Turn sideways
Do you intend to play your video on a TV or on a larger screen? Then position your iPad sideways, in landscape mode. This way, your image will fill the entire screen.

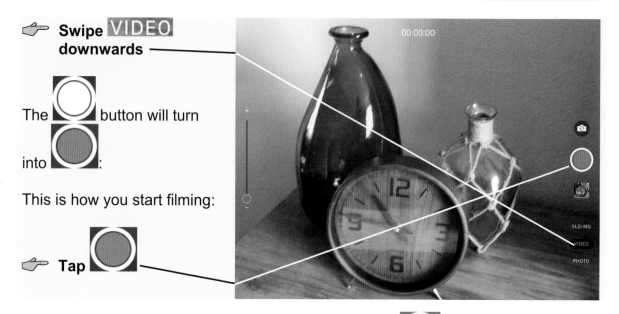

☞ **Swipe** VIDEO **downwards**

The ◯ button will turn

into ● :

This is how you start filming:

☞ **Tap** ◯

While you are shooting the film, the button will turn into ◼. This is how you stop filming:

☞ **Tap** ◼

You can reset the *Camera* app for taking pictures:

☞ **Swipe** PHOTO **upwards**

 **If desired, turn the iPad a quarter turn until it is in upright position again**

 **Go back to the home screen** ✋[8]

6.3 Viewing Photos

You have taken a number of pictures with your iPad. You can view these photos with the *Photos* app. This is how you open the app:

☞ **Tap** Photos

You may see a window about new options in *Photos*:

☞ **If necessary, tap** Continue

💡 **Tip**

Transfer photos to the iPad with iTunes
You can also use *iTunes* to transfer photos taken with your digital camera to your iPad. Very handy, if you want to show your favorite pictures to others. In *section 6.6 Copy Photos and Videos to Your iPad Through iTunes* you can read how to do this.

You will see the collections of your pictures, grouped by location:

You may see a different screen, because the groups may be arranged differently.

You are going to the screen where the albums have been arranged in a more orderly way:

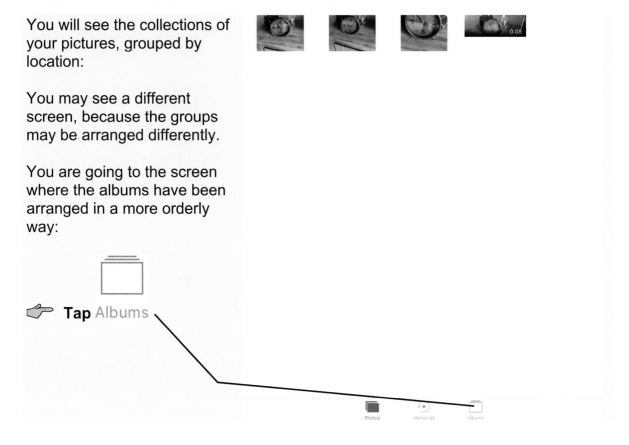

☞ **Tap** Albums

In the *Albums* view, the photos have been arranged into piles:

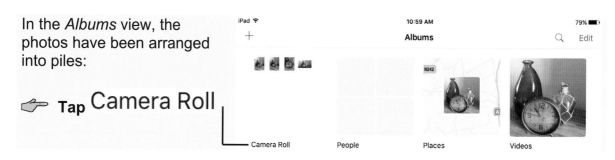

☞ **Tap** Camera Roll

You will see the thumbnails of the pictures you have taken:

In this example you can also see a video, in between the photos: ——

☞ **Tap the first photo**

The photo will be displayed on a full screen. This is how you scroll to the next photo:

☞ **Swipe across the photo, from right to left**

You will see the next photo. You can go back to the previous photo:

 Swipe across the photo, from left to right

You can also zoom in on a photo:

 Move your thumb and index finger apart, on the screen

You will zoom in on the photo:

Note: the picture might become a bit blurry when you zoom in.

 Tip
Move away
You can move the photo you have just zoomed in on, by dragging your finger across the screen.

This is how you zoom out again:

 Move your thumb and index finger towards each other, on the screen

You will again see the regular view of the photo.

 Tip
Delete a photo
You can easily delete a photo you have taken with the iPad from your iPad:

☞ **If necessary, tap the photo**

☞ **In the top right of your screen, tap** 🗑

☞ **Tap** Delete Photo

☞ **Tap** OK

These photos will be stored in the album *Recently Deleted*. The photos or videos will be erased 30 days after being marked for deletion. Each item shows the days remaining. You can restore an item like this:

☞ **Open the folder** Recently Deleted

☞ **In the top right of your screen, tap** Select

If you would like to recover all items:

☞ **Tap** Recover All

☞ **Tap** Recover

To recover one or multiple items:

☞ **Tap one item or more photos or videos**

☞ **Tap** Recover

You can also view a slideshow of all the pictures on your iPad. Here is how to do that:

☞ **If necessary, tap the photo**

At the top right corner of the screen:

☞ **Tap**

☞ **Tap** Slideshow

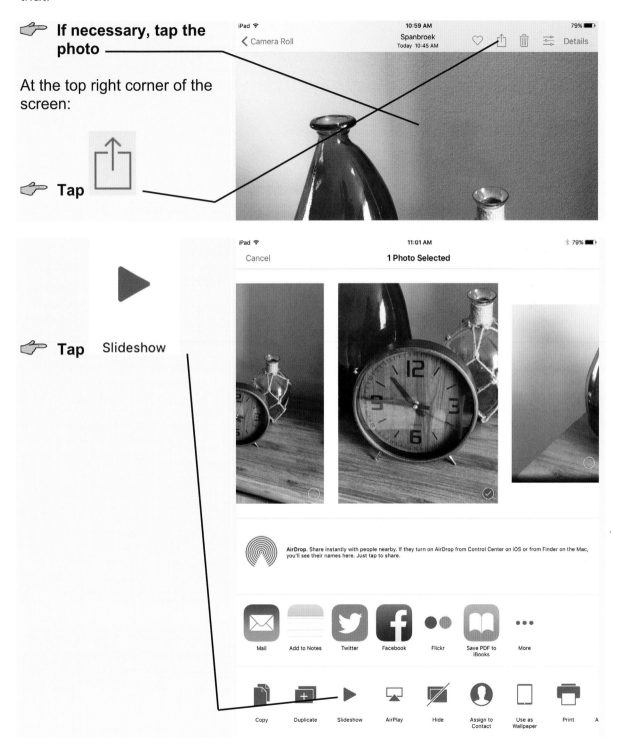

The slideshow starts immediately:

you can set various options:

☞ **Tap the photo**

☞ **Tap Options**

Here you can set the theme for the slideshow: ————

If you have stored music on your iPad, you can play music during the slideshow: ————

Here you can set if you want to repeat the slideshow: ————

With the slider ⭕ you can change the tempo: ————

This is how you pause the slideshow:

☞ **Tap ❚❚**

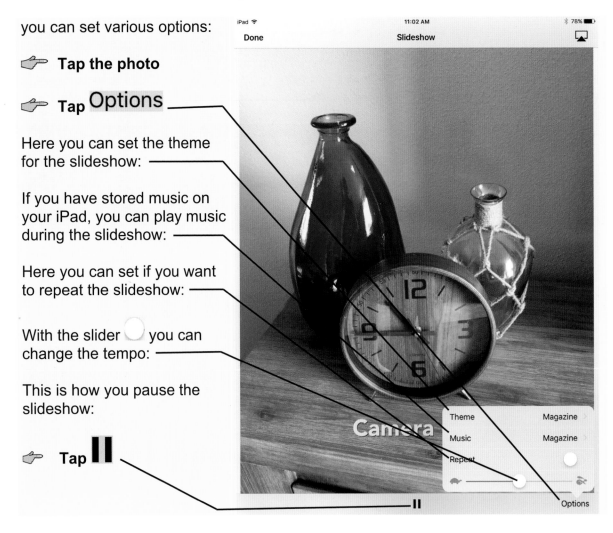

If you have also made a video, this will be played during the slideshow.

The last photo that was displayed during the slideshow will freeze and remain on screen. Unless you activated the **Repeat** option.

☞ **Tap Done**

☞ **Tap ‹ Camera Roll**

6.4 Play a Video Recording

In *section 6.2 Shooting Videos* you have shot a short video with your iPad. You can view this video with the *Photos* app as well:

☞ **Tap the video**

☞ **If necessary, turn your iPad a quarter turn, so it is in the horizontal position**

You will see your video. To play the video:

☞ **Tap**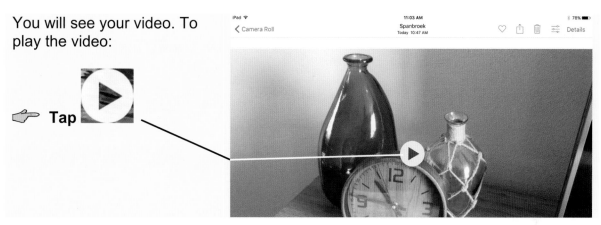

The video will fill the screen:

☞ **Tap the screen**

You can see a pause button:

With this slider, you can fast forward or rewind the video:

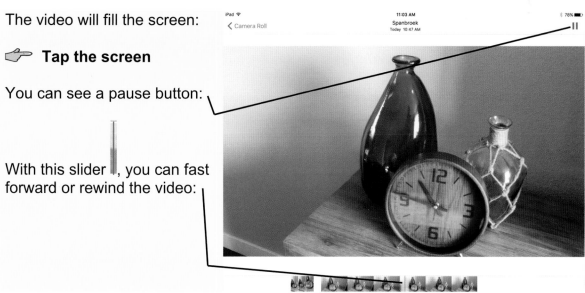

To go back:

👉 **Tap** ❮ Camera Roll

👉 **Tap** ❮ Albums

☞ **Go back to the home screen** 🐾⁸

☞ **Turn the iPad a quarter turn until it is in upright position again**

6.5 Copying Photos and Videos to the Computer

You can use *File Explorer* to copy the photos you have made with your iPad to your computer. This is how you do it:

☞ **Connect the iPad to the computer**

☞ **If necessary, close *iTunes*** 🐾¹¹

☞ **If necessary, close the *AutoPlay* window** 🐾¹¹

You can open *File Explorer* from the desktop:

⊕ **Click**

Your iPad will be detected by *Windows*, as if it were a digital camera:

⊕ **Click** 🖥 This PC

⊕ **Double-click your iPad name**

Naturally, your own iPad will have a different name than shown here.

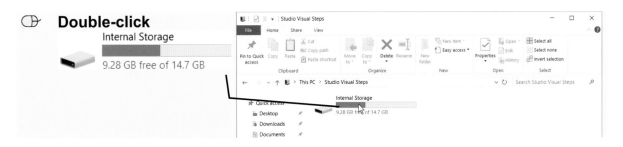

The photos are stored in a folder called *DCIM*:

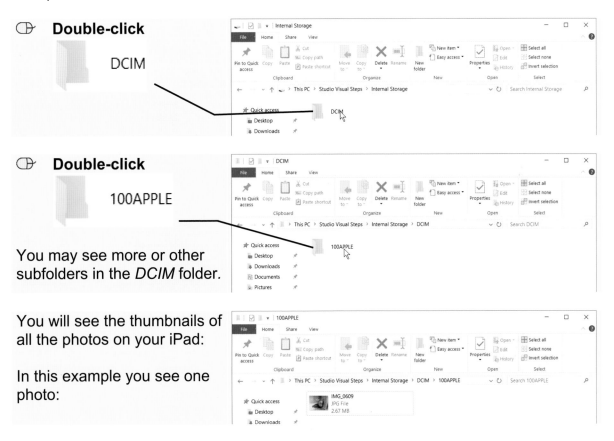

Double-click

DCIM

Double-click

100APPLE

You may see more or other subfolders in the *DCIM* folder.

You will see the thumbnails of all the photos on your iPad:

In this example you see one photo:

You can copy these photos to your computer, for example, to your *Pictures* folder:

Press **Ctrl** **and** **A** **simultaneously**

The photo(s) will be selected:

If you drag the photo(s) to a folder on your computer, they will be copied:

 Drag the photo(s) to a folder, for example, Pictures _____

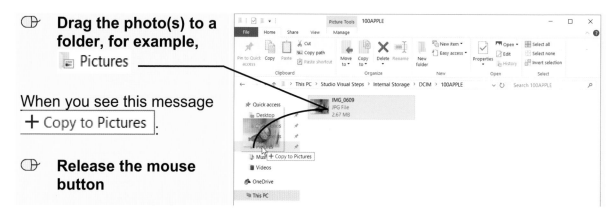

When you see this message .

 Release the mouse button

Now the photos have been copied to your computer.

Please note:
This method will only work if you copy photos from your iPad to your computer. You cannot transfer photos from your computer to your iPad in this way. In the next section you can read how to do this with *iTunes*.

☞ **Close** *File Explorer* 🐾11

6.6 Copy Photos and Videos to Your iPad Through iTunes

Your iPad is a useful tool for showing your favorite pictures and videos to others. Actually, you can also use the photos on your computer. This is done by synchronizing the folder containing the photos and videos with your iPad, through *iTunes*.

The iPad is still connected to the computer. Open *iTunes*:

☞ **Open** *iTunes* **on your computer** 🐾12

 Click [ ]

 Click 📷 **Photos**

In this example, the photos from the *(My) Pictures* folder will be synchronized. You will select a folder with your own pictures:

☞ **Check the box ☑ by**
    Sync Photos

The `Pictures ⬦` folder has
already been selected:

In this example we will not
synchronize all the subfolders
of the *(My) Pictures* folder:

☞ **Check the radio button**
    ⦿ next to
    Selected folders

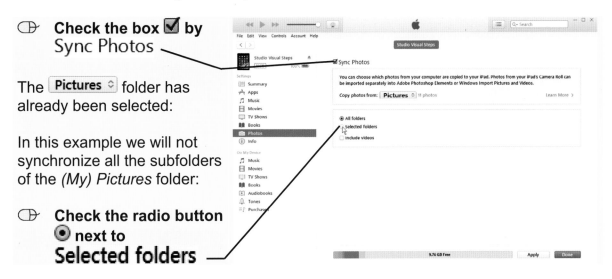

💡 **Tip**
Video's
If you also want to synchronize the videos stored in this folder:

☞ **Check the box ☑ by Include videos**

Select the folder(s) you want to synchronize with your iPad. You will see different folders from the ones in this example, of course:

☞ **Check the box ☑ by**
    the desired folder(s),
    for example
    📁 **Barcelona**

☞ **Click** [**Apply**   ]

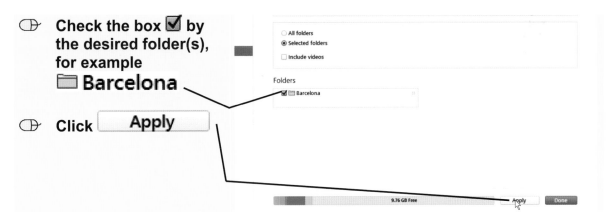

The synchronization is started:

You will see the progress of the synchronization:

When you see the *Apple* logo the synchronization operation has finished:

☞ **Safely disconnect the iPad from the computer** 🐾⁹

☞ **Close *iTunes*** 🐾¹¹

The photos are transferred to your iPad.

☞ **Open the *Photos* app** 🐾⁸⁰

At the bottom of the screen

👉 **If necessary, tap**

Albums ——————

The pile with the synchronized photos has been given the same name as the folder on your computer:

👉 **Tap the album** ——

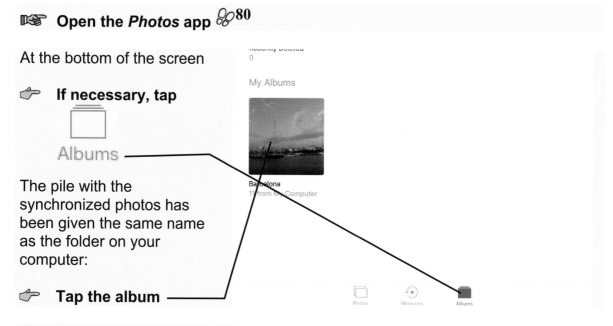

The pictures are shown:

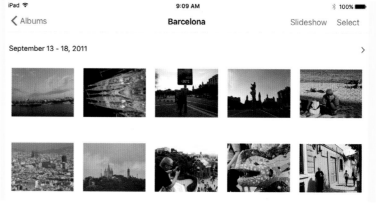

You are going back to all the albums. In the top left-hand corner of the screen:

☞ **Tap**

6.7 Automatically Enhance a Photo

Sometimes, a photo can be too dark or too light. The auto-enhance function will let you make a 'ruined' photo look better in just a short while. This function adjusts the exposure and saturation of the photo. Just try it:

☞ **Open a photo** ✂81

The photo in this example looks bleak and blurred:

☞ **If necessary, tap the photo**

☞ **Tap**

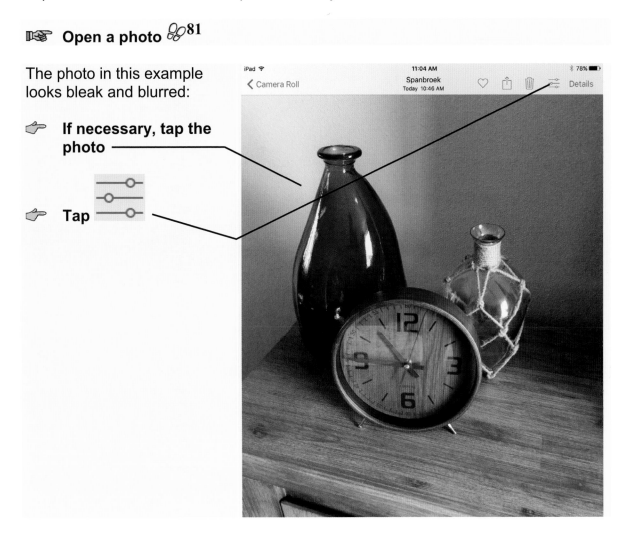

To automatically enhance the photo:

☞ **Tap**

Now the photo looks much clearer and much livelier:

If you tap 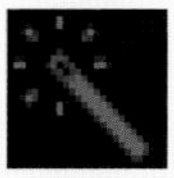 once again, you will see the original photo again.

To save the photo:

☞ **Tap** Done

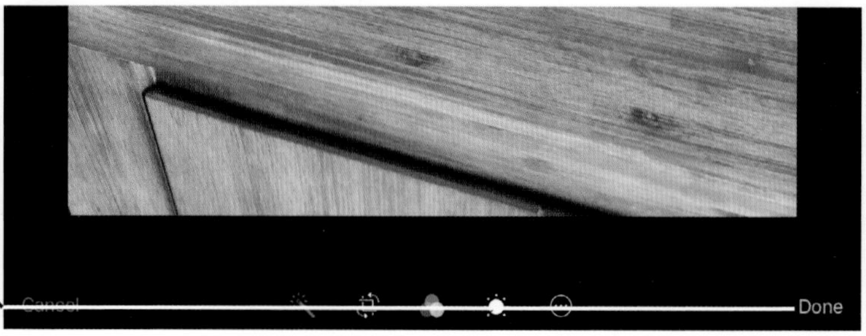

To go back to the album:

☞ **Tap the album, for example**
   ❮ Camera Roll

The photo is saved.

Please note:

If you have transferred photos from your computer to your iPad you need to tap Duplicate and Edit before you can edit the photo. Then a copy of the photo will be saved on the iPad.

If you want to view the picture you have saved, you do this:

☞ **Tap the name of the album at the top, for example,** ❮ Barcelona

☞ **Tap** ❮ Albums

☞ **Tap** ❮ Camera Roll

You will see the edited photo.

6.8 Crop a Photo

By cropping photos you can bring forward the most important part of the photo, or get rid of less pretty parts of the photo. You are going to crop a photo:

☞ **Open a photo** 🦶❝81

☞ **If necessary, tap the photo**

☞ **Tap** ⚙️

At the bottom of the screen:

☞ **Tap** 🔲

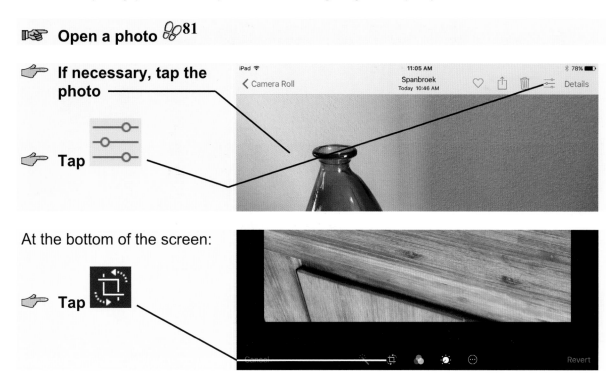

You will see a clear frame with nine boxes, all across the photo:

You can move this frame:

☞ **Drag the frame to the desired position**

You will see that the view of the photo is immediately adjusted to the frame.

☞ **Drag the bottom left-hand corner to the top right-hand corner a bit**

Now the height/width ratio of the photo is no longer correct. Select the desired ratio:

☞ **Tap**

The iPad's screen has a 3x4 ratio:

☞ **Tap 3:4**

If desired, you can still straighten the photo by swiping your finger over

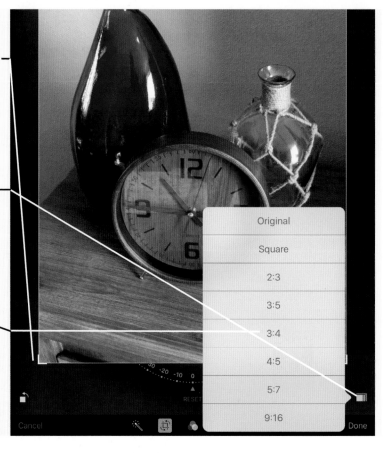

The cropped photo has been adjusted to the selected image ratio.

If necessary you can still move the photo, so the desired object is placed in the frame on the right spot.

With the RESET button you can restore the photo: ———

You may need to practice a bit in order to crop the photo as it should be.

To save the photo:

☞ **Tap** Done

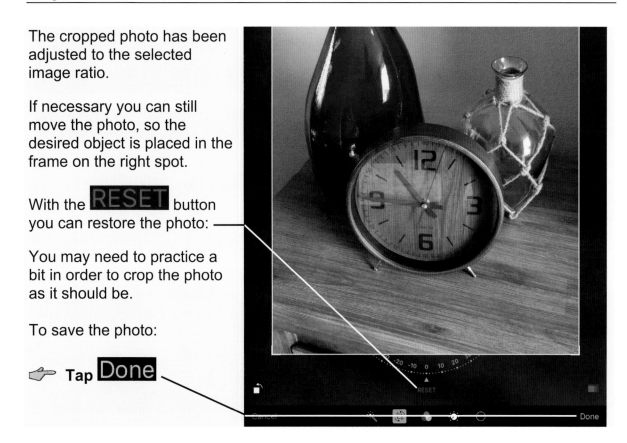

6.9 Correcting Contrast and Exposure

You can also correct the contrast and exposure of a photo. In this example we will use the same photo. Just try it:

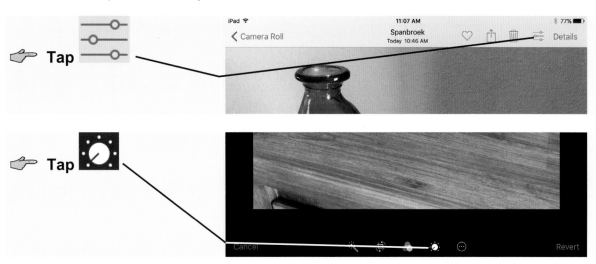

☞ **Tap**

☞ **Tap**

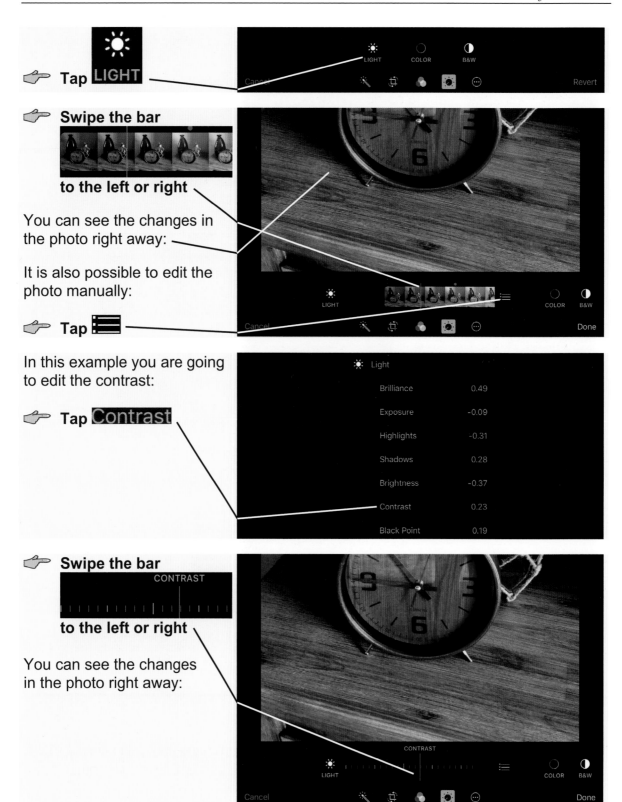

☞ Tap **LIGHT**

☞ **Swipe the bar**

to the left or right

You can see the changes in the photo right away:

It is also possible to edit the photo manually:

☞ Tap

In this example you are going to edit the contrast:

☞ Tap **Contrast**

☞ **Swipe the bar**

to the left or right

You can see the changes in the photo right away:

6.10 Use Filters

You can also apply a filter to a photo. This will often produce a creative effect. In this example we will again use the same photo.

☞ **Tap**

At the bottom of the screen you will see the filter options:

☞ **Tap a filter, for**

example

To save the changes:

☞ **Tap Done**

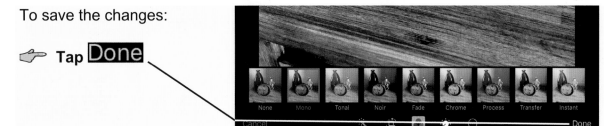

You are going back to the album with the photos. In the top left-hand corner of the screen:

☞ **Tap the album, for example** ‹ Camera Roll

6.11 Sending a Photo by Email

In the *Tips* from Chapter 2 *Sending Emails with Your iPad* you have learned how to add an attachment to an email. There is another method available for photo attachments with the *Photos* app. You can easily add one or more photos to an email using the share option in this app.

☞ **Open a photo** 🐾⁸¹

☞ **If necessary, tap the photo**

☞ **Tap** ⬆️

☞ **Tap** Mail

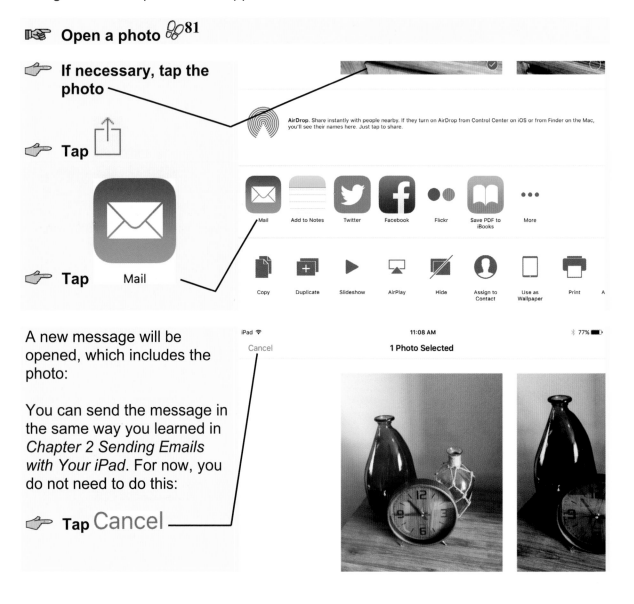

A new message will be opened, which includes the photo:

You can send the message in the same way you learned in *Chapter 2 Sending Emails with Your iPad*. For now, you do not need to do this:

☞ **Tap** Cancel

You will be asked if you want to save the draft:

👉 **Tap** Delete Draft

You will see the photo once again.

👉 **Tap** Cancel

6.12 Printing a Photo

If you use a printer that supports the *AirPrint* function, you can print the photos on your iPad through a wireless connection.

This is how you print a photo from your iPad:

👉 **If necessary, tap the photo**

👉 **Tap**

👉 **Tap** Print

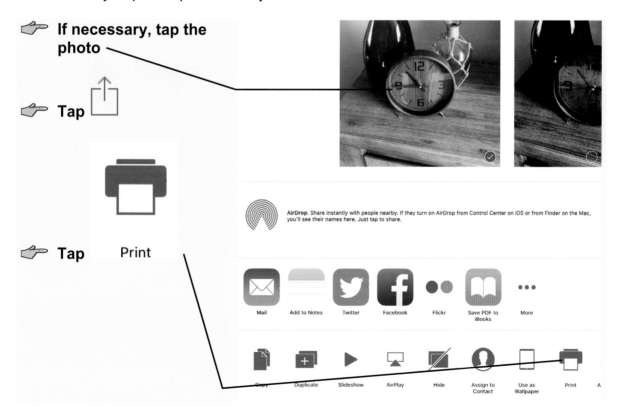

Select the right printer:

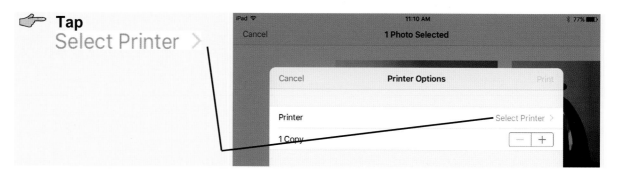

☞ **Tap**
Select Printer >

☞ **Tap the printer you want to use**

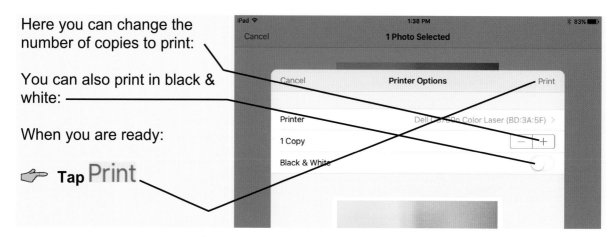

Here you can change the number of copies to print:

You can also print in black & white: ————

When you are ready:

☞ **Tap** Print

The photo will be printed.

☞ **Tap** Cancel

☞ **Go back to the home screen** 👣 8

☞ **If you want, put the iPad into sleep mode or turn it off** 👣 1

In this chapter you have learned more about the *Camera* and *Photos* app. In the next few exercises, you can practice all the things you have learned.

6.13 Exercises

To be able to quickly apply the things you have learned, you can work through these exercises. Have you forgotten how to do something? Use the numbers next to the footsteps 👣¹ to look up the item in the appendix *How Do I Do That Again?*

Exercise 1: Take Pictures

In this exercise you are going to use the *Camera* app to take pictures.

☞ If necessary, wake the iPad up from sleep or turn it on. 👣²

☞ Open the *Camera* app. 👣**82**

☞ Choose an object or a person for your photo.

☞ Focus on a part of the object 👣**83** and take a picture. 👣**84**

☞ Zoom in on the object 👣**85** and take a picture. 👣**84**

☞ Go back to the home screen. 👣**8**

Exercise 2: View Pictures

In this exercise, you will be going to view the photos on your iPad.

☞ Open the *Photos* app 👣**80** and open a photo. 👣**81**

☞ Scroll to the next photo 👣**86** and scroll back to the previous photo. 👣**87**

☞ Start the slideshow and select the *Origami* transition. 👣**88**

☞ Stop the slideshow. 👣**89**

☞ Zoom in on the photo you are viewing 👣**85** and zoom out again. 👣**90**

☞ Go back to the home screen. 👣**8**

☞ If you want, put the iPad into sleep mode or turn it off. 👣**1**

6.14 Background Information

Dictionary

AirDrop	A function that lets you quickly and easily share photos and other files with others next to you using Wi-Fi or Bluetooth.
AirPrint	An iPad function that allows you to print through a wireless connection, on a printer that supports *AirPrint*.
Camera	An app for taking pictures and shooting videos. With this app you can use both the front and back cameras on the iPad.
Camera Roll	The name of the photo folder where the photos on your iPad are stored. For instance, the photos you made with your iPad or those that were downloaded from an attachment or a website.
Digital zoom	A digital zoom function that enlarges a small part of the original picture. You will not see any additional details; all it does is make the pixels bigger. That is why the photo quality will diminish.
Family Sharing	Share photos directly with family members.
Photo Booth	An app that lets you take pictures with funny effects, such as an X-ray or kaleidoscope photo.
Photos	An app the lets you view the photos on the iPad.
Slideshow	Automatic display of a collection of pictures.
Transition	An animated effect that is displayed when browsing through the photos in a slideshow.
Videos	An app that allows you to buy or rent movies from the *iTunes Store*.
Zoom in	Take a closer look.
Zoom out	View from a distance.

Source: iPad User Guide, Wikipedia

6.15 Tips

  Tip

Change the Location Services setting in Settings app

You can change the settings and turn off Location Services for the camera in the *Settings* app.

☞ **Open the *Settings* app** ✇⁶

☞ **Tap** ✋ **Privacy**

☞ **Tap** ◤ **Location Services**

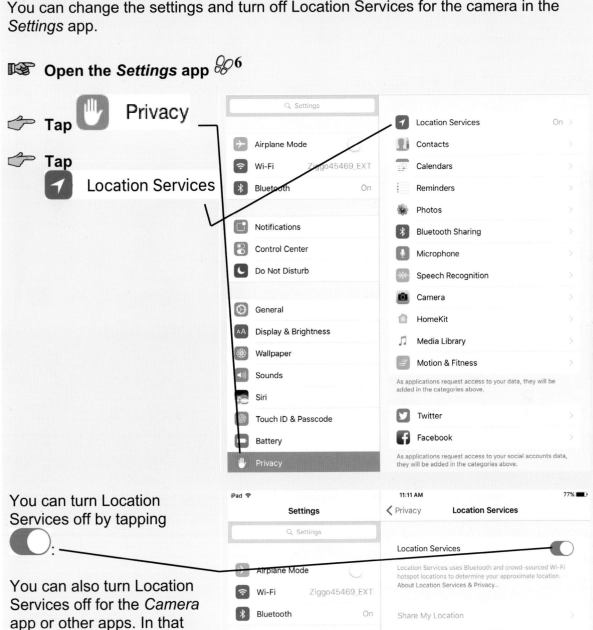

You can turn Location Services off by tapping ⬤:

You can also turn Location Services off for the *Camera* app or other apps. In that case you need to tap the app and tap Never >.

Tip

Self-portrait
You can also use the camera at the front of the iPad. For instance, for taking a picture of yourself. This is how you switch to the front camera:

 Tap

Now you will see the image recorded by the front camera:

You can take a picture in the same way as you previously did with the back camera. Only, the front camera does not have a digital zoom option.

This is how you switch to the back camera again:

  Tap

 Tip

Directly transfer photos to your iPad with the Camera Connection Kit
A very useful accessory to your iPad is the *Camera Connection Kit*. This is a set of two connectors that lets you quickly and easily transfer photos from your digital camera to your iPad. You can buy this *Camera Connection Kit* for about $29 (as of October 2016) at your Apple store.

Tip

Use photo as wallpaper

You can also use your own photo as a background for the lock screen or the home screen. This is how to do that:

☞ **Open a photo** 👣**81**

👉 **Tap** ⬆️

👉 **Tap** Use as Wallpaper

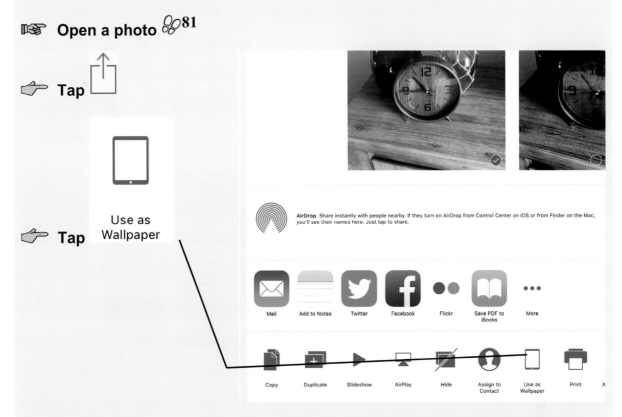

Now you can choose whether you want to use this photo as wallpaper for the lock screen, the home screen, or both:

If you wish, you can move or scale the photo:

When you are done:

👉 **Tap one of the options, for example**
Set Lock Screen

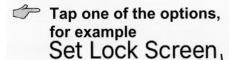

Tip

Different displays

In the *Photos* app you can display your photos in various ways:

☞ **Open the *Photos* app** **80**

At the bottom of the screen:

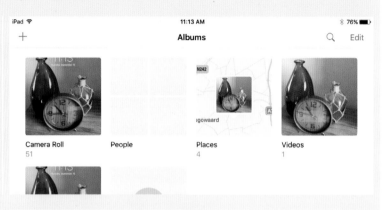

☞ **Tap** Albums

In the *Albums* view the photos have been ordered and stacked:

At the bottom of the screen:

☞ **Tap** Photos

In the *Moments* view you will see all the photos, below and next to each other, sorted by date and location:

By tapping **‹** Collections the view will become a bit more compacted. And in the next view, the **‹** Years, view, it will become even more compacted:

You can view the pictures that were taken with the Location Services turned on and look at them on the map:

☞ **Tap a location**

- Continue on the next page -

Drag upwards the screen

You will see a map showing the location(s) where the photo(s) were taken:

To go back to the recent view:

 Tap <

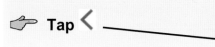

💡 **Tip**

The Videos app

With the *Videos* app you cannot shoot videos or playback your own videos. This app allows you to buy or rent movies from the *iTunes Store*. More about that in the *Tips* in the end of *Chapter 7 Entertainment*.

💡 **Tip**

Organize your photos in albums

You can create albums for your photos directly on your iPad. When you add a photo to a new album, you are actually adding a link to the photo from the Camera Roll album to the new one. By sorting your photos into albums, it makes it easier to find a series of photos about a specific subject later on. You can create a new album like this:

 Tap Albums

You will see the albums on your iPad:

To create a new album:

👉 **Tap** +

- Continue on the next page -

⌨ **Type a name**

☞ **Tap** Save

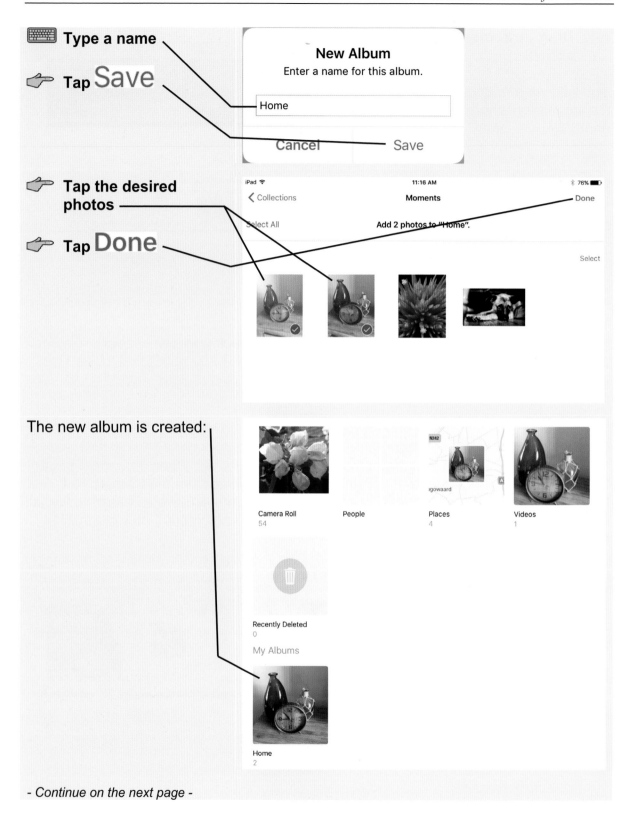

☞ **Tap the desired photos**

☞ **Tap** Done

The new album is created:

- Continue on the next page -

If you want to delete an album on your iPad, you need to do this. You will only delete the album; the photos will still be stored on your iPad.
Please note: you can only delete the albums you have created on your iPad yourself.

☞ **Tap** Edit

☞ **By the album, tap**

☞ **Tap** Delete

☞ **Tap** Done

Tip
Photo Booth
The *Photo Booth* app allows you to add eight different types of effects to your photo right as you are taking the picture. You can use both cameras on the iPad with this app. This is how you open the *Photo Booth* app:

☞ **Tap** Photo Booth

You will see examples of the different effects:

☞ **Tap an effect, for example** Kaleidoscope

You will see a larger image of this effect. Now you can take a picture:

☞ **Tap**

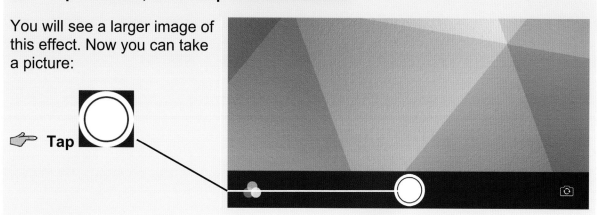

With ⟳ you can switch to the back camera. With ◉ you can display the opening screen of the *Photo Booth* app.

Tip

Delete synchronized photos and videos
If you have second thoughts and you do not want to save one or multiple synchronized photos on your iPad you will need to delete these through *iTunes*. You can do this in several ways. If you want to delete just a few pictures, this is what you need to do:

☞ **Delete or move the unwanted photo from the synchronized folder on your computer**
☞ **Synchronize the folder with your iPad once more, just like you have done in *section 6.6 Copy Photos and Videos to Your iPad Through iTunes***

Synchronizing means that the content of the iPad folder will be made equal to the content of the folder on your computer. The photos that have been deleted or moved will also disappear from the iPad. You can also delete one or more synchronized folders:

⊕ **Uncheck the box ☑ by the folder you no longer wish to synchronize, for example,**
🗀 Barcelona

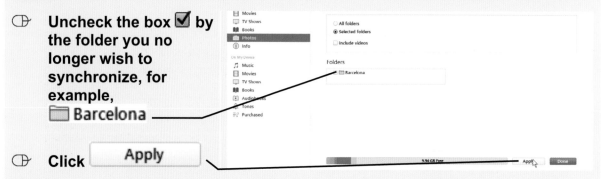

⊕ **Click Apply**

The synchronization operation is started and the folder is deleted from your iPad.

If you do not want to synchronize any photos at all with your iPad, you can delete all the photos, like this:

⊕ **Uncheck the box ☑ by**
Sync Photos

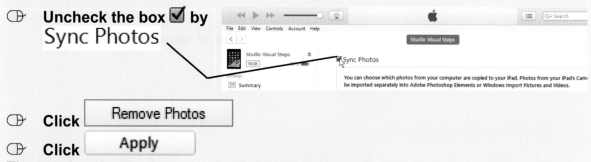

⊕ **Click Remove Photos**
⊕ **Click Apply**

The synchronization operation is started and all synchronized photos will be deleted.

Tip

Upload a video to YouTube

You can also directly upload a video from your iPad to *YouTube*. This is how you do it:

☞ **Open the *Photos* app** 👣**80**

☞ **Open the video**

👉 **Tap** [⬆️]

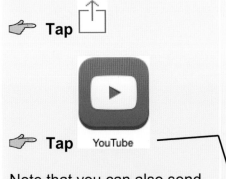

👉 **Tap** YouTube

Note that you can also send a video by email. This is done in the same way as sending a photo. But keep in mind that videos take up a lot of space, and may be too large to send them by email.

If you want to upload to *YouTube* you need to sign in with your *YouTube* account. Next, you enter the information for the video. If you do not yet have a *YouTube* account you can create such an account at www.youtube.com.

Tip

Different video formats
The iPad only supports a limited number of video file formats: .M4V, .MP4 and .MOV. The video you want to play may have a different format, such as.MPG or .AVI, for example. In that case you can do one of two things.

First, you can convert the video to a different format by using your computer. You can use the free *WinFF* program for this, for example. The downside of converting a video file is that it is very time-consuming.

Another option is to download an app that is capable of playing all sorts of video file formats, such as the *Movie Player*, *GoodPlayer* or *CineXPlayer* app. These paid apps can be purchased in the *App Store*.

  Tip

Photostream, AirDrop and Family Sharing
If you use *iCloud* you can use *Photostream* to share your photos on your iPad, computer (Mac or *Windows*), or on other devices, such as your iPhone or iPod touch.

Photostream will automatically send copies (through Wi-Fi) of the photos on your iPad to other devices on which *iCloud* has been set up, and on which *Photostream* has been activated.

The photos that are added to *Photostream* from an iPad will include all the photos taken with your iPad, the photos that have been downloaded from email, text, or *iMessage* messages, and the screen prints you have made. With *Photostream* you can exchange up to 1000 of your most recent pictures with your iPad, iPhone, iPod touch, and computer.

Through *Photostream* you can easily share photos as well. The friends who use *iCloud* on a device where *iOS 6* or higher is installed, or on a Mac computer with *OS X Mountain Lion* or higher will be able to see the photos right away, in the *Photos* app or in *iPhoto*. Anyone who does not use an *Apple* device but a *Windows* computer, for instance, will be able to view the shared photos on the Internet. Your friends can also comment on your photos.

Another useful function is *AirDrop*. This function lets you quickly and easily share photos and other files with others next to you using Wi-Fi or Bluetooth. It is also possible to share photos directly with family members. You can do this with *Family Sharing*.

7. Entertainment

Your iPad is equipped with an extensive music player, the *Music* app. If you have stored any music files on your computer, you can transfer this music to your iPad, through *iTunes*. In the *iTunes Store* you can also purchase songs or entire albums.

With the *iBooks* app, you can turn your iPad into a pleasant e-reader with which you can read digital books. Because you can change the size of the font and adjust the background lighting, you will no longer be dependent on the lighting conditions of your surroundings when you want to read a book.

In the *iBookstore* (an online book store) you can buy the newest books and transfer them to your iPad in seconds. If you want to learn to know *iBooks* a bit better you can practice downloading and reading a free ebook in this chapter.

In this chapter you will learn how to:

- add music to the *iTunes* Library;
- synchronize music with your iPad;
- buy music on your iPad;
- play music on your iPad;
- download a book in the *iBookstore*;
- read a book with the app *iBooks*.

7.1 Adding Music to iTunes

Your iPad comes with a very extensive music player, called the *Music* app. If you have stored any music files on your computer, you can use *iTunes* to transfer these files to your iPad.

☞ **Open *iTunes* on your computer** ᎒᎒12

You will see the *iTunes* window. This is how you add the folder containing the music files to the Library:

⊕ **Click** File

⊕ **Click**
    Add Folder to Library...

If you want to add a single
file, or multiple files, select
Add File to Library... .

In this example we have used the folder containing the sample files that come with *Windows*, but you can use your own music files if you want:

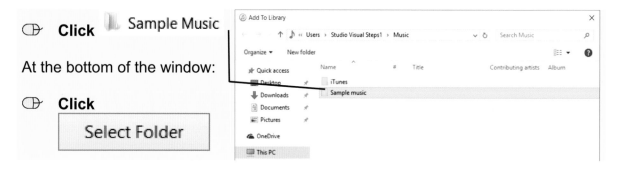

⊕ **Click** Sample Music

At the bottom of the window:

⊕ **Click**
    Select Folder

You may see this window:

⊕ **If necessary, click**
    Convert

After a while, these songs will appear in your *iTunes* program. You will see the albums. You can also select a different view:

⊕ **Click** ♪ Songs

The songs will be shown.

7.2 Synchronizing Music with Your iPad

Once the songs have been transferred to *iTunes*, it is very simple to add them to your iPad. Select the songs you want to transfer:

☞ **If necessary, wake the iPad up from sleep or turn it on** 👣²

☞ **Connect your iPad to the computer**

⊕ **Click the first song**

⌨ **Press** Shift **and hold it down**

⊕ **Click the last song**

⌨ **Release** Shift

The songs have been selected. Now you can copy the songs to your iPad:

⊕ **Drag the selected songs to the left-hand side of the window to** ⬜ Studio Visual Steps

The mouse pointer will turn into 🖱️**3**:

You will see a progress bar
indicating the progress of the
update:

View the contents of the iPad:

⊕ **Click** 🔲

⊕ **By** On My Device,
click 🎵 **Music**

You will see that the songs
have been copied to your
iPad:

Now you can disconnect the iPad and close *iTunes*:

☞ **Safely disconnect the iPad** 👣⁹

☞ **Close** *iTunes* 👣¹¹

7.3 Buying Music on Your iPad

You can also add music files to your iPad right away, by purchasing songs in the
iTunes Store.

This is how you open the *iTunes Store* from the home screen:

☞ **Tap** iTunes Store

You will see the home page of the *iTunes Store*:

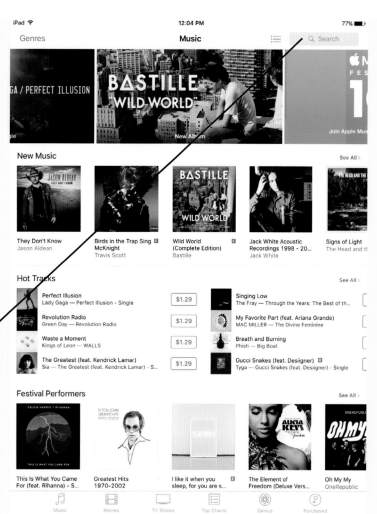

The *iTunes Store* changes almost daily. The home page and the current artist or album selection will be different from the screenshots shown in this book.

The *iTunes Store* works in a similar way to the *App Store*.

You can search for a song:

 Tap the search box

Please note:

The appearance of a web page by a web store, including the *iTunes Store*, will often change. The *iTunes Store* is actually a website that is opened on your iPad. The screen that you see will very likely be different from the screenshots you see in this book.

You might see a message about setting up *Family Sharing*. You can skip that for now:

 Tap Not Now

You can search for an artist:

 Type: adele

 Tap Search

You will see the available material for this singer:

Her songs: ————

Her albums: ————

Music videos : ————

Ringtones: ————

View the tracks on the album called '21':

Tap 21
Adele

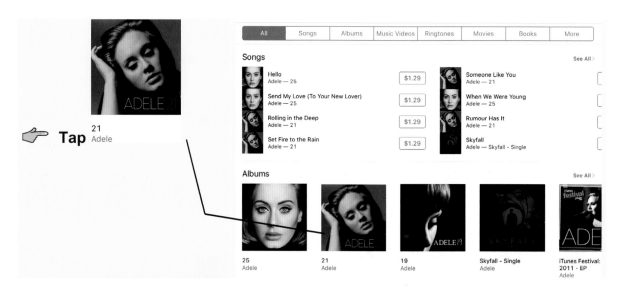

Before you decide to purchase a track you can listen to a sound fragment of thirty seconds. This is how you can listen to the fragment:

 Tap the first song title

The fragment will be played.

If there are more songs on the album, you can listen to a few more songs.

To view all the tracks on the album:

 Swipe upwards over the window

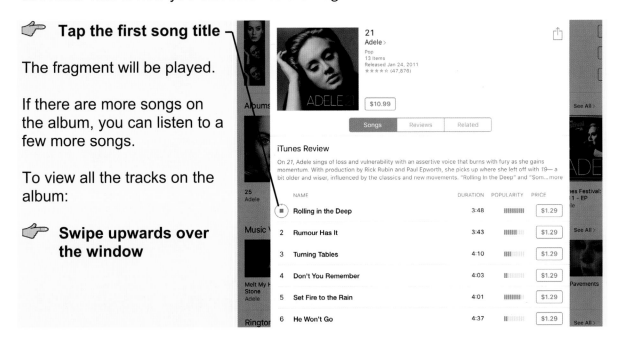

If you want to buy a song, you can use the same method as for buying an app, as explained in *Chapter 5 Downloading Apps*. You can also use your prepaid *iTunes* credit from an *iTunes Gift Card* to buy music.

Please note:

To follow the examples in the next section, you need to have an *Apple ID*. You also need to have some prepaid credit or you need to have a credit card linked to your *Apple ID*. For more information, read *Chapter 5 Downloading Apps*.

Please note:

In the following example, we will actually purchase a song, which will cost $1.29. Follow these steps literally, only if you really want to buy this song.

You are going to buy the song:

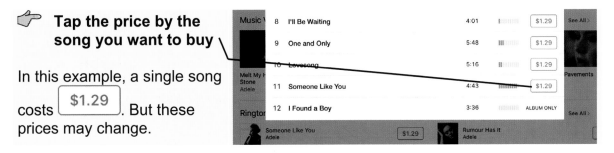 **Tap the price by the song you want to buy**

In this example, a single song

costs $1.29 . But these prices may change.

☞ **Tap** BUY SONG

☞ **Sign in with your *Apple ID*** 👣**72**

The song will be downloaded:

☞ **Tap** Downloads

You will see the progress of the download operation:

After the song has been downloaded, the button Downloads disappears. You can view your purchases in the *Music* app:

☞ **Go back to the home screen** 👣**8**

☞ **Tap** Music

When you open the *Music* app for the first time you will see a screen concerning a free trial of *Apple Music*. To go to the *Music* app:

☞ **Tap** Not Now

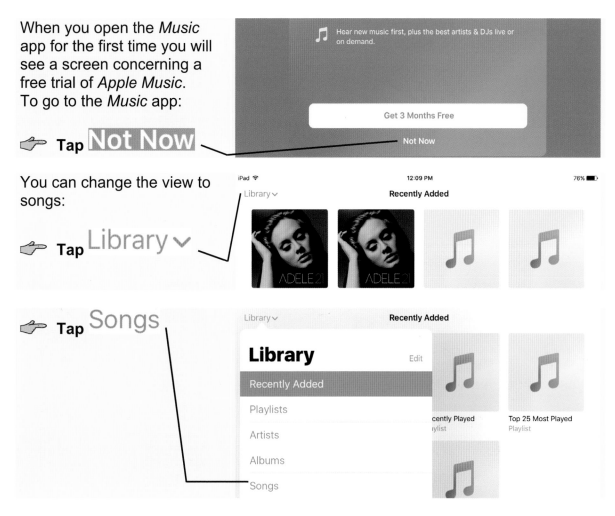

You can change the view to songs:

☞ **Tap** Library ⌄

☞ **Tap** Songs

You will see all the music currently stored on your iPad.

7.4 Playing Music with the Music App

This is how you play a song:

☞ **Tap a song title, for instance,** Someone Like You

The song is played:

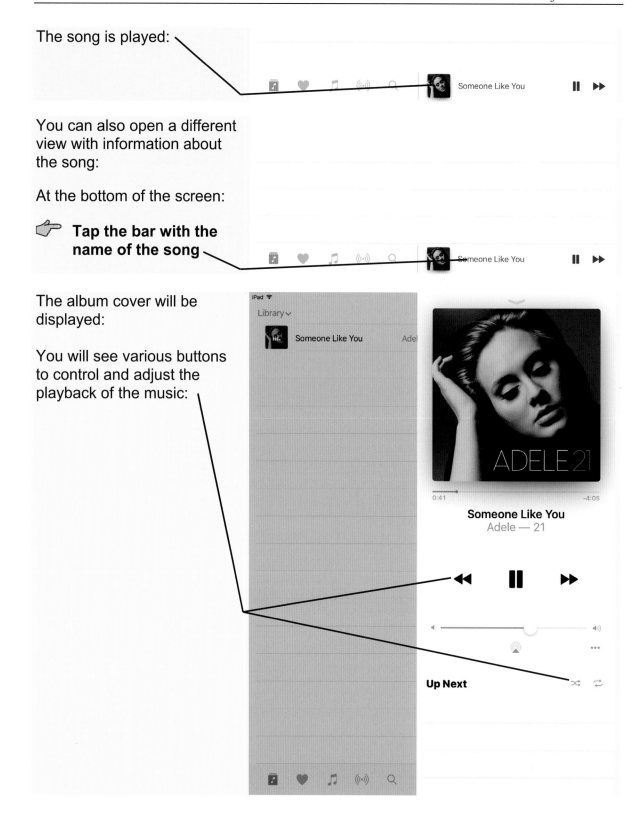

You can also open a different view with information about the song:

At the bottom of the screen:

☞ **Tap the bar with the name of the song**

The album cover will be displayed:

You will see various buttons to control and adjust the playback of the music:

This is how all the buttons work:

∨ Go back to the overview of all the songs in the Library.

  Drag the playback bar to go to a specific place in the song.

  With this option you can 'like' a song.

◄◄ This button has multiple functions:
- tap once: skip to the beginning of the current song.
- tap twice: skip to the previous song.
- press and hold your finger gently on the button to fast backward.

►► This button has multiple functions:
- tap once: skip to the next song.
- press and hold your finger gently on the button to fast forward.

❚❚ Pause.

► Play, or resume play.

≔ View the songs on the album (if these songs are stored on your iPad).

—○— Volume control.

⤨ Shuffle: play in random order.

⟲ Repeat, there are three options:

- ⟲ : do not use repeat.

- ⟲ : all songs will be repeated.

- ⟲¹ : the current song will be repeated.

  Share song.

• • • Add song to playlist, show in *iTunes Store* or delete song.

You can return to the previous screen like this.

☞ **Tap next to the window**

During playback, you can quit the *Music* app and do something else:

☞ **Go back to the home screen** ✔ 8

The music is still being played. You can display the *Music* app control buttons in any of the other apps:

☞ **Drag your finger upwards on the screen**

You will see the Control Center:

☞ **Swipe from right to left over the Control Center**

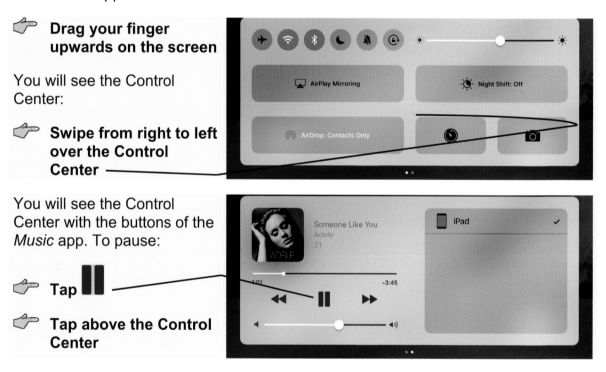

You will see the Control Center with the buttons of the *Music* app. To pause:

☞ **Tap ❚❚**

☞ **Tap above the Control Center**

Now you will see the home screen again.

7.5 Downloading a Book with the iBooks App

The *iBooks* app will turn your iPad into an e-reader with which you can read digital books.

To open the app *iBooks*:

👉 **Tap** iBooks

You might see the following window:

👉 **If necessary, tap OK**

Welcome to iBooks
Your purchased books in iCloud now appear in your library. You can also view them all in the Purchased Books collection.

OK

You might be asked whether you want to synchronize the content of *iBooks* with various other devices:

👉 **If necessary, tap Don't Sync**

Sync iBooks
Would you like to use your Apple ID to sync your bookmarks, notes, and collections between devices?

Don't Sync | Sync

In the *iBookstore* (a book store) you will find free books as well as paid books. Open the *iBookstore*:

At the bottom of the screen:

👉 **Tap Featured**

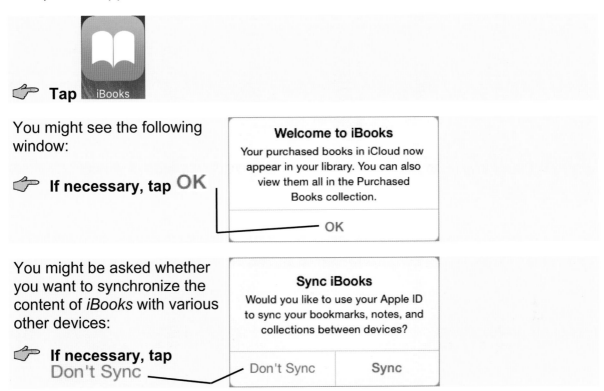

You will see the *iBookstore* home page, where new and remarkable editions are highlighted:

This is how you go to the lists of popular free and paid books:

👉 **Tap Top Charts**

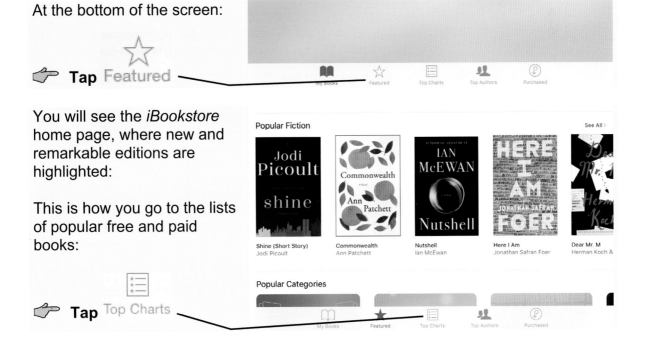

Popular Fiction   See All >

Shine (Short Story)   Commonwealth   Nutshell   Here I Am   Dear Mr. M
Jodi Picoult   Ann Patchett   Ian McEwan   Jonathan Safran Foer   Herman Koch &

Popular Categories

You will see the best sold and most frequently downloaded digital books:

If you want to view the rest of the list:

☞ **Drag the list upwards**

You can also search for an author or a title:

☞ **Tap the search box**

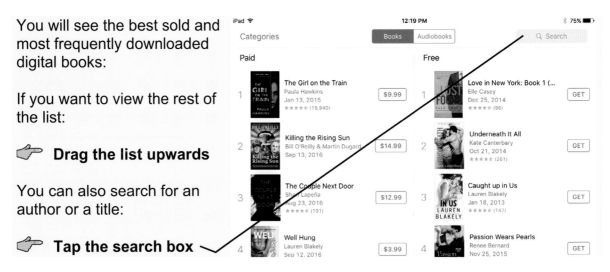

Many classic books are no longer subject to copyright, which means they can now be offered as a free e-book:

⌨ **Type:** `Great expectations`

☞ **Tap** Search

You will see the search results. You are going to download this free book:

☞ **Tap the book you want to download, for**

example

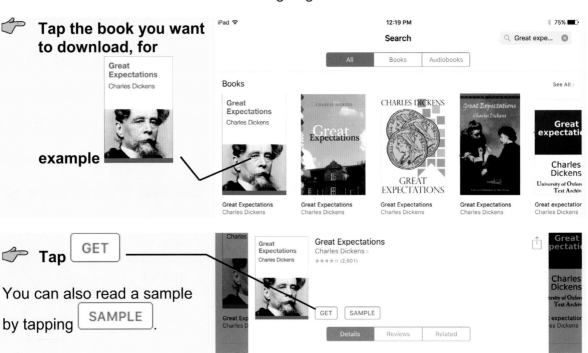

☞ **Tap** GET

You can also read a sample by tapping SAMPLE .

☞ **Tap** GET BOOK

You will see the following window. For now:

☞ **Tap No**

☞ **Sign in with your *Apple ID*** ✇72

💡 **Tip**

Purchase a book

In the *iBookstore* you can make good use of your *iTunes* credit to purchase books. You can buy a book in the same way as you buy an app, a song, or a movie.

At the bottom of the screen:

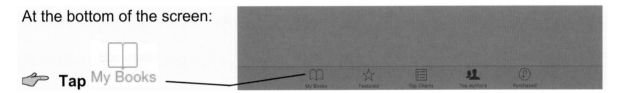

☞ **Tap** My Books

The book will be downloaded and stored in your own library:

7.6 Reading a Book with the iBooks App

After the download operation has finished you can open the book:

☞ **Tap the book**

You will see the book's title page:

With the ‹ button you go
back to your library: ⟍

With ☰ you can view the
chapters in the book: ⟋

To leaf to the next page:

👉 **Swipe from right to left
over the screen**

You can also leaf through the
pages more quickly:

👉 **Tap the right-hand
margin of the page**

If the toolbars have
disappeared:

👉 **Tap the middle of the
page**

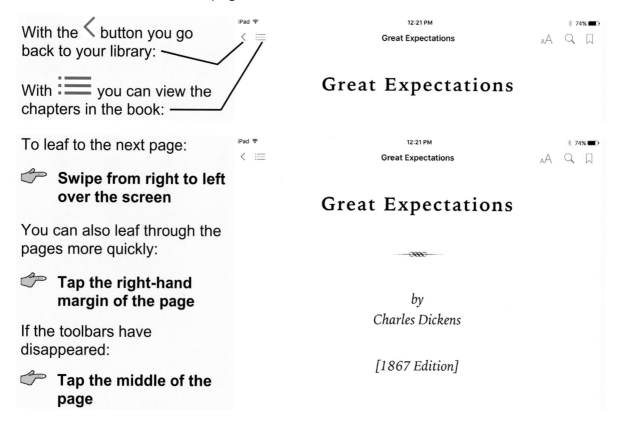

You scroll quickly back to the first page of the book:

👉 **Tap the left-hand margin of the page twice**

You will see the book's title page again. You can easily change the *iBooks* settings:

👉 **Tap A𝖠**

With the slider ◯ you can
adjust the brightness of the
screen:

With the ᴬ and **A**
buttons you can change the
font size:

By **Fonts** you can select a
different font for the book with
the › :

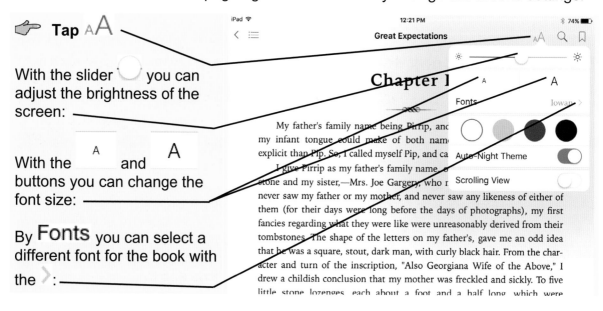

The ⬤ view renders the page a light beige, with dark brown letters:

The ⬤ and ⬤ views use a grey or black background with white letters:

Auto-Night Theme

enables night mode on the iPad automatically when it becomes dark:

Scrolling View lets you

hide the slider at the bottom of the screen:

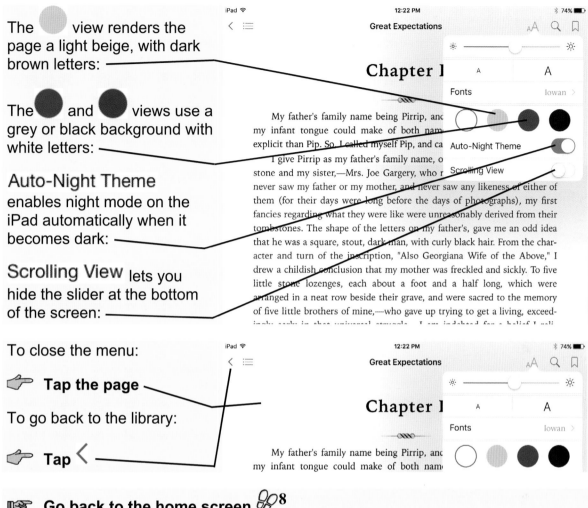

To close the menu:

👉 **Tap the page**

To go back to the library:

👉 **Tap** ❮

 Go back to the home screen 👣8

💡 **Tip**

Continue reading
When you close the *iBooks* app, the app will remember and mark the page where you stopped reading. When you start *iBooks* again, the book will be opened on the correct page. This will also happen if you are reading multiple books at once. If you use the button ❮ to go back to the library once you have opened a book, and open another book, *iBooks* will mark your page in the first book. As soon as you open the first book again you will see the correct page right away.

👉 **If you want, put the iPad into sleep mode or turn it off** 👣1

In this chapter you have learned how to download and play music files, and how to download eBooks and read them on your iPad. In the *Tips* at the back of this chapter we will give you an extra tip for this app, and for the *Videos* app too.

7.7 Exercises

To be able to quickly apply the things you have learned, you can work through these exercises. Have you forgotten how to do something? Use the numbers next to the footsteps $\theta\theta^1$ to look up the item in the appendix *How Do I Do That Again?*

Exercise 1: Listen to Music

In this exercise you are going to listen to the music on your iPad.

🖙 If necessary, wake the iPad up from sleep mode or turn it on. $\theta\theta^2$

🖙 Open the *Music* app. $\theta\theta^{91}$

🖙 Play the first song. $\theta\theta^{92}$

If the album cover is not displayed in full screen mode:

🖙 Tap the bar with the name of the song.

🖙 Turn up the volume. $\theta\theta^{93}$

🖙 Skip to the next song. $\theta\theta^{94}$

🖙 Repeat the current song. $\theta\theta^{95}$

🖙 Disable the repeat function. $\theta\theta^{96}$

🖙 Enable the shuffle function. $\theta\theta^{97}$

🖙 Skip to the next song. $\theta\theta^{94}$

🖙 Disable the shuffle function. $\theta\theta^{98}$

🖙 Go back to the Library. $\theta\theta^{99}$

🖙 Pause playback. $\theta\theta^{100}$

🖙 Go back to the home screen. $\theta\theta^8$

🖙 If you want, put the iPad into sleep mode or turn it off. $\theta\theta^1$

7.8 Background Information

Dictionary

Apple ID	A combination of a user name and a password. For example, you need an *Apple ID* to use *FaceTime* and to purchase and download music from the *iTunes Store* or apps from the *App Store*.
E-reader	A device with which you can read digital books. With the *iBooks* app you can turn your iPad into an e-reader.
iBooks	An app that lets you read digital books (eBooks).
iBookstore	A bookstore that goes with the *iBooks* app. Here you can download lots of books, free and at a price.
Library	In *Music*: an overview of all the songs you have stored on your iPad. In *iBooks*: a book case containing all the books you have purchased and downloaded.
Music	An app that plays music.
News	An app where you can select magazines or topics that you are interested in. The app shows all the news stories that you are interested in, all in one place.
Playlist	A collection of songs, ordered in a certain way.
Podcast	An episodic program, delivered through the Internet. Podcast episodes can be audio or video files and can be downloaded with the *iTunes Store*.
Theme	In *iBooks*: the way in which a page is displayed.
Videos	An app that lets you rent, buy and play video films.

Source: User Guide iPad

7.9 Tips

 Tip

Create a playlist
Another useful function in the *Music* app is the option for creating playlists. In a playlist, you can collect and sort your favorite songs, in any way you want. When you are done, you can play this list over and over again. Here is how to create a new playlist in the *Music* app:

☞ **Tap** Library ⌄, Playlists

☞ **Tap** New

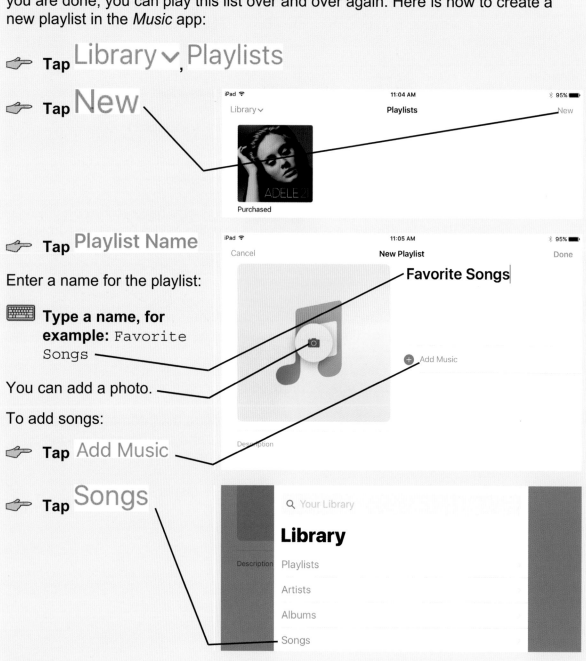

☞ **Tap** Playlist Name

Enter a name for the playlist:

⌨ **Type a name, for example:** Favorite Songs

You can add a photo.

To add songs:

☞ **Tap** Add Music

☞ **Tap** Songs

- Continue on the next page -

Now you can add songs to the playlist:

☞ **Next to the songs you want to add, tap** ⊕

☞ **Tap** Done

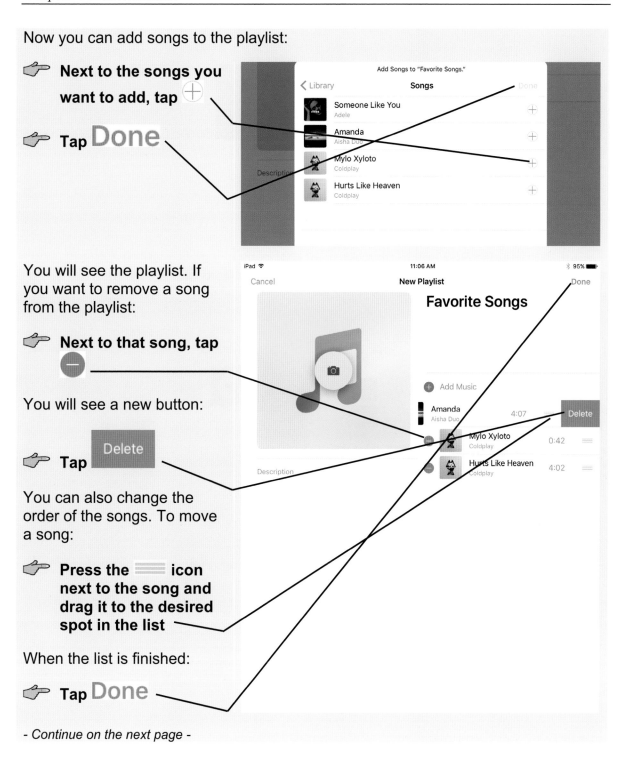

You will see the playlist. If you want to remove a song from the playlist:

☞ **Next to that song, tap** ⊖

You will see a new button:

☞ **Tap** Delete

You can also change the order of the songs. To move a song:

☞ **Press the ☰ icon next to the song and drag it to the desired spot in the list**

When the list is finished:

☞ **Tap** Done

- Continue on the next page -

You will see all the playlists:

Your playlist will now appear in the overview of playlists:

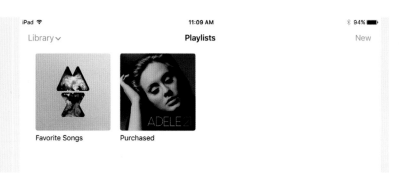

 Tip
Delete songs from the iPad
If you have stored some songs on your iPad that you no longer want to listen to, you can delete them from your iPad. If necessary, in the bottom of the screen:

☞ **Tap**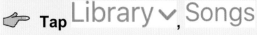

By the song you would like to delete:

☞ **Keep your finger pressed on the song**

A menu appears:

☞ **Tap**
Delete from Librar

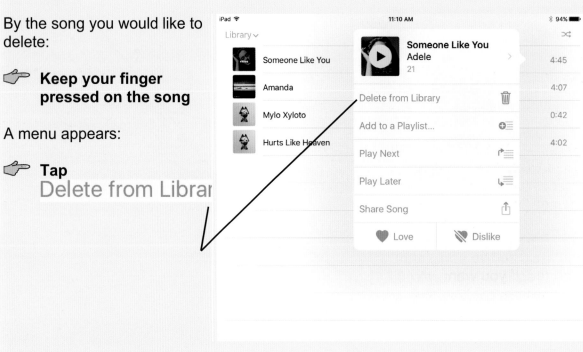

You will have to confirm this:

☞ **Tap**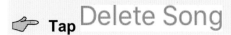

Tip

Import CDs into iTunes
You can also transfer songs from a CD to you iPad. But first, you will need to import
these songs into *iTunes*. From there you can transfer the songs to your iPad, as
described in *section 7.2 Synchronizing Music with Your iPad*.

☞ **Insert a music CD from your own collection into the CD/DVD drive on
your computer**

You will see a list of song
titles (tracks):

iTunes will ask if you want to
import the CD:

☞ **Click** ⬚ Yes ⬚

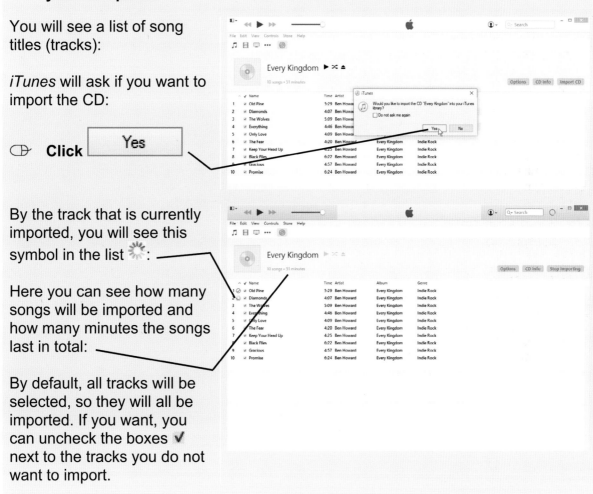

By the track that is currently
imported, you will see this
symbol in the list ☀:

Here you can see how many
songs will be imported and
how many minutes the songs
last in total:

By default, all tracks will be
selected, so they will all be
imported. If you want, you
can uncheck the boxes ✔
next to the tracks you do not
want to import.

After the CD has been imported, you will hear a sound signal. All tracks are now
marked with a ⊘. This means this import operation has been successfully
concluded. Now the songs have been added to the *iTunes* Library.

Tip

Delete a book

Digital books are actually quite small files. An average e-book takes up less than 500 KB of disk space. But if you still want to delete a book from your library, this is how you do it:

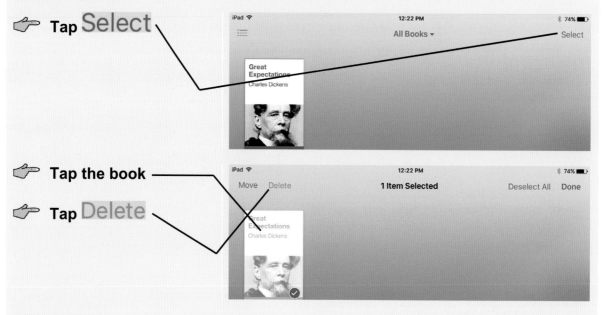

☞ **Tap** Select

☞ **Tap the book**

☞ **Tap** Delete

If you are sure:

☞ **Tap** Remove Download

 Tip

Your subscriptions in the News app

In the *News* app you can show all the stories you're interested in, all in one place.

☞ **Tap** News

You will see a couple of windows:

☞ **Tap**  Next

- Continue on the next page -

When you open this app for the first time, you need to pick at least one favorite in order to continue:

Tap three favorite topics

At the bottom of the screen:

Tap Continue

You will see the following screen where you are asked if you want the app to access your location. For now:

Allow "News" to access your location while you use the app?

Your location is used to show local weather in the For You feed

Don't Allow   Allow

Tap Don't Allow

The articles of your favorite topics are shown:

iPad 🛜   12:23 PM   * 74% 🔋

THURSDAY SEPTEMBER 15

TOP STORIES ⊙

Vox

A brutal new batch of polls for Clinton shows Trump winning in several swing st...

This race is looking a whole lot closer all of a sudden.

5h ago

QUARTZ
A banned chemical in antibacterial soap is still lurking in practically everything else America...
4h ago

The New York Times
Hillary Clinton and Donald Trump Give More Details on Their Health
14m ago

NATIONAL GEOGRAPHIC
Capturing the Wild Power of the Sea
2h ago

THE WALL STREET JOURNAL.
Behind Monsanto Deal, Doubts About the GMO Revolution
56m ago

Tip

Rent or purchase a movie on your iPad
In the *iTunes Store* you can buy much more than just music. You can rent or buy movies and view them on your iPad. The movies are arranged in various categories or genres, such as children's movies, action films, and comedies.

☞ **Open the app *iTunes Store* ✃101**

☞ **Tap** Movies

☞ **Tap a movie**

At the top you can see the price for purchasing or renting a movie: ————

Here you can see some details about the movie: ————

Many movies are offered in HD (*High Definition*) and SD (*Standard Definition*). HD is more expensive than SD. On the small iPad screen, HD will not be fully appreciated.

If you purchase a movie for your iPad it will be yours to view as often as you like. If you rent a movie you will need to watch it within 30 days. Also, after you have started watching the movie you will need to watch the entire movie within 48 hours. Within these 48 hours you are allowed to watch the movie several times. After that period the movie will be automatically removed from your iPad. If you do not start the movie within 30 days, the movie will be removed as well.
When you buy or rent a movie for your iPad you will not be able to transfer this movie to other devices, such as your computer, iPhone, iPod touch, or Apple TV. This will only be possible if you purchase or download the movie through *iTunes*, on your computer.

- Continue on the next page -

Buying or renting a movie is similar to buying music, for instance:

☞ **Buy or rent the movie, if you wish**

You can watch the rented movie in the app that is one of the standard apps installed to your iPad. The screen of this app can be compared to the screen you see when you watch a video in the *Photos* app. The playback sliders are very similar too.

Through the *iTunes Store* you can also purchase TV Shows. This works much the same way.

💡 Tip
Podcast
You can use the Podcast app to search for podcasts. Podcasts are episodes of a program available on the Internet. There are thousands of podcasts available. These can be anything from a recorded broadcast of a particular radio program, lecture, live musical performance, and many other types of events. You can download a podcast like this:

☞ **Tap** Podcasts

At the bottom of the screen:

☞ **Tap** Featured

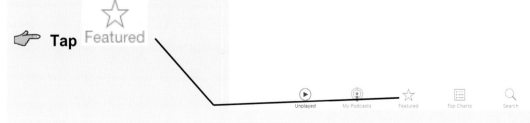

- Continue on the next page -

You will see a page with many different podcasts. You can see more information by tapping an individual podcast:

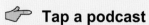 **Tap a podcast**

To download an episode:

 Tap ⬇

Note that you can also subscribe to the podcast. Whenever a new episode is available, your iPad will download it automatically:

When the download is completed, you can view the podcast by tapping My Podcasts. To play an episode you need to tap the podcast first to see the episodes you have downloaded. Then you can play it by clicking it.

8. Communication

Are you a keen *Facebook* and/or *Twitter* user? Then you should not forget to install the free apps for these social networks to your iPad.

Moreover, *Facebook* and *Twitter* have already been integrated in several of the standard apps on your iPad. You can quickly paste items on your *Facebook* wall or send tweets from within other apps. A link from *Safari*, a photo from *Photos*, a location from the *Maps* app: with just a few taps you can share these items with your friends or followers. The events you have applied on *Facebook* will also be entered in your calendar at once, and your *Facebook* friends will be included in the *Contacts* app.

With the free *Skype* app you can hold video conversations with contacts that also use *Skype* on their computer or smartphone. If you already use *Skype* on your computer or notebook, you will find that Skyping with your iPad is very easy and pleasant.

In this chapter you will learn how to:

- sign in with *Facebook* and *Twitter* and install the free apps;
- use the *Facebook* app;
- use the *Twitter* app;
- make use of *Facebook* and *Twitter* within standard iPad apps;
- hold a video conversation with *Skype*.

 Please note:

In this chapter we have assumed you already have a *Facebook*, *Twitter*, and *Skype* account. If you do not yet have such an account, you can create these accounts through www.facebook.com, www.twitter.com, and www.skype.com, if you wish. Of course you can also just read through this chapter.

8.1 Signing In with Facebook

In the *Settings* app you can sign in with *Facebook* and use your *Facebook* account. Afterwards, you will no longer need to sign in with the standard iPad apps that make use of your *Facebook* account.

☞ **If necessary, wake the iPad up from sleep or turn it on** ᛞᛞ²

☞ **Open the *Settings* app** ᛞᛞ⁶

👉 **Drag the list on the left side upwards**

👉 **Tap** 𝐟 **Facebook**

You need to sign in:

⌨ **Type your user name**

⌨ **Type your password**

👉 **Tap** Sign In

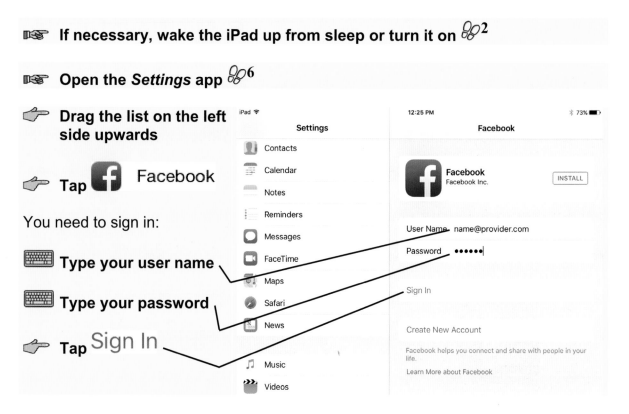

You will see a window with additional information:

👉 **Tap** Sign In

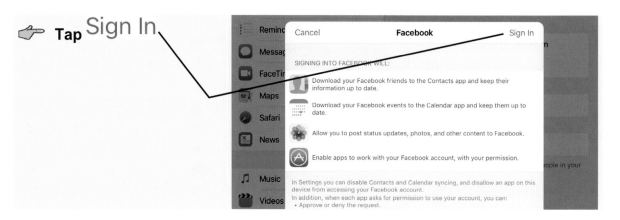

Right away, you will be asked whether you want to install the free *Facebook* app:

☞ **Tap** If necessary, sign in with your *Apple ID* 🐾 **72**

The *Facebook* app will now be installed on your iPad. In the next section you can read how to use this app.

8.2 Using the Facebook App

You will open the *Facebook* app:

☞ **Tap** Facebook

The app has remembered that you have just signed in through the *Settings* app:

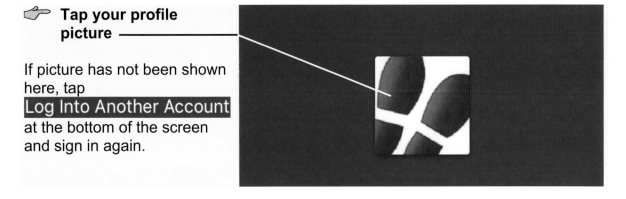

☞ **Tap your profile picture** ————

If picture has not been shown here, tap
Log Into Another Account
at the bottom of the screen and sign in again.

Facebook will ask for permission to send you push messages:

👉 **Tap** OK

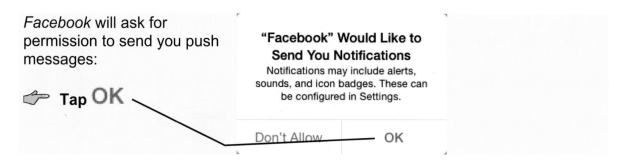

"**Facebook" Would Like to Send You Notifications**
Notifications may include alerts, sounds, and icon badges. These can be configured in Settings.

Don't Allow   OK

In the news feed you will see notifications posted by your friends, and by well-known people or companies you follow. The messages you post on your own page will appear in your friends' news feeds.

With ✒️ Status you can post a status message on your own *Facebook* page:

With 📷 Photo you can select a photo or take a picture and post it on your page, with a covering text:

With 📍 Check In you can post a notification on your page with information on your current location:

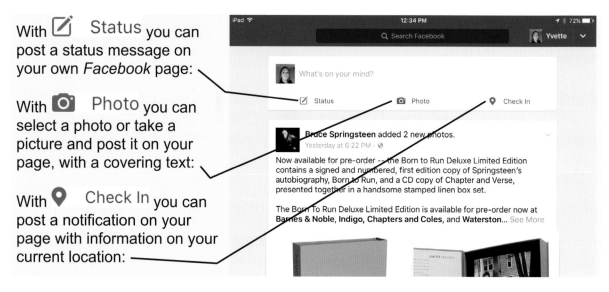

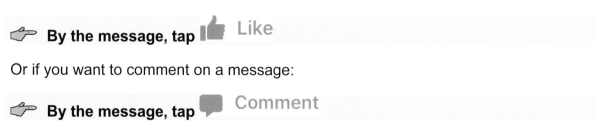

If you like a message:

👉 **By the message, tap** 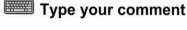 Like

Or if you want to comment on a message:

👉 **By the message, tap** 💬 Comment

⌨️ **Type your comment**

👉 **Tap** Post

This is how you can view your own wall. At the top right-hand side:

☞ **Tap your name**

You will see the messages in your timeline:

With **About** you can view the personal information you are sharing on *Facebook*: ——

With **Friends** you can access your list of friends: ——

With **Photos** you can view the photos you have uploaded to *Facebook*: ——

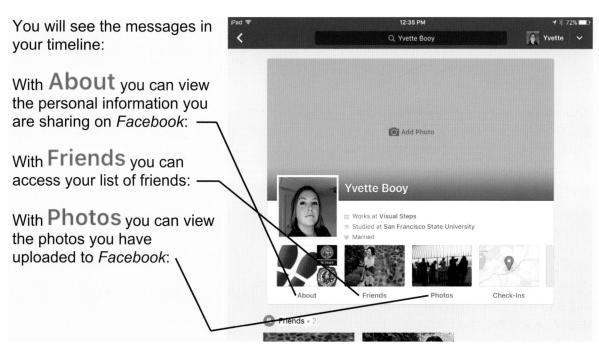

If someone comments on your timeline message, or comments on a message on which you have commented too, the 🌐 button at the bottom of the screen will turn into 🌐①. In the same way you can tell that there are friendship requests by 👥, and use Messenger with 💬.

Take a look at the other options in the menu:

☞ **At the bottom of the screen, tap** More

You can use the search box to look for acquaintances or pages:

Friends opens your list of friends:

With Events you can see upcoming events you are interested in and upcoming birthdays:

At the bottom you will find buttons for the help and settings functions:

If you stay signed in, new notifications will be retrieved as soon as you open the *Facebook* app. If you prefer to sing out, you can do it like this:

 **Tap** Log Out

When you are sure you want to log out:

☞ **Tap** Log Out

🖙 **Go back to the home screen** �🐾**8**

8.3 Signing In with Twitter

In the *Settings* app you can sign in with *Twitter*. Afterwards, you will no longer need to sign in with the standard iPad apps that make use of your *Twitter* account.

🖙 **Open the *Settings* app** �🐾**6**

☞ **Drag the list on the left side upwards**

☞ **Tap** 🐦 **Twitter**

You need to sign in:

⌨ **Type your user name**

⌨ **Type your password**

☞ **Tap** Sign In

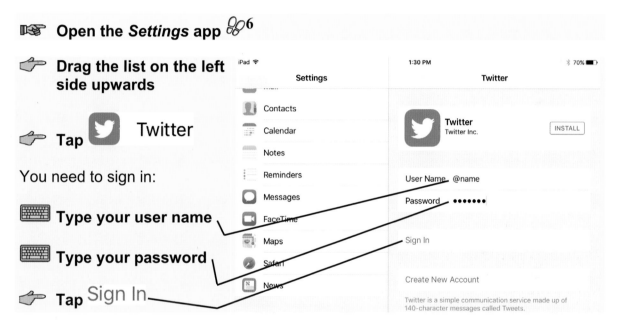

Right away, you will be asked whether you want to install the free *Twitter* app:

☞ **Tap** Install

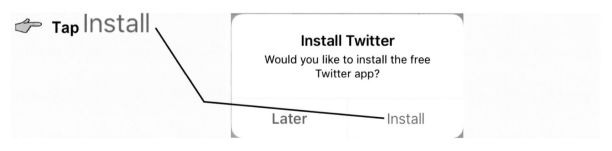

Install Twitter
Would you like to install the free Twitter app?

Later   Install

🖙 **If necessary, sign in with your *Apple ID*** ⌀⌀**72**

The *Twitter* app will now be installed on your iPad. In the next section you can read how to use this app.

8.4 Using the Twitter App

You will open the *Twitter* app:

☞ **Tap** Twitter

Twitter will also ask for permission to send you push notifications:

☞ **Tap** Allow

You will see a window about *Twitter* using your current location:

☞ **Tap** Allow

You might see a message with information about getting started. For now this will not be necessary:

☞ **If necessary, tap**

You will see your timeline, containing the most recent tweets by the people or companies you follow. Your own tweets will appear in your followers' timelines.

You see the Home page:

This is how you load the new tweets:

☞ **Swipe downwards, across the messages**

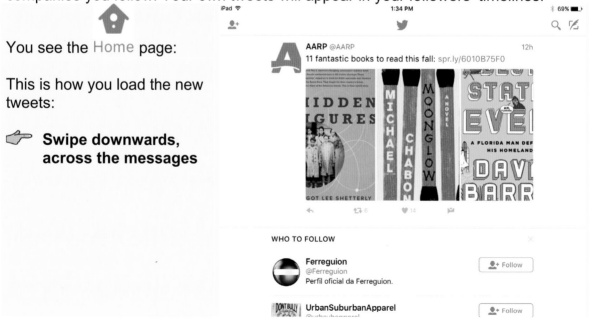

These are the functions of the buttons in the menu:

Home

This opens the *Twitter* home page. Here you can see the most recent tweets by people or companies you follow, as well as your own tweets.

Notifications

Here you can open an overview of all the replies you have received through a tweeted reply. You will also see all the tweets in which your user name is mentioned.

Messages

Here you can see received messages and send private messages to others.

Me

This button takes you to the page with your profile information. This page also contains links to the timeline with the tweets you have sent, the accounts you follow, and your own followers. This page is visible to everyone.
Here you can access your private messages too. These are only visible to you.

By Notifications and Home, the ■ indicates that there are new notifications or

tweets. At the top of the status bar you see . You can use this to search for tweets, by their subject or by their name.

This is how to send a new tweet:

☞ **In the top right-hand corner, tap**

Twitter will also ask for permission to access your photos:

☞ **Tap** OK

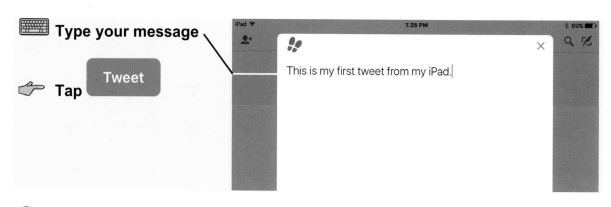

⌨ **Type your message**

☞ **Tap** [**Tweet**]

💡 **Tip**

Add items to your tweet
You can add various items to your tweet:

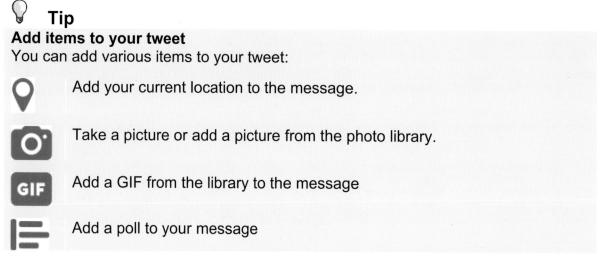

📍 Add your current location to the message.

📷 Take a picture or add a picture from the photo library.

🄶🄸🄵 Add a GIF from the library to the message

▤ Add a poll to your message

Your tweet will appear at the top of your timeline. Your followers will see your tweet in their own timeline.

☞ **Go back to the home screen** 👣**8**

8.5 Using Facebook and Twitter in Other Apps

Facebook and *Twitter* have been integrated in the standard *Photos*, *Safari*, and *Maps* apps on your iPad, among other things. In this section you will discover a number of options for these apps.

It is very easy to share a photo through *Facebook* or *Twitter* while you are working in the *Photos* app:

☞ **Open the *Photos* app** 👣**80**

☞ **Open a photo** 👣**81**

☞ **Tap** 📤

☞ **Tap** Twitter **or**

Facebook

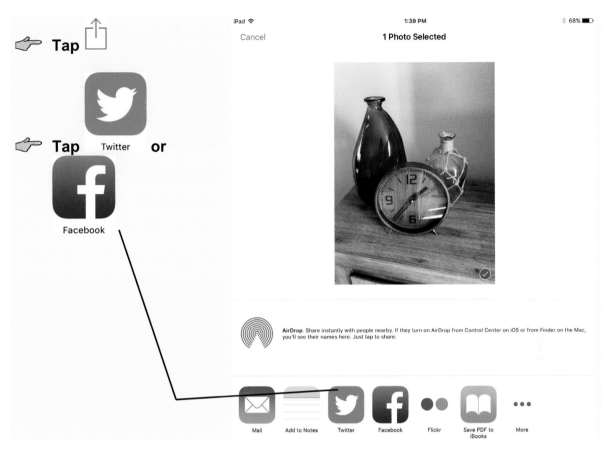

⌨ **Type your message**

☞ **Tap** Post

👉 **Go back to the home screen** 👣⁸

In the same way, you can share a link to an interesting web page while you are using *Safari*:

👉 **Open the** *Safari* **app** 👣³²

👉 **Open a random web page** 👣³³

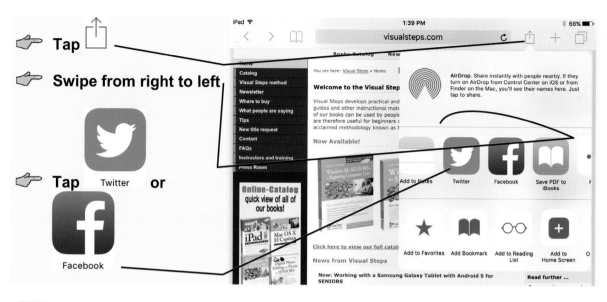

👉 **Tap** ⬆️

👉 **Swipe from right to left**

👉 **Tap** Twitter **or**

Facebook

⌨️ **Type your message**

👉 **Tap Post**

👉 **Go back to the home screen** 👣⁸

8.6 Skyping on Your iPad

With *Skype* you can hold video conversations on your iPad, with contacts who use *Skype* too. You will only be charged for the cost of the Internet connection on your iPad, the call itself is free. *Skype* is a service that is used all over the world. Not just on iPads and iPhones, but on *Windows* computers and notebooks too, as well as on *Android* and *Windows* smartphones.

👉 **Download the free *Skype for iPad* app** 👣65, 70, 71, 72

Open the *Skype* app:

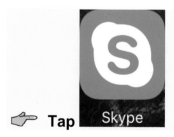

👉 **Tap** Skype

Please note:

It is possible to use *Skype* to hold video conversation through the mobile data network (3G/4G). However, if your subscription has a restriction on the amount of MBs used for Internet traffic, this may lead to unexpected high costs. In such a case it is recommended to only hold video conversations when there is a Wi-Fi connection available.

You might see a window about push notifications:

 **Tap Allow**

Before you can start using *Skype* you will need to sign in with your *Skype* name and password. You can also use a *Microsoft* Account:

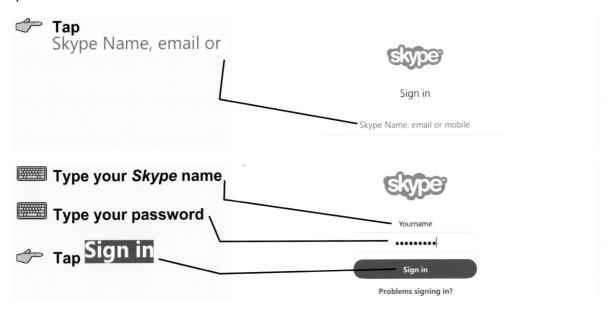

Skype would like access to the microphone and camera:

☞ **Tap** →

You might see information about a new version of *Skype*:

 ☞ **Tap Skip**

After you have signed in you will see the *Recent* page:

If you have previously used *Skype* on your computer, you will see your recently conversations on the left:

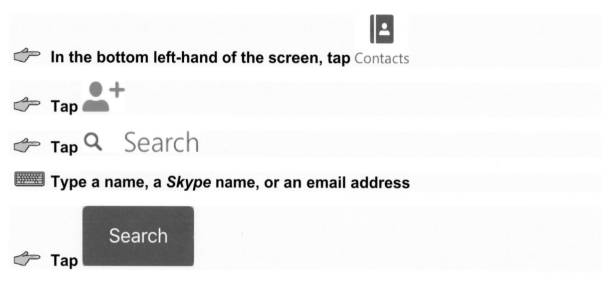

You do not yet have any contacts? This is how you add contacts:

☞ **In the bottom left-hand of the screen, tap** Contacts

☞ **Tap**

☞ **Tap** 🔍 Search

⌨ **Type a name, a *Skype* name, or an email address**

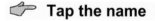

☞ **Tap** Search

If you have found your contact:

☞ **Tap the name**

☞ **Tap** 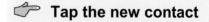 Send contact request

💡 **Tip**
Receive a contact request
As soon as your contact opens *Skype*, he will see that a contact request has been received. This is what to do next, which you can do too if you yourself have received a contact request:

☞ **Tap the new contact**

To accept the contact:
At the bottom of the screen:

☞ **Tap**  Accept

Tip

Skype test call

Before you start a video call you can hold a test conversation without using video.

☞ **Tap**

☞ **Tap**

First, you will hear a brief explanation. Then you will hear a 'ping'. Now you can speak right away, just say a few words. After a while you will hear another 'ping'. And then you will hear your own voice with the recorded message.

Was the explanation unclear? Then turn up the volume on your iPad with the volume controls:

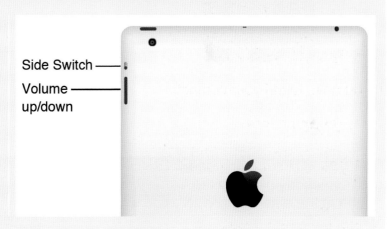

Side Switch ———

Volume ———
up/down

Was your own voice difficult to hear? Speak a bit louder and/or bring your face closer to the iPad.

If you have added a contact that uses a computer with a webcam, or a smartphone with a camera, you can hold a video conversation with this contact. Establishing a successful connection depends on whether the other person is online.

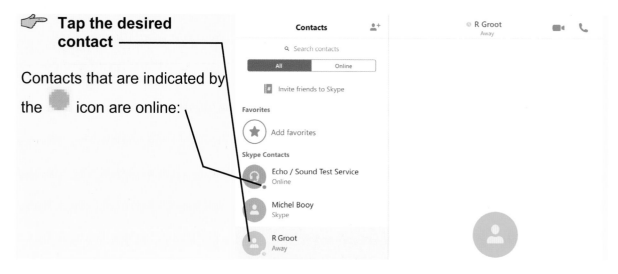

☞ **Tap the desired contact**

Contacts that are indicated by the ⬤ icon are online:

To start the video call:

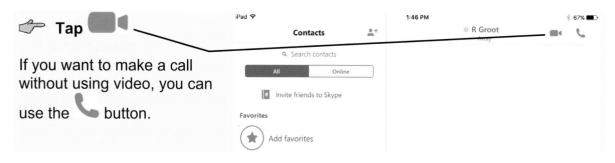

☞ **Tap** 📹

If you want to make a call without using video, you can use the 📞 button.

Now you will hear a ringtone, until somebody picks up the phone at the other end:

♀ **Tip**

Video call or voice call

If somebody calls you, you can choose between a video call and a 'regular' phone call. If you select ▣, the camera on your iPad is activated. The ▣ option will only establish a sound connection. If the person calling you has chosen to use the video call option, his camera will be activated. You will be able to see him, but not the other way round.

Of course, you can also refuse a call by tapping the ▣ button.

Please note: if you begin a video chat and have clicked a contact, the content from your iPad's front facing camera becomes visible to your contact.

After the connection has been established you can hold a conversation and see each other. You will see a large image of your contact, through the camera lens. In the bottom right-hand corner you will see the image recorded by the camera on the front of your iPad.

☞ **Hold the conversation**

If you tap the screen of the iPad during a video call you will see a number of buttons. This is what they do:

 Display the menu bar on the side.

 This button can be used to switch between using the camera on the front or on the back of the iPad.

 Open a window to communicate with your contact through written messages (chatting).

 With this button you can choose to turn the camera on or off.

 Mute the sound of the microphone.

 Add participants to conversation.

 End the call.

If you want to end the call:

 Tap the screen

 **Tap**

If you want to stop using *Skype* you need to do more than just go back to the home screen. If you do this, *Skype* will still remain active in the background. You will still be signed in and available for receiving video calls, even if your iPad is in sleep mode.

☞ **Go back to the home screen** 𝒦𝒫 **8**

☞ **Scroll to the second page** 𝒦𝒫 **66**

Open the *Skype* app on your iPad:

 **Tap**   Skype

You are still signed in. When you go back to the home screen, your status will change to *offline*, either right away or after the time period you just set. You will no longer be available for (video) calls, but still be signed in with *Skype*.
You can also sign out completely with *Skype*. At the bottom of the screen:

☞ **Tap** My info

☞ **Tap** ⤷ Sign out

Now you will see the *Skype* login screen again.

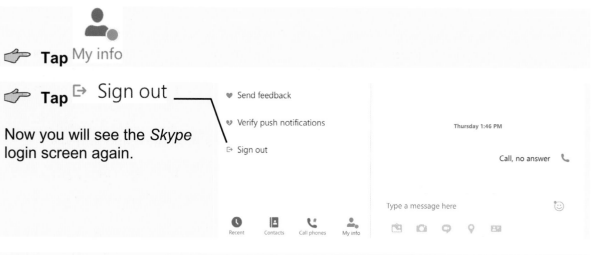

☞ **Go back to the home screen** 𝒦𝒫 **8**

☞ **If you want, put the iPad into sleep mode or turn it off** ✂¹

You have reached the end of this book. In this book you have learned how to work with the iPad. Now you have gathered sufficient knowledge to start working with the multitude of options and apps.

8.7 Visual Steps Website and More Books

By now we hope you have noticed that the Visual Steps method is an excellent method for quickly and efficiently learning more about computers, tablets, other devices and software applications. All books published by Visual Steps use this same method.
In various series, we have published a large number of books on a wide variety of topics including *Windows*, *Mac OS X*, the iPad, iPhone, Samsung Galaxy Tab, Kindle, photo editing and many other topics.

On the **www.visualsteps.com** website you will find a full product summary by clicking the blue *Catalog* button. For each book there is an extensive description, the full table of contents and a sample chapter (PDF file). In this way, you can quickly determine if a specific title will meet your expectations. You can order a book directly online from this website or other online book retailers. All titles are also available in bookstores in the USA, Canada, United Kingdom, Australia and New Zealand.

Furthermore, the website offers many extras, among other things:
- free computer guides and booklets (PDF files) covering all sorts of subjects;
- frequently asked questions and their answers;
- information on the free Computer Certificate that you can acquire at the certificate's website **www.ccforseniors.com**;
- a free email notification service: let's you know when a new book is published.

There is always more to learn. Visual Steps offers many other books on computer-related subjects. Each Visual Steps book has been written using the same step-by-step method with short, concise instructions and screenshots illustrating every step.

Would you like to be informed when a new Visual Steps title becomes available? Subscribe to the free Visual Steps newsletter (no strings attached) and you will receive this information in your inbox.
The Newsletter is sent approximately each month and includes information about
- the latest titles;
- supplemental information concerning titles previously released;
- new free computer booklets and guides;
When you subscribe to our Newsletter you will have direct access to the free booklets on the **www.visualsteps.com/info_downloads.php** web page.

8.8 Background Information

Dictionary

Account	An account grants the user access to a service. It consists of a user name and a password. If you want to use *Skype*, *Facebook*, and *Twitter* you need an account.
Android	An operating system for mobile phones and tablet computers, the counterpart of the *iOS* manufactured by Apple.
Contacts	The people you have agreed to communicate with.
Facebook	A popular social network site, with a free iPad app.
FaceTime	An app that lets you hold free video conversations through the Internet, with contacts all over the world. One of the limitations of *FaceTime* is that you can only connect to other iPad, iPhone, iPod touch and Mac users.
Messages	An app that lets you send free *iMessages* through the mobile data network (3G of 4G), or through Wi-Fi, to other Mac, iPhone, iPad and iPod touch users. If you send a message through 3G/4G you need to pay a fee for the data traffic, but a text message usually takes up no more than140 bytes.
Skype	An app that lets you hold free (video) conversations through the Internet, with contacts all over the world. *Skype* is not just used on iPads and iPhones, but also on *Windows* computers and notebooks, and on *Android* and *Windows* smartphones too.
Status	You can use this option to indicate whether you are available to take a (video) call. With the Status option in *Facebook* you can post a status message on your own *Facebook* page:
Twitter	A popular social network site with a free iPad app. Users post short messages (tweets) of no more than 140 characters.
Video call	A conversation with a contact, through a video and sound connection.

Source: iPad User Guide, Skype Help, Wikipedia

8.9 Tips

 Tip

Adjust status

By changing your status you can indicate whether you are available to take calls. This is how you do it:

☞ **Tap** My info

☞ **Tap** Status

You will see five possible status options:

☞ **Tap the desired status**

 Tip

Make video calls with FaceTime

You can use the *FaceTime* app to make video calls with the iPad. To use *FaceTime* you will need an Internet connection and an *Apple ID*. The person you want to talk with will also need to have an *Apple ID*, and needs to be signed in with an iPad, iPhone, iPod Touch or Mac computer. This limits the use of the *FaceTime* app, since you cannot hold video calls with people who do not have such a device.

☞ **Tap** FaceTime

- Continue on the next page -

You may need to sign in first:

⌨ **Type your email address**

⌨ **Type your password**

☞ **Tap Sign In...**

Now you will see the image of your iPad's front camera:

You can start *FaceTime* by entering a name, email address or phone number:

You can also select one of your contacts:

☞ **Tap** ⊞

This is how you start a video conversation with a contact:

☞ **Tap the name of your contact**

For video calling:

☞ **Tap** 📹

For voice calling you need to tap 📞.

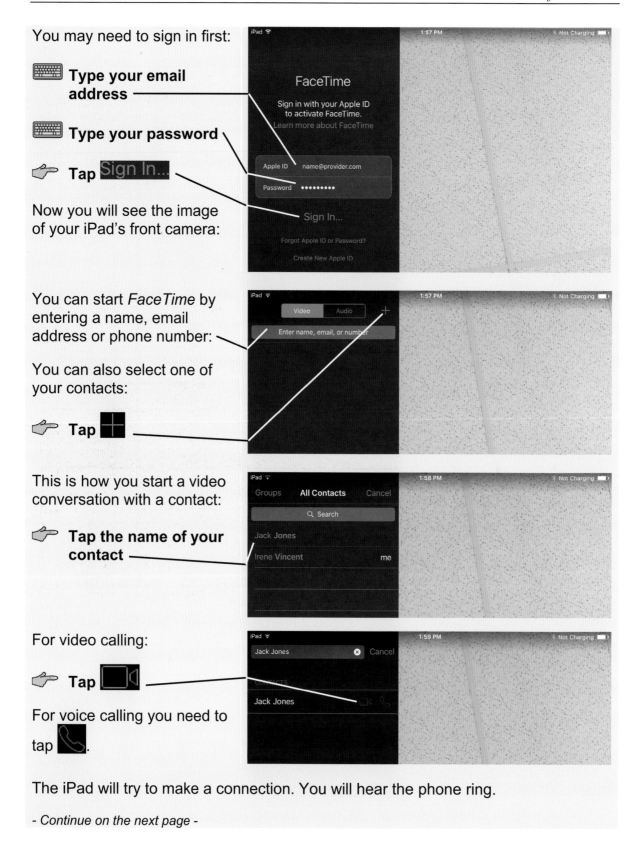

The iPad will try to make a connection. You will hear the phone ring.

- Continue on the next page -

Please note: The contact needs to be online, and needs to have added your name and email address to his contacts.

Once the connection has been made, you will be able to see and hear your contact:

In this way you can hold a video conversation with contacts all over the world.

Use the 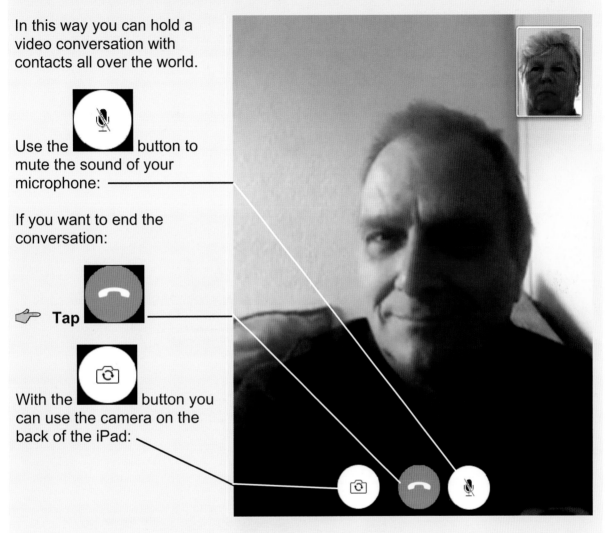 button to mute the sound of your microphone:

If you want to end the conversation:

☞ **Tap**

With the button you can use the camera on the back of the iPad:

Tip: you can also open the *FaceTime* app from within the *Contacts* app. Simply tap the ⬜◁ button that you see by your contact's information.

Tip
Send messages with the Messages app

With the *Messages* app you can send iMessages (text messages) through Wi-Fi or the mobile data network, to other people who own an iPad, iPhone, iPod Touch or Mac computer. To be able to use the *Messages* app you will need to have an *Apple ID*.

This is how you can send messages with the *Messages* app:

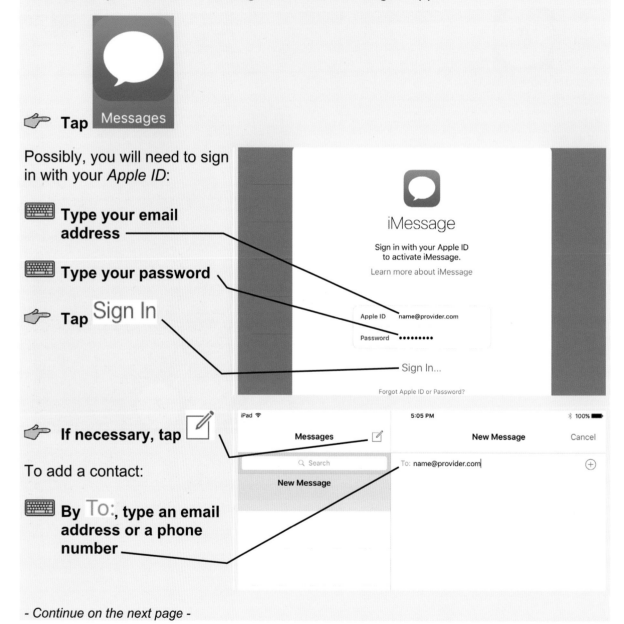

👉 **Tap** Messages

Possibly, you will need to sign in with your *Apple ID*:

⌨ **Type your email address**

⌨ **Type your password**

👉 **Tap** Sign In

iMessage

Sign in with your Apple ID to activate iMessage.

Learn more about iMessage

Apple ID   name@provider.com

Password   ●●●●●●●●

Sign In...

Forgot Apple ID or Password?

👉 **If necessary, tap** 📝

To add a contact:

⌨ **By** To:, **type an email address or a phone number**

iPad 🔉   5:05 PM   🔋 100% ▪

Messages   New Message   Cancel

🔍 Search   To: name@provider.com   ⊕

New Message

- Continue on the next page -

At the bottom of the screen:

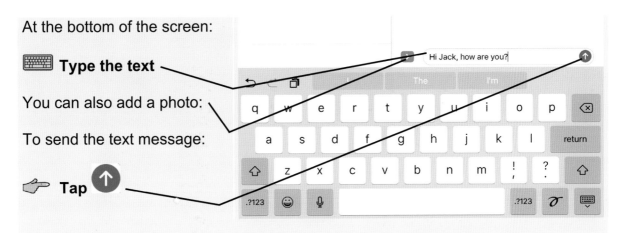

🖮 **Type the text**

You can also add a photo:

To send the text message:

☞ **Tap** ⬆

As soon as the message has been sent you will hear a sound signal.

You will immediately see whether the message has been delivered:

☞ **Go back to the home screen** 👣8

When a reply is received you will hear a sound signal and see a message on the login screen:

- Continue on the next page -

If the iPad is unlocked you will see a badge on the app icon:

When you open the app you will see the answer displayed below your message:

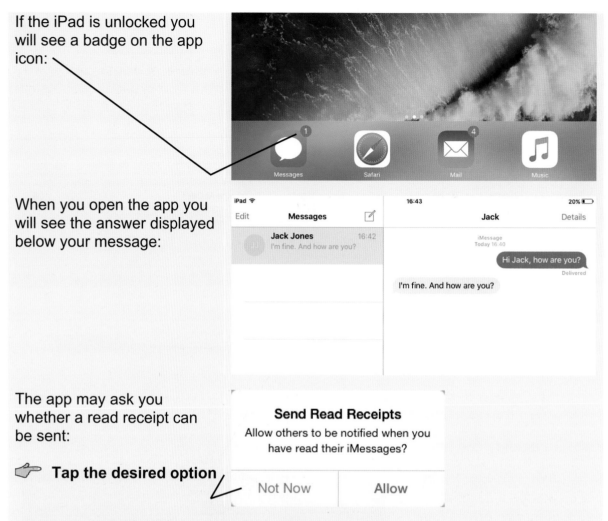

The app may ask you whether a read receipt can be sent:

☞ **Tap the desired option**

Send Read Receipts

Allow others to be notified when you have read their iMessages?

Not Now	Allow

When you reply to such a message, it will be placed below the answer you have just received. This way, you can view the whole conversation with this contact, with the messages neatly placed one below the other.

Tip

Calendar and Contacts

You will never have to forget a birthday again, because your *Facebook* friends' birthdays will be entered in your calendar. When you accept an invitation to an event on *Facebook*, or indicate you will be present at a certain event, this event will be entered in your calendar as well.

☞ **Tap** Calendars

You will see that separate calendars have been added for *Facebook* events and birthdays:

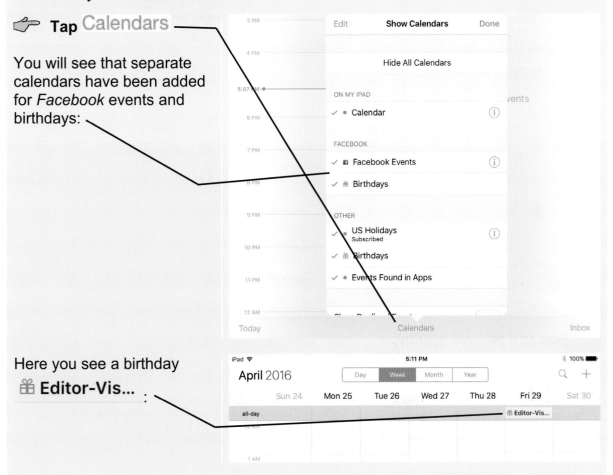

Here you see a birthday

🎁 **Editor-Vis...** :

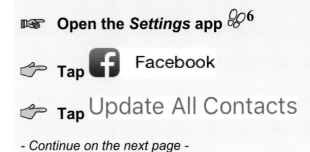

By default, your *Facebook* friends will be added to the *Contacts* app. If you grant *Facebook* access to your contacts' information for just once, the photos of existing contacts will be updated by using their *Facebook* profile photos. This is how you do it:

☞ **Open the *Settings* app** 👣⁶

☞ **Tap** 📘 Facebook

☞ **Tap** Update All Contacts

- Continue on the next page -

If you do not want the *Calendar* and/or *Contacts* apps to use your *Facebook* account, you can turn it off:

By ☰ Calendars

or 👤 Contacts ,

tap ⬤

Now the *Facebook* calendar and/or the contact data will be deleted.

Appendix A. How Do I Do That Again?

In this book actions are marked with footsteps: ✎¹ Find the corresponding number in the appendix below to see how to execute a specific operation.

✎**1** **Turn to sleep mode or turn off the iPad**

Turn to sleep mode:
● Press the Sleep/Wake button

Turn off the iPad:
● Press the Sleep/Wake button until you see

● Swipe  to the right

✎**2** **Turn on the iPad or wake up from sleep mode**
Wake up from sleep mode:

● Press the Home button

Or:
● Press the Sleep/Wake button

● Swipe across the screen from left to right

Turn on the iPad:
● Keep the Sleep/Wake button depressed until you see the *Apple* logo

● Swipe across the screen from left to right

If you have set up a four-digit code:
● Enter the code

✎**3** **Open *Notes* app**

● Tap **Notes**

✎**4** **Type a text**
● If necessary, tap the screen

● Type the text

✎**5** **Delete a note**

● Tap 🗑

● Tap OK

✎**6** **Open *Settings* app**

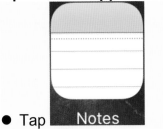

● Tap Settings

✎**7** **Turn off Wi-Fi**

● Tap Settings

- Tap  Wi-Fi

- By Wi-Fi, tap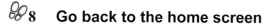

8   Go back to the home screen

- Press the Home button

9   Safely disconnect the iPad
- Next to the iPad's name, click
⏏

- Disconnect the iPad

10   Turn on Wi-Fi

- Tap Settings

- Tap 🛜 Wi-Fi

- By Wi-Fi, tap

11   Close a window on a pc
- Click ✕

12   Open *iTunes* on computer
On a Windows 7 pc:
- Click

- Click ▶   All Programs

- Click ▮ iTunes

- Click 🎵 iTunes

On a Windows 10 and 8.1 pc, on the desktop:

- Double-click

13   Select a word
- Press your finger on the word

- Use the magnifying glass to check if the cursor is positioned on the word

- Release your finger

- Tap

14   Open *Mail* app

- Tap   Mail

15   Open new email message

- Tap 🖊

16   Type email address
- Tap To:

- Type your email address

17   Add a subject
- Tap Subject:

- Type the subject

18 Type text in email message
- If necessary, tap the blank area where you want to type your message
- Type the text

19 Do not accept suggestion
- Tap the correction that is put between brackets

20 Delete word
- Tap ⟨×⟩ several times, until the word has been deleted

21 Go to new line
- Tap return

22 Copy selected word
- Tap Copy

23 Paste copied word
- Tap the spot where you want to paste the word
- Tap

24 Send an email
- Tap Send

25 View incoming message
- Tap ‹ Inbox (1)
- Tap the message

26 Delete a message
- Tap 🗑

27 View contents of *Trash* folder
- Tap ‹ Inbox
- Tap ‹ Mailboxes or the name of your email account
- Tap 🗑 Trash

28 Permanently delete message
- Tap Edit
- Tap the message
- Tap Delete

29 Return to *Inbox* folder
- Tap ‹ Mailboxes
- Tap ▱ Inbox

Or:
- Tap the name of your account and then tap ▱ Inbox

30 Check for new email
- Swipe your finger downwards over the left side of the screen

31 Close a tab
- By the tab, tap ⊗

⧉32 **Open *Safari* app**

- Tap

⧉33 **Open a website**
- Tap the address bar

- If necessary, tap ⊗

- Type the web address

- Tap

⧉34 **Scroll downwards**
- Drag your finger upwards across the screen

⧉35 **Quickly scroll downwards**
- Swipe your finger upwards across the screen, moving fast

⧉36 **Return to top of web page**
- Tap the status bar twice

⧉37 **Zoom in**
- Double-tap the page

Or:
- Spread two fingers on the screen

⧉38 **Zoom out**
- Double-tap the page

Or:
- Move two fingers towards each other on the screen

⧉39 **Add a bookmark**

- Tap

- Tap Add Bookmark

- Tap Save

⧉40 **Open a link**
- Tap the link

⧉41 **Open link in new tab**
- Put your finger on the link

- Tap Open in New Tab

⧉42 **View recently used apps**

- Press the Home button twice

⧉43 **Switch to a recently used app**
- Tap the desired app

⧉44 **Add info for contact**
- Tap the desired field, for instance, ⊕ add email

- Type the data

⧉45 **Add contact**
- Tap ✛

- Tap a field

- Type the data

- Repeat this action for all the fields you want to use

● Tap Done

🐾46 **Open *Contacts* app**

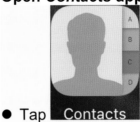

● Tap Contacts

🐾47 **Open contact to edit data**
● Tap the desired contact

● Tap Edit

🐾48 **Change a field label**
● Tap the name of the label

● Select the name you want from the list and tap it

🐾49 **Save changes**
● Tap Done

🐾50 **Open *Calendar* app**

● Tap Calendar

🐾51 **Select *Day* view**
● Tap Day

🐾52 **Go to today**
● Tap Today

🐾53 **Skip to the day after tomorrow**
● Swipe from right to left over the screen until you see the desired day

🐾54 **Open new event**
● Tap +

Or:
● Press your finger on the desired date and time

🐾55 **Add name and location of event**
● Tap the desired field

● Type the data

🐾56 **Change start and end time**
● Tap Starts

● Turn the scroll wheels to change the start time

🐾57 **Open *Maps* app**

● Tap Maps

🐾58 **Search for current location**
● Tap ◁

● If necessary, tap Allow

🐾59 **Change view**
● Tap ⓘ

● Tap the desired view

🐾60 **Search for location**
● Tap the search box

● If necessary, tap ⊗

● If necessary, tap the keyword you want to use

● Tap Search

Ø61 Map out a trip
● Tap Directions

● Enter the start and end point of the route

● Tap Route

Ø62 Display full set of directions for walking a route

● Tap Walk

Ø63 Open *Spotlight*
On the home screen:
● Swipe downwards across the screen a bit, halfway the screen

Ø64 Search in *Spotlight*
● Type the desired keyword

Ø65 Open *App Store*

● Tap App Store

Ø66 Scroll to the second page
● Swipe across the screen from right to left

Ø67 Move app to another screen
● Drag the app to the left or right border of the screen

When you see the other screen:
● Release the app

Ø68 Jiggle apps
● Press your finger on a random app for a few seconds

Ø69 Remove app from folder
● Drag the app out of the folder

Ø70 Search for apps in *App Store*
● Tap the search box

● If necessary, tap ⊗

● Type your keyword

● Tap Search

Ø71 Download free app
● Tap GET

● Tap INSTALL

Ø72 Sign in with your *Apple ID*
● Type your password

● Tap OK

Or, if you had signed out:
● Tap

● Type your email address

● Type your password

● Tap OK

73 Scroll to home screen
- Swipe across the screen from left to right

74 Move an app
- Drag the app to the desired location

75 Store apps in a folder
- Drag an app across another app

76 Close folder
- Tap below the folder

77 Stop apps from jiggling

- Press the Home button

78 Open a folder
- Tap the folder

79 Delete an app from the iPad
- By the app you want to delete, tap
- Tap Delete

80 Open *Photos* app

- Tap Photos

81 Open a photo
- If necessary, tap the option to go back to the overview of the photos, for example the name of the folder ‹ Barcelona or ‹ Camera Roll
- Tap the photo

82 Open *Camera* app

- Tap Camera

83 Focus
- Tap the object you want to focus on

84 Take a picture

- Tap

85 Zoom in
- Move your thumb and index finger apart, on the screen

86 Skip to the next photo
- Swipe across the screen from right to left

87 Skip to the previous photo
- Swipe across the screen from left to right

88 Start slideshow

- Tap

- Tap Slideshow

To set various options:
- Tap the photo

- Tap **Options**

- change the desired options

89 **Stop slideshow**
- Tap the screen

- Tap ❚❚

90 **Zoom out on a photo**
- Move two fingers towards each other on the screen

91 **Open *Music* app**

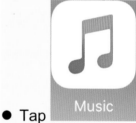

- Tap

92 **Play a song**
- Tap the song

93 **Turn up the volume**
- Drag the slider on the volume control to the right

94 **Skip to the next song**
- Tap ▶▶

95 **Repeat current song**
- Tap ↻

- Tap ↻

96 **Disable repeat**
- Tap ↻ or ↻¹

97 **Enable shuffle**
- Tap ⤭

98 **Disable shuffle**
- Tap ⤭

99 **Go back to the Library**
- Tap ⌄

100 **Pause playback**
- Tap ❚❚

101 **Open *iTunes Store* app**

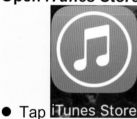

- Tap iTunes Store

102 **Open website**
From the desktop:

- Click or

- Type the web address in the address bar

- Press

Appendix B. Download and Install iTunes

In this appendix you can read how to download and install *iTunes*. *iTunes* can be downloaded (for free) from the *Apple* website, the manufacturers of the iPad and *iTunes*.

 Please note:

In this book we will install version 12.5.1 of the *iTunes* program. But there may be a more recent version of this program, by the time you start using this book. In that case, just look for buttons that resemble the buttons we describe in this appendix.

The first step is to download the *iTunes* program. You will find this program on the *Apple* website.

☞ **Surf to www.apple.com/itunes/download** ✇102

You might see a message about an add-on:

⊕ **If necessary, click** ✖

run the following add-on: 'Apple' from 'Apple Inc.'.   What's the risk?   Allow ▾ ✕

Apple will ask if you want to sign up for product news and special offers. But you do not need to enter your e-mail address to download *iTunes*:

⊕ **Uncheck the boxes** ☑

☞ **If necessary, select your location**

⊕ **Click** Download now

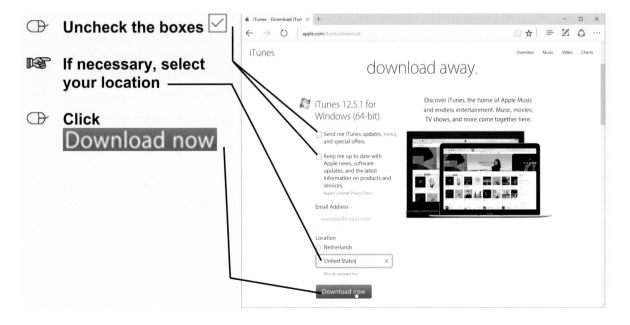

☞ **If necessary, click** `Save`

☞ **Click** `Run`

A progress bar indicates the amount of time left for the program to be downloaded.

In a few moments, you will see the installation window with information about *iTunes*:

☞ **Click** `Next >`

In the next window you can select the installation options for *iTunes*:

In this example, a shortcut will be added to the desktop and *iTunes* will be the default player for playing audio files.

You can also change the language, if you want:

☞ **Click** `Install`

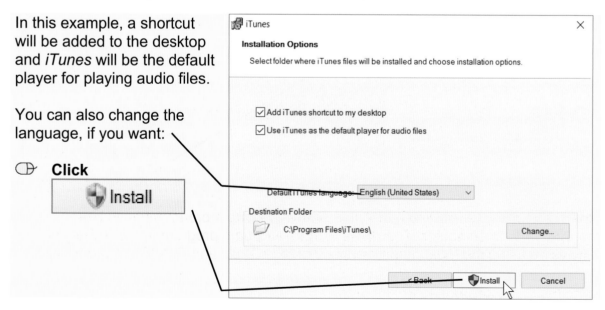

Your screen now turn dark. You will be asked for permission to continue with the installation.

☞ Give permission to continue

Now the *iTunes* program will be installed and if needed, the *QuickTime* program also. *QuickTime* is the multimedia platform from the Apple Corporation; you will need this program if you want to use *iTunes*. This may take several minutes. You will see the progress of the installation process in the window.
Your screen may turn dark once again. You will be asked for permission to continue with the installation:

☞ Give permission to continue

The installation process continues:

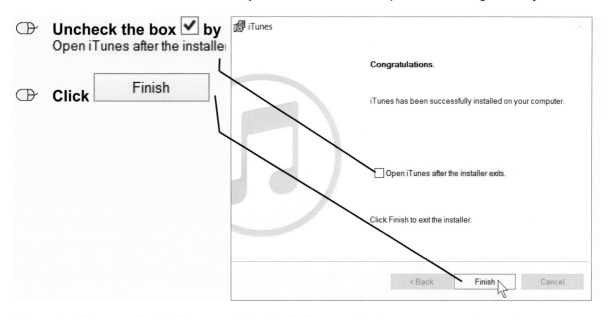

After the installation has finished, you do not need to open *iTunes* right away:

☞ **Uncheck the box ✔ by** Open iTunes after the installer

☞ **Click** Finish

Now the *iTunes*, *QuickTime* and *Apple Software Update* programs have been installed to your computer. The *Apple Software Update* program ensures that you will always be using the most recent versions of the *iTunes* and *QuickTime* programs.

☞ Close all windows 11

Appendix C. Opening a Bonus Chapter

On the website accompanying this book you will find several bonus chapters in PDF format. You can open these files (on a pc) with *Adobe Reader,* free software that lets you open, view and print PDF files. Here is how to open these files from the website:

☞ **Go to www.visualsteps.com/ipad10** $\mathscr{QP}$**102**

Go to the page with the bonus chapters:

☞ **Click**
Bonus Chapters

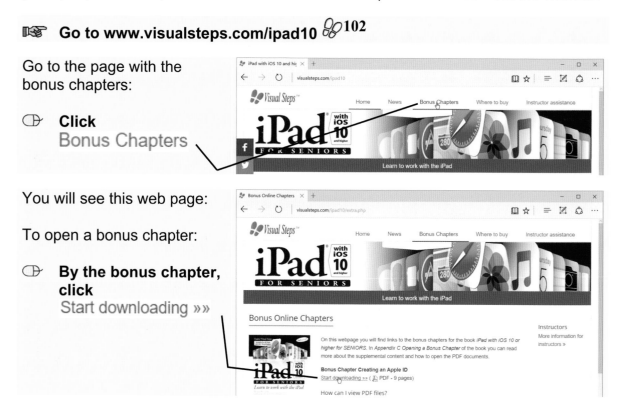

You will see this web page:

To open a bonus chapter:

☞ **By the bonus chapter, click**
Start downloading »»

The PDF files are protected with a password. To open the PDF files you will need to enter this password:

⌨ **Type:** 81822

☞ **Click** OK

You will see the bonus chapter. You can read the chapter. Use the scroll bars to go to the previous and next page. You can also print the file by clicking the 🖶 button.

☞ **Close all windows** $\mathscr{QP}$**11**

Appendix D. Index

Photo Editing on the iPad for SENIORS

There is so much you can do with an iPad. But one of the best applications is surely working with photos! There are many apps available that come with a variety of tools for enhancing your photos. You can spruce up the photos you took from a memorable event or vacation for example, and share them with others. And what about making a collage, slideshow or photo album?

> *HAVE FUN AND BECOME A PHOTO EDITING EXPERT ON YOUR IPAD!*

This user-friendly book shows you in a jiffy how to create and edit all of these types of projects. A number of photo editing apps are easy to use and free to download. They offer lots of preset filters, plus useful tools to crop, repair, lighten, darken or sharpen your photos. And if you want additional editing capability, you can purchase an app for a small amount with even more great features. You will learn how to use these apps with clear step-by-step instructions. You can get started right away with exercise pictures that can be downloaded from our website.

With the knowledge and experience you gain, you will soon be able to edit your own photos and turn them into works of art. It will surprise you how much is possible with photos on the iPad!

Author: Studio Visual Steps
ISBN 978 90 5905 731 9
Book type: Paperback, full color
Nr of pages: 312
Accompanying website: www.visualsteps.com/photoipad

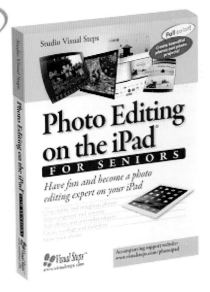

Full color!

Learn how to:
- Crop, rotate and straighten photos
- Adjust exposure and contrast
- Add effects, text and other objects
- Create a collage and slideshow
- Share your photos

Suitable for: all iPads.

Windows 10 for SENIORS

Windows 10 for Seniors is the ideal book for seniors who have worked with an earlier version of Windows on a desktop or laptop computer and want to get started right away with Windows 10. All of the most important topics are covered, such as using the Internet safely, sending and receiving email and working with files and folders. You will also learn how to organize and view photos and videos and listen to music in Windows 10.

Step by step, in your own tempo, you will get acquainted with the new and renewed programs in Windows 10. You will get familiar with the new Start menu and learn how to adjust the settings to make Windows 10 easier and more comfortable to work with. The book contains additional exercises to repeat and reinforce everything you have learned. Instructional videos are also available on the website that accompanies this book. They explain how to perform specific tasks.

In no time at all you will become comfortable and at ease with Windows 10!

Author: Studio Visual Steps
ISBN 978 90 5905 451 6
Book type: Paperback, full color
Nr of pages: 320 pages
Accompanying website:
www.visualsteps.com/windows10

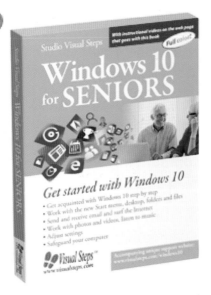

Learn how to:
- Get acquainted with Windows 10 step-by-step
- Work with the new Start menu, desktop, folders and files
- Send and receive email and surf the Internet
- Work with photos and videos, listen to music
- Adjust settings
- Safeguard your computer

Suitable for:
Windows 10 on a desktop or laptop computer